Election '94
South Africa

ELECTION '94

South Africa

The campaigns, results and future prospects

Edited by
ANDREW REYNOLDS

ST. MARTIN'S PRESS   New York

For my father
who taught me about stories
for my mother
who taught me about people
and for my sister
who has always been my friend.

First published 1994 in Southern Africa by David Philip Publishers (Pty) Ltd, 208 Werdmuller Centre, Claremont 7700, South Africa

Published 1994 in the United States of America by St. Martin's Press, Scholarly and Reference Division, 175 Fifth Avenue, New York NY 10010

Published 1994 in the United Kingdom by James Currey, 54B Thornhill Square, Islington, London N1 1BE

© 1994 David Philip Publishers

ISBN 0-86486-276-8 (David Philip)
ISBN 0-312-12375-2 (St. Martin's Press)
ISBN 0-85255-388-9 (James Currey)

Printed by Clyson Printers (Pty) Ltd, 11th Avenue, Maitland, South Africa

CIP data is available upon request from the British Library.

Library of Congress Cataloging-in-Publication data applied for.

Contents

Contributors

Andrew Reynolds is the author of *Voting for a New South Africa* (1993) which outlined the electoral system choices for the new South African constitution. He gained his Masters degree from the University of Cape Town and is currently a doctoral candidate at the University of California, San Diego, studying the impact of electoral laws upon emerging democracies. He was born and brought up in London, U.K.

Robert Mattes holds a Ph.D. in political science from the University of Illinois, Urbana-Champaign. He is presently a Visiting Lecturer in the Department of Political Studies at the University of Cape Town and recently served as a political analyst with South Africa's Independent Electoral Commission. His general research interests centre around democratic institutions, focusing on the impact of public opinion and survey research on democratic government.

Hermann Giliomee is a Professor of Political Studies at the University of Cape Town. Among many other works he is the co-author of *From Apartheid to Nation Building* (1989) and *Negotiating South Africa's Future* (1989) [both with Lawrence Schlemmer]. He is a frequent contributor to the *Cape Times* and journals dealing with South African politics.

Tom Lodge is an Associate Professor in the Department of Political Studies at the University of the Witwatersrand, Johannesburg. He is the author of *Black Politics in South Africa since 1945* (1991) and co-author of *All, Here, and Now* (1991). Born in Manchester, U.K., he was educated in Nigeria, Malaysia, and Britain, receiving a D.Phil. from the University of York.

Georgina Hamilton graduated from the University of Toronto and has a Masters degree from the School of Oriental and African Studies, London. She is the co-author [with Gerhard Maré] of *An Appetite for Power: Buthelezi's Inkatha and South Africa* (1987). She is currently a freelance writer based in Durban.

Gerhard Maré has degrees from the Universities of Natal and Witwatersrand. He is a Senior Lecturer in the Department of Sociology and the Centre for Industrial and Labour Studies at the University of Natal. He is the author of *Brothers Born of Warrior Blood: Politics and Ethnicity in South Africa* (1991).

David Welsh is Professor of Southern African Studies at the University of Cape Town. He was educated at the University of Cape Town (where he obtained a Ph.D.) and Oxford University. He is the co-editor of *South Africa's Options: Strategies for Sharing Power* (1979) [with F. van Zyl Slabbert] and numerous chapters and articles analysing political development in South Africa.

Johann van Rooyen was educated in law and political studies at the Universities of Stellenbosch and Cape Town. He taught politics at Rhodes University in 1989 before resuming full-time research on the white right-wing in South Africa. He has lectured and written extensively on this subject, for which he also received a Ph.D. from the University of Cape Town in 1992. He is currently involved with independent research in Canada pertaining to the comparative nature of Afrikaner and Quebec nationalism. He is the author of *Hard Right: South Africa's New White Power* (1994).

Saths Cooper is Director of the Family Institute and a board member of the Institute for Multi-Party Democracy. He is a psychologist by training and was formerly President of the Azanian People's Organisation. He was an originator of the National Forum and a key analyst for the SABC during its Election '94 coverage.

Daniel Silke is a Research Assistant at the Institute for the Study of Public Policy at the University of Cape Town. He gained a Masters degree from UCT, having completed a study of the electronic media entitled 'The Broadcasting of Politics in South Africa'. He writes regularly for the Argus group of newspapers in Cape Town and Durban.

Robert Schrire is Professor of Political Studies at the University of Cape

Town, and Director of the Institute for the Study of Public Policy. He is the editor of the Critical Choices for South Africa series and *Leadership in the Apartheid State: From Malan to de Klerk* (1994). He holds a Ph.D. from the University of California.

Timothy Sisk is a programs officer at the United States Institute of Peace in Washington D.C., specialising in comparative ethnic, racial, national and religious conflict resolution. He completed his Ph.D. at George Washington University doing fieldwork as a Fulbright scholar at the University of Stellenbosch. He is the author of the book *Democratization in South Africa: The Elusive Social Contract* (1994).

Benjamin Pogrund was born in Cape Town and studied at the Universities of Cape Town and Witwatersrand. He was Deputy Editor of the *Rand Daily Mail* until the newspaper was closed in 1985, when he went to Britain. He has been a Visiting Lecturer at the Graduate School of Journalism at City University, London, and is currently in the foreign department at the *Independent* newspaper, London. He is the author of *Sobukwe and Apartheid* and *Nelson Mandela*.

Arend Lijphart is a Professor of Political Science at the University of California, San Diego, and a leading expert on consociationalism and the politics of power-sharing in divided societies. His published works include *Power Sharing in South Africa* (1985), *Democracy in Plural Societies* (1977) and he is co-editor of *Choosing an Electoral System* (1984) [with Bernard Grofman].

Illustrations

Abbreviations

ACDP	African Christian Democratic Party
ADM	African Democratic Movement
ANC	African National Congress
APLA	Azanian People's Liberation Army
AV	Alternative Vote
AVF	Afrikaner Volkfront (Afrikaner People's Front)
AVU	Afrikaner Volksunie (Afrikaner People's Union)
AWB	Afrikaner Weerstandsbeweging
AZAPO	Azanian People's Organisation
BCM	Black Consciousness Movement
CCB	Civil Co-operation Bureau
CODESA	Convention for a Democratic South Africa
COSAG	Concerned South Africans Group
COSATU	Congress of South African Trade Unions
CP	Conservative Party
DP	Democratic Party
FA	Freedom Alliance
FF	Freedom Front
FPTP	First Past the Post
GNU	Government of National Unity
HNP	Herstigte Nasionale Party
HSRC	Human Sciences Research Council
KLA	KwaZulu Legislative Assembly
KNEON	KwaZulu-Natal Electoral Observer Network
IDASA	Institute for Democracy in South Africa
IEC	Independent Electoral Commission
IFP	Inkatha Freedom Party
IMC	Independent Media Commission

MF	Minority Front
MK	UMkhonto weSizwe
MP	Member of Parliament
MPD	Institute for Multi-Party Democracy
MPF	Multi-Party Forum
NA	National Assembly
NEON	National Electoral Observer Network
NIC	Natal Indian Congress
NP	National Party
NUSAS	National Union of South African Students
OAU	Organisation of African Unity
OFS	Orange Free State
PAC	Pan Africanist Congress
PFP	Progressive Federal Party
PR	Proportional Representation
PWV	Pretoria–Witwatersrand–Vereeniging
R	Rand (South African unit of currency)
RAU	Rand Afrikaans University
RDP	Reconstruction and Development Programme (of the ANC)
SABC	South African Broadcasting Corporation
SACP	South African Communist Party
SADF	South African Defence Force
SAP	South African Police
SASO	South African Students Organisation
STV	Single Transferable Vote
SWAPO	South West African People's Organisation
TEC	Transitional Executive Council
UCT	University of Cape Town
UDF	United Democratic Front
UN	United Nations
UNISA	University of South Africa
UP	United Party
UWC	University of the Western Cape
UWUSA	United Workers Union of South Africa
Wits	University of the Witwatersrand
ZCC	Zion Christian Church

Preface

On the 27th of April 1994, a 58-year-old domestic worker named Primrose Ngabane left her place of work in Rondebosch, Cape Town, and set off to reach the sprawling township of Guguletu to cast her vote in a general election. Despite being less sure of foot after many years of hard work, she nevertheless walked the mile to the bus stop in Mowbray and then crammed in the back of a 'black taxi' with many other prospective voters for a half an hour journey to the house of her cousin. Upon reaching the house, she linked up with the older members of her extended family to walk the further mile to the makeshift polling booth which had been set up inside a local primary school the day before. After queuing along with hundreds of others, she finally made it inside the school building where an official designated by the Independent Electoral Commission handed her a multi-coloured ballot paper with the names, initials and symbols of 19 political parties along with a photograph of each party's leader. She hesitated for a moment and then placed her cross beside the name of the second-last party listed on the ballot – the National Party led by Frederik Willem de Klerk.

As Primrose was heading south in her taxi along the main road in Rondebosch, she was passed by one Jansie van der Merwe who was driving her new Golf in the other direction, headed for the Constantia polling station. Here Jansie, surrounded by hundreds of other whites, went through the same procedure as Primrose and, after a few moments of studying the ballot paper, made a large X beside the smiling face of Nelson Mandela and thus cast her vote for Mandela's party, the African National Congress.

The most remarkable, and moving, thing about both actions was not for whom Primrose and Jansie decided to vote but more the fact that they had never been allowed even the possibility of such actions before that day in April 1994. Primrose, although a woman in her late fifties, had never been allowed to vote before; Jansie (a veteran voter of three South African general elections) had never been given the opportunity for voting for a party which was not rooted in the whites–only constitutional dispensation.

Those two crosses were among the most special in the history of democratic ballots and those two crosses are what this book is really all about.

In writing, editing and producing this story of the first non-racial South African elections at breakneck speed, I owe a great debt to many people. All the contributors have, I believed, managed to craft in a very short space of time chapters which are both interesting and informative and at the same time capture the exciting, confusing, chaotic, joyful and intriguing aspects of this election campaign and its aftermath.

I am blessed to have colleagues who have lived through, and in many cases influenced, the most tumultuous times in modern South African history. Benjamin Pogrund was scuttling back and forth between townships and the offices of the *Rand Daily Mail*, the PAC and the government in the 1960s, while at the same time trying to evade government prosecution for his honest journalistic descriptions of the dehumanising conditions that were inflicted upon both white and black prisoners in the government's jails. He is also the author of, what I believe to be, the best biography ever written of a South African political leader: *Sobukwe and Apartheid*.

Hermann Giliomee was my supervising professor at the University of Cape Town and my window into the world of Afrikaner political thought. His important books have consistently searched for a peaceful settlement to the problems of South Africa while always stressing the crucial need for democratic accountability and the protection of all rights, not just majority ones. David Welsh, too, has helped to make this country a better place by arguing for universal democracy long before others were willing to seize the nettle. Through his writing, lecturing and work as a DP adviser to the negotiations, he has been able to fan the flames of liberal democratic principles in the new South Africa.

Many of us overseas rely upon the incisive interpretations of everyday South African events which are channelled through the world media from people such as Robert Schrire, Tom Lodge, Saths Cooper and Gerhard Maré. It is hard to explain the relief that a political scientist in America feels when, listening to the midnight BBC world service news or reading the morning newspaper, one of these leading scholars appears and explains the intricacies of the most recent South African political event.

I am also indebted to those writers whom I have only come to know and form friendships with in the course of this book project. Georgina Hamilton and Bob Mattes proved to be stars in my eyes when they agreed to contribute to *Election '94* at the very shortest of notice, and Daniel Silke offered those fascinating insights into the voting process which can only come from someone so deeply involved in election as part of a party organisation. Bob Mattes also supplied a very welcome sounding board throughout the process, especially when we tried to work out the results by analysing the turnout, even before the votes had begun to be counted. He is quite clearly emerging as one of the leading experts on electoral politics in Southern Africa and I greatly look forward to working with him in the future.

I am happy to be writing alongside two political scientists, and friends, who, like me, are in the early stages of their academic careers and keen students of the new South Africa. Tim Sisk is my kindred spirit in the United States and (although we live on different sides of the continent) is always available to discuss the latest wrinkle. Johann van Rooyen has done what few have even attempted before, and produced a book on the white Right in South Africa which critically analyses their behaviour while describing the all-important motivations of the Afrikaner which underpin their attitudes and strategies. I am sure his book *Hard Right* will become one of the definitive works in the field.

Finally, I must pay tribute to my supervising professor, colleague and friend at the University of California, San Diego, Arend Lijphart. No one has made a larger contribution to the advancement of comparative political science and the understanding of divided societies than this one man. Apart from all the best-selling textbooks he has written, constitutions he has influenced and students he has trained, the best tribute to Arend is that his door is always open regardless of whether the caller is a lowly undergraduate or visiting cabinet minister. I fundamentally believe that the adoption of aspects of his democratic consociationalism, or power-sharing, in South Africa has set the foundations for a prosperous and far more stable future South Africa.

My research in South Africa in 1994 was supported by a grant from the American National Sciences Foundation (SBR-9321864) which was, in conjunction with Arend Lijphart, obtained by Bernie Grofman of the University of California, Irvine. No student could wish for a more supportive benefactor than Professor Grofman or a more well-respected authority on minority voting rights and the politics of implementing stable democracy. It is to the great benefit of the fragile states in Southern Africa that he is turning his thoughts to ways to help mitigate the problems that these embryonic democracies will undoubtedly face.

Lastly, I must thank all the people who have helped, advised and befriended me during my frequent stays in South Africa. Once again Boone and Nan Wilson have been a great support, as have the Van Aswegens and my unofficial translator (and official friend) Annie Leatt. Russell Martin, Jeremy Boraine, Ingrid Küpper and Bridget Impey of David Philip Publishers have worked over and above the call of duty to produce and distribute this book in such a short time, and I must thank Matthew Kentridge and Wilmot James who helped along the way. I would probably never have even begun my journey through South African politics had it not been for Tony Lewis, Margie Marshall, Hillary Marshall and Francis Wilson back in Boston in 1990, and I salute their part in the history of this country which ultimately led up to the first democratic elections. Finally, Shirlane Douglas managed to show me the vote and the workings of the Independent Electoral Commission while at the same time running an exemplary polling operation in the heart of Cape Town. The success of the election in this area was a fitting tribute to her efficiency, patience and belief in South African democracy.

My wife Jennifer has proved to be, as always, my ever-present support mechanism despite being half the world away. I thank the innovators of computerised e-mail for keeping us both sane!

In the end the production of this book was much like the running of the election itself, with myself playing the part of Judge Kriegler and the IEC, the contributors fulfilling the role of keen voters and the publishers prodding us sympathetically along in the manner of international observers. There ensued a combination of great excitement, chaos, administrative pitfalls, satisfying successes and a pleasing lack of physical violence. Some of the contributors came on board very late (no fault of theirs). For others the pressure of time and logistical problems meant that we had to give them an extra day of writing. Interestingly, a number of the authors split their chapters between two different parties while the majority plumped for one subject only. It took us a number of days to reconcile what the contributors had sent us, with what we sent out to them, but in the end we were able to compile a full book which related quite closely to what we had imagined. At the end of they day I think we actually got the book out on the shelves quicker than the IEC gave us the results, but I do not wish to cast aspersions.

Sadly, through some as yet unexplained disappearance, we lost 57 million books somewhere in the greater Southern African area. I am confident that they will turn up, if not at this election, possibly at the next one in five years' time. However, despite all these problems, I can confirm this book is 'substantially' perfect and a fair reflection of the 1994 South African elections.

In a more serious vain: The immediate future for South Africa, although characterised by great optimism, is strewn with pitfalls, and no one can confidently predict the successes of the first parliament or government of national unity. But South Africa has taken a huge step in the right direction and few can deny that this beloved land is a better country as a result of all the people having had their say on 26, 27 and 28 April 1994.

Andrew Reynolds
Rondebosch, May 1994

Note to Readers

The terminology used to describe South Africa, her people, and her diverse cultures has always been fraught with difficulties, and one would hope that in the new South Africa such debates about language will become less prevalent; but I am not overly confident about this happening. However, when talking about South Africa one often needs to differentiate in order to describe distinct and equally powerful cultural identities and traditions. I myself use the terms 'white South Africans' to describe, English, Afrikaners and others of European descent; 'black South Africans' to describe indigenous peoples such as the Xhosa and Zulu, Venda and Sotho; 'Indian South Africans' to describe those of Indian descent; and 'coloured South Africans' to refer to that community which is collectively of Khoi or San or mixed race descent. Other contributors may use the term 'Africans' to describe black South Africans; and while I do not wish to criticise anyone else's language use, to me an African can be black, can be brown, can be white, can be pale or dark. If the events of April 1994 taught us anything, it was that 'Africanness' comes from the content of the heart and not the colour of the skin.

1

The Road to Democracy: From 2 February 1990 to 27 April 1994

ROBERT MATTES

To understand South Africa's first universal franchise election and its preceding campaign, we must begin not in 1994 or even 1993, but in February 1990. This is not because of the usual need for introductory chapters to look at the general background or context of the event in question – a sort of 'how did we get here from there?' story. Rather, we need to begin in 1990 because how South Africa got to 'here' from 'there' has deeply affected what the campaign and elections of 1994 looked like. In other words, how the elections were conducted and contested cannot be understood without reference to the negotiations that led to those elections.

In turn, the ever-looming spectre of the first elections profoundly shaped those constitutional negotiations by casting a long, retrospective shadow over the entire transition process. As the philosopher John Rawls has pointed out, negotiations would produce the fairest result if they could be conducted behind a 'veil of ignorance' about how the various parties might benefit from their outcome. All parties would then attempt to protect the position of the least well-off, since it could well be any of them.[1] However, if they could consider how the outcome might affect their fortunes, negotiators would probably choose the procedures best suited to their own particular interests. And, if they were not equally strong at the outset, the strongest parties would be able to negotiate outcomes most favourable to themselves.

In retrospect, Rawls provides an accurate description of the South African transition to democracy. The political parties' positions (on matters ranging from the timing of the elections and the rules under which they would be conducted, to the nature of the government to be elected) were linked, among other things, to estimates of how much support they could expect, when and where that support might arise, and under what conditions such support would be forthcoming. Consequently, the parties seen to have the most political strength in terms of popular support as well as international legitimacy, bureaucratic muscle and military might (the NP and the ANC) were able to secure elections and a constitutional framework which were in their favour and to the disadvantage of parties deemed to be weaker and smaller.

KEY FEATURES OF THE CAMPAIGN AND ELECTION

A Liberal Democratic Constitutional Framework

The first important thing to note about South Africa's 1994 elections, so obvious that it will probably be missed, is that they put into power a government which would rule within a largely liberal democratic constitutional framework. This was not always a hard and fast certainty. Certainly, before the ANC's publication of its constitutional guidelines in 1988, there were strong strains in that organisation that would eschew the negotiations route and pursue total liberation, or a revolutionary transfer of power to the masses, most likely in the form of a 'one-party democracy'. Why did the African National Congress (ANC), upon return from exile in 1990, choose the electoral uncertainty of a multi-party democracy, even as its fellow liberation organisations, AZAPO and the PAC, remained committed to revolutionary liberation?

Undoubtedly, the loss of Soviet military support and the collapse of the one-party model throughout Eastern Europe exercised major influences on ANC thinking. Equally important, however, was the ANC's awareness that the electoral path, in fact, did not entail all that much uncertainty. As Donald Horowitz has pointed out, the positions of these liberation movements were all consistent with what was known at the time about their relative shares of popular support: all available evidence indicated that the ANC would be by far the biggest of the three, as well as the largest party in the country. Horowitz called this a classical coincidence of interest and behaviour: the extraparliamentary organisation with the most support chose a strategy of negotiation; the organisations that found themselves weak opposed negotiation, the result of which ironically entrenched their weakness.[2]

More important, this election did not elect members for ethnically defined legislatures nor were there any 'group rights' entrenched in the interim constitution. This was because, in 1990, the National Party (NP) abandoned its long embrace of ethnically defined constitutionalism as it, for the first time, began to factor the possibility of significant non-white electoral support into its thinking.

This is why President F. W. de Klerk's dramatic speech of 2 February

1990 must be seen as the first campaign 'event' of the 1994 election. Unbanning the liberation movements, releasing their key leaders from prison or allowing them to return from exile, lifting restrictions on domestic organisations, and formally beginning a process leading toward negotiations, did not signal the NP's surrender of power to the liberation movement. Rather, it signalled the arrival of a much more confident and important player in the transition process. For in ensuing months, surveys indicated that De Klerk, and to a lesser extent the NP, had attained an astonishing degree of popularity among black South Africans.[3] For the first time, the NP saw the possibility of electoral success, organisational survival, and even political influence within a new dispensation. Rather than relying on 'group rights,' the NP could survive and prosper if it were assured of gaining a certain proportion of seats in the legislature. But obtaining these seats to defend the Bill of Rights and gaining a significant share of cabinet seats, or taking advantage of any devolution of power by controlling some non-racial regional and local governments, would clearly require the support of non-white voters.[4]

Thus, it was the very possibility of such alliances and increased black support that reinforced the NP's belief that the transition offered the prospect of continued influence even in a qualified majority-rule system.[5] This enabled the NP to make the fundamentally important shift in constitutional thinking away from a design featuring 'group' protection to one utilising proportional representation, federalism, bicameralism and, most important, super-majority thresholds to check majorities and safeguard minorities.[6] As Minister for Constitutional Development, Gerrit Viljoen, proclaimed in November 1990, 'I now have a complete new vision of the future ... it is possible for us to be part of the majority instead of only thinking of ourselves as a minority which needs special protection.'[7]

Why 1994?

A second important, but also overlooked, element of these elections was that they were held only in 1994, a full four years after De Klerk's watershed speech. South Africa's transition to democracy differed from the democratisation wave of the 1980s in many ways, chief among which was its timing. The search for electoral advantage appears to be an important reason why.

In their classic work on transitions to democracy, Phillipe Schmitter and Guillermo O'Donnell demonstrated a general pattern whereby high levels of uncertainty about the actual support of the various parties actually *hastened* the movement toward elections. This was because reformist regimes often moved quickly toward elections in order to channel popular pressures, and in the hope of achieving victory over a divided and unorganised opposition. However, as Schmitter and O'Donnell pointed out, the optimism of reformist regimes was usually illusory, as transitions are 'littered with examples of authoritarian soft-liners who overestimated their popular support'.[8]

For its part, the reformist South African regime moved towards elections much more slowly than the general model would suggest. The NP preferred elections later rather than sooner, while it was the ANC who preferred them sooner rather than later. One key reason behind the government's hesitance appears to be its regular access to detailed intelligence about public opinion from state-supported survey organisations, such as the Human Sciences Research Council, and through the South African Communications Service. While the NP did come to entertain hopes of doing surprisingly well, this data gave the NP much more certainty about its electoral prospects and dampened any early illusions they might have had about winning a general election over a divided and disorganised opposition liberation front. This prevented it from taking that blind leap in the dark that has characterised reforming regimes in so many other transitions.

The government also appears to have concluded, on the basis of polling data, that it was in its interest to prolong the transition process as long as possible in the hope of reducing popular support for the ANC through attrition. Surveys in the early 1990s indicated that the ANC's electoral prospects were much weaker than might have been realised in a world without polls. Thus, as formal constitutional talks got under way at the Convention for a Democratic South Africa (CODESA) in early 1992, an NP strategist confident about his party's ability to gain black support suggested that the longer the transition, the greater the NP's advantage. He pointed out that the ANC had not returned from exile to take power like other revolutionary movements, and argued that a longer interregnum would only increase disillusion (though he also conceded that this strategy ran the risk of greater instability).[9]

This appears to be one reason that the NP, in no hurry to reach agreement by the planned second plenary session of CODESA in May, stuck to extremely tough bargaining positions that ultimately derailed the talks. The NP needed time to increase its electoral support (especially its black support), build alliances, and stoke black disillusionment with the ANC.[10] In fact, several CODESA participants claimed that the NP counselled its allies prior to the May deadlock to stall the proceedings because the government needed six more months to run an election campaign in black areas, as well as to retain control of the SABC during this critical period.[11] Whether or not the NP's beliefs were accurate, it was true that by the time of the breakdown, ANC strategists conceded that their estimated support had been revised to around 50 per cent, significantly down from the two-thirds they believed they could have easily won in 1990.[12]

Yet while the ANC wanted elections sooner, it did not want them before they were organisationally ready to run a campaign.[13] And while the NP preferred elections later, it was prepared to have them sooner if held on its terms. For instance, January 1992 proposals indicated that the NP was ready to call for elections as long as they would elect an interim government of national unity that would double as a constitution-making body, and – here was the catch – would last for a decade or more while the constitution was negotiated.[14] In April, De Klerk was prepared to move rapidly to a vote if it were for a collective interim executive, consisting of the three to five top vote-getters, and if it were held *ahead* of elections for the interim legislature (a suggestion which was consistent with polls at the time that revealed that the President was far more popular among blacks than his party).[15]

Thus, the timing of the election was initially a function of jockeying between the parties' electoral interests. However, as the talks wore on, setting the election date came to be seen by both the ANC and NP as important to the very survival of the transition process. In fact, the date came to be seen by the ANC, and gradually the NP, as so important that it had to be set even before the rest of negotiations were finished.

In April 1993 the government proposed separating the fruitless talks about a Transitional Executive Council (which would administer the country until the elections for an interim government) from negotiations about the nature of that interim government, arguing that the details of elected bodies had to be agreed before an election date could be set. However, the ANC feared that the government wanted to draw it into co-operation on the TEC while negotiations for an election date dragged on, possibly turning the TEC into a *de facto* interim government and avoiding elections entirely.[16] Thus, by the end of the month, the ANC demanded that an election date be announced before any other issues were settled. But a senior government official pointed out that agreeing 'to an election date would be like signing our own death warrant. The ANC and its allies could stall on the issues until after the election and then the new government could do just as it liked.'[17]

Yet by June, the government had agreed to set a date (27 April 1994). This was because they, like the ANC, had now become convinced that their constituency support base was dangerously slipping away.[18] Government officials came to believe that the longer the talks dragged on, the more support they would lose to the CP and the Inkatha

Freedom Party (IFP), and there would be a corresponding loss in legitimacy and increase in violence as well. As one cabinet minister admitted, 'The worst scenario is if the major parties reach agreement but lose control over their own constituencies.'[19] In the final analysis, if initial NP policy had been to delay and let the ANC twist in the wind, it seems to have backfired, as violence wrecked consumer and investor confidence, and De Klerk's poll ratings plummeted.[20]

The Ground Rules

Another outstanding feature of this election was that, unlike previous white elections which were fought along the lines of the Anglo-American constituency-based plurality system, this one was conducted under proportional representation (PR). More specifically, parties ran lists of candidates (200 national, and 200 from the nine regions for the National Assembly, as well as nine separate provincial lists for each provincial legislature). Thus voters were only able to select a party, not specific candidates. Moreover, voters could not differentiate between their choice for the regional and national lists for the National Assembly, nor (until late in the campaign) could they differentiate between those choices and their choice for the provincial list (the so-called single – as opposed to double – ballot).

Interestingly, the ANC's initial preference, when it returned from exile, was the plurality system. ANC constitutional expert Kader Asmal then equated PR (the long-standing choice of the Democratic Party and more recent preference of the NP) with 'the ineluctable need of the racial oligarchy to maintain its power'. He concluded, quite erroneously, that PR had 'a built-in mechanism to ensure that no party obtains over 50 per cent of the seats; they inevitably give rise to coalitions through the over-representation of minority interests.'[21] Significantly, a review of available surveys from 1981 until July 1990 indicated that the ANC would win plurality, but not majority, support. This, according to Horowitz, was 'perfectly consistent' with its choice of the Anglo-American model because 'With widespread electoral support and a fair number of three- or four-way contests, a party like the ANC could secure a very substantial majority of seats on a mere plurality of votes.'[22]

The ANC did shift to PR in October 1990 after a meeting with party officials and constitutional scholars, where Asmal read a paper now advocating PR with two separate lists (200 national, 200 regional).[23] One obvious reason for the shift was that drawing small, non-racial constituencies in a country whose demographics had been so warped by the Group Areas Act would have been extremely difficult, if not impossible. Another reason may have been the ANC's willingness to be fair towards minority parties.[24] But if the ANC had made this shift while it still believed that it was only a plurality (and not a majority) party, that would have been a true act of compromise and sacrifice in the interests of fairness. However, this shift was certainly helped along by the knowledge that the ANC would not be hurt politically by doing so. Newer poll reports in 1990 and 1991 had begun to show majority support for the ANC.[25] Thus, the ANC's shift was greased by the knowledge that any additional representation gained by minority parties with PR (over and above what they might have got with plurality) would be harmless so long as the ANC maintained disciplined control over 51 per cent of the legislative seats in parliament.

More important, even though the major parties did come to agree on some form of PR, the first South African election did not necessarily have to be based on that particular type of PR (which was the type advocated by the ANC). Negotiators might have chosen a form of PR that encouraged cross-racial appeals so that the election did not end up resembling an ethnic census.[26] Negotiators might have chosen forms of PR that built in strong constituency links to promote individual accountability and voter control over party nominations.[27] They might have opted for a series of purely regional PR elections which would have focused voter attention on party candidates and regional issues (whereas a national list forces attention on the leaders and 'presidentialises' the contest).[28] These options were not totally ignored. In fact, negotiators at a technical subcommittee of the multi-party talks charged with reporting on an appropriate electoral system called in a wide range of experts and focused a great deal of debate on systems which would have combined PR with smaller constituencies and some form of candidate choice. But when debate shifted to the working-group level, ANC representative Frene Ginwala weighed in and in effect unilaterally imposed the ANC plan while the NP stood by.

Why did the ANC place so much emphasis on the regional/national list form of PR, and why did the NP acquiesce? One reason is that this form of PR (especially in conjunction with the single ballot), probably the simplest voting system possible, benefited ANC mobilisation of its support base because citizens were able to vote wherever they were, and vote for well-known symbols and pictures of national leaders from the liberation struggle (rather than go through complicated registration procedures to establish constituency residence, and then search multiple ballots for the names of not-so-well-known candidates).[29] The list system also assisted both parties by providing central party control over the nomination of candidates, and thus helped ensure their loyalty in parliament. It also would enable both parties to 'parachute' key officials, who stood little chance of being elected in any specific constituency, into competitive spots on the party list – this especially aided the ANC, whose senior white and Indian SACP members would have no hope of being elected in largely white or Indian districts and would have encountered stiff black nationalist PAC campaigns in largely black districts.[30] Thus, as R. W. Johnson argued, this system had great appeal to centralising party elites both in the ANC–SACP alliance and in the NP.[31] More important, it does not appear that the NP, with the exception of Deputy Minister of Constitutional Affairs, Tertius Delport, ever devoted much thought to the issue of a voting system (beyond knowing that proportional representation was good for minorities). One senior cabinet minister even derisively referred to such considerations as *'sommetjies maak'* (making sums).[32]

In the end, the ANC was able to gain an electoral system that most favoured itself and least favoured the smallest parties. It obtained virtually the simplest type of PR voting system and enabled the party to focus symbolic attention on Mandela, the struggle and racial disparity. It obtained (initially) a single ballot, which limited opportunities to build strong regional sources of opposition to the national government. And it also obtained a clause in the interim constitution that (by giving party leaders the ability to throw any MP out of parliament who 'ceased' to be a member of that party) would prevent internal splits and virtually freeze the ANC's initial successes until the next election.[33]

Constituent Assembly, Interim Government and Power-sharing

The 1994 election selected a legislature, but it also simultaneously created a body which (when sitting with the Senate) would write South Africa's final constitution. And besides an interim legislature elected by proportional representation, it also generated an interim proportional cabinet (De Klerk's much-touted 'power-sharing').

As stated earlier, the ANC was fairly sure in 1990 and 1991 that it would be the largest, if not majority, party in the country. It is no coincidence, then, that it steadfastly demanded that the new constitution be written by a popularly elected assembly. On the other hand, it made perfect sense that the NP initially desired that an 'all-party conference' (where all parties with identifiable support would have an equal voice) would either write the constitution or produce detailed guidelines which would severely constrain any body writing it.

Because it was adamant that the government would not preside over the elections, and because it wanted to send the government into retirement as quickly as possible, the ANC also wanted an unelected but sovereign interim government of national unity, which would rule until the first elections, and possibly during the writing of the constitution.[34] The NP government generally criticised this approach on the grounds that it would create a vacuum of constitutional authority. In contrast, it wanted 'interim arrangements' which would co-opt the ANC and other parties at legislative and executive levels, yet leave itself in power for as long as possible.[35]

The main ANC goal in the final draft of the interim consitution was to secure majority rule through a parliamentary system where the majority party in the legislature would form 'the government' or executive. In contrast, NP proposals generally envisaged at least a plural executive comprising all parties in proportion to their strength in the legislature (with some agreed threshold for inclusion) and, at most, a small collegial presidency consisting of the three to five top vote-getters. Either form would operate along consensual lines with regard to policy-making.

The competition among these few goals was the main feature of the negotiations process. The most significant proposal, put forward by the NP at the start of constitutional talks in early 1992, combined the ANC's desire for an elected constitution-making body and an interim authority, with its own desire for a constitutional transition and, most important, its determination that ANC popular support would not allow it to dominate the process. It called for CODESA to write an interim constitution that would bind any transitional authorities. That constitution would provide an elected interim government which would also draft the final constitution, would last for five to ten years, and would provide for power-sharing (a rotating, three-person presidency from the three largest parties with an enforced coalition cabinet, and a bicameral parliament with the regions represented equally in the upper house). While the ANC initially rejected it, the basic framework of an elected constitutional body doubling as an interim government (with possible power-sharing features) continually recurred as the basis for compromise over the next few years.

CODESA 2. The NP proposal certainly provided the basis for initial negotiations at CODESA. And as CODESA's working groups rushed so as to be able to report back to the next planned plenary session in May (CODESA 2), general agreement was reached that the interim constitution, to be drafted by CODESA, would provide for a National Assembly which would draft the final constitution, a Senate, and a multi-party cabinet.

However, two important points of difference remained unresolved. First of all, while the ANC had argued that 66.7 per cent approval in the Constitutional Assembly would be sufficient for all decisions, it appeared ready to compromise at 70 per cent and even 75 per cent for matters affecting the Bill of Rights. The government, however, demanded that constitutional clauses relating to regionalism also require 75 per cent. The second point of difference concerned the Senate, which the government wanted to be co-equal to the Assembly in the constitutional process.

However, with top government negotiator Gerrit Viljoen away on sick leave, a relatively inexperienced junior minister was thrust into the centre of negotiations. As the CODESA 2 deadline approached, the government dropped its insistence on retaining the role of the Senate, but only if *all* other thresholds relating to the constitution were raised to 75 per cent. At that point, the ANC pulled back to re-evaluate and only then realised that, through the combination of the absence of time limits or deadlock-breaking mechanisms with extremely high threshold levels, it had come close to agreeing to what could have been an indefinite period of 'interim' government. Within a few days, the ANC withdrew all its compromise positions, retreating to 66.7 per cent and rejecting any role for the Senate. It also now demanded rigid time-frames and a deadlock-breaking mechanism, and called for the interim constitution to be limited to preparing for elections.[36] By mid-June, following the massacre at Boipatong township of ANC-supporting citizens, negotiations were formally over.

Why was so much at stake over a few percentage points? One main reason appears to have been that while current estimates of popular support indicated that the ANC might not necessarily be a majority party,[37] they also showed that the NP could not yet count on controlling a one-third veto by itself. Senior government and NP sources indicated that they had worked on a 30 per cent estimate during CODESA 2.[38] NP demands appear to have come on the heels of the HSRC's latest poll results, which gave the ANC only 40–45 per cent of the vote, but also only gave the NP approximately 20 per cent.[39] 'That', commented the *Cape Times*, 'is why the percentages are so finely calculated: they rest on each side's perception of what vote it can be sure of mustering during the period of interim government.'[40]

Mass Action. Thwarted in the talks, and facing mounting disgruntlement among its ranks, the ANC retreated. The 17 June massacre at Boipatong was the final straw, and the ANC formally suspended negotiations. Now came the opportunity for the ANC to unload the heavy artillery: its popular power. It adopted a strategy that Cyril Ramaphosa called 'rolling mass action', consisting of specifically targeted strikes, boycotts, stayaways and occupations, all of which were designed to induce government concessions at the negotiating table.

Mass action was to do this, first of all, by demonstrating substantial evidence of mass support for the ANC. If the government was becoming more confident as a result of polls showing a decline in ANC support, the ANC could show the government that it did indeed control effective popular support.[41] Secondly, it would also induce concessions by threatening to wreck the economy and driving a wedge between business and government. Yet mass action was also a way for the ANC to repair its links with its branches and grassroots, as well as with the allied labour union COSATU, from whom it had run well ahead in the rapid pace of the negotiations.[42]

As mass action wore on, the ANC-SACP-COSATU alliance presented the government with fourteen demands. Key among these were an interim government and rapid movement to a constitutional assembly. But as stayaways and work stoppages culminated in August, there was no sign of government movement. In August, Mandela narrowed the list to three 'core' demands, calling only for the government to take steps to curb the violence, and to commit itself to an interim government of national unity as well as to a sovereign, elected constituent assembly.

In early September, alliance plans to take the struggle to the 'puppets of apartheid' backfired when ANC demonstrators attempting to march into Bisho, the capital of the nominal Republic of Ciskei, were gunned down by homeland troops. Senior ANC leaders who had remained on the sideline throughout the middle of the year, while the militants ran their course, re-emerged to save the transition from disaster. Following a meeting between the Finance Minister, Derek Keys, and ANC finance director, Trevor Manuel, at which Keys painted an extremely grim picture of the state of the economy, Mandela said the ANC was eager to re-start negotiations to save the country from disaster. He whittled down his core demands even further, stating that the government only need make good on previous promises about hostels, political prisoners and dangerous weapons so that he could show some results to those frustrated with negotiations.[43]

Thus, rather than forcing the government to change its positions, it appears that the ANC returned to talks because it had nowhere else to go.[44] While the government did move away from its hardline positions of CODESA 2, it had already begun to do so *before* mass action began, in June. In fact, by early July government positions almost mirrored those taken earlier at CODESA 2 by the ANC.[45]

The Record of Understanding and the Strategic Perspective. By early

September, resumed bilateral negotiations between the new government negotiator, Roelf Meyer, and Cyril Ramaphosa had reached agreement in principle on an elected Constitutional Assembly with specified time-frames and deadlock-breaking mechanisms. This was codified in a Record of Understanding, which also met all three of Mandela's final demands on security measures. Whether this constituted an ANC victory is doubtful, however. As Steven Friedman pointed out, the three security concessions were basically meaningless and the procedural concessions were sufficiently vague to warrant continued disagreement for the next several months.[46]

Shortly thereafter, the ANC indicated that it was ready to implement a set of ideas recently floated by senior negotiator and former SACP leader, Joe Slovo. Slovo, an ANC-SACP stalwart, was apparently chosen to do so because these ideas represented what was perhaps the biggest ANC concession of the entire transition – the concession to a pro-portional power-sharing cabinet, something Mandela had explicitly ruled out just one year earlier. In fact, since Mandela had returned from prison, one of his most consistent themes had been a call for majority rule where 'The party that commands the majority runs the country', or what he called 'normal democracy as the world knows it.'[47]

Slovo argued that there could be no total victory for either side in the negotiations. Instead, the liberation movement's objectives depended on the relative 'balance of forces' at each stage of the struggle. Arguing that while this balance was not static, as had been demonstrated by the success of mass action, the liberation movement could not expect to funda-mentally affect the balance of power between itself and the government in the near future (especially in view of state control of the SADF, SAP and the civil service). Thus, he urged that the movement's immediate objectives should focus on establishing a democratic constitution-making process, and ending the NP monopoly on power, as soon as possible.[48] In order to get such agreement, Slovo argued that this might require entrenched power-sharing for a fixed time period, guaranteeing regional government powers, granting amnesty for certain political crimes, and guaranteeing the contracts of civil servants.

What was called the 'strategic perspective' was finally adopted by the ANC's National Executive on 18 November, though not without open division in the ranks. In an open letter, ANC information director, Pallo Jordan, argued that the ANC and the government had entered negoti-ations with such 'diametrically opposed immediate and long-term objectives' that 'one or other party to the dispute must go under'. 'Negotiations in such a situation' were 'aimed at liquidation of one of the antagonists as a factor in politics.'[49] In response, Slovo accused Jordan of fighting struggles in his head rather than on the ground, and criticised the 'triumphalists' who wanted to drag matters out until the government capitulated.[50] However, a key question was whether the ANC could afford politically to wait until it was able to 'liquidate' its negotiating partner. This was because, according to some polls, the ANC had suffered a crucial decline in popular support throughout mid-1992. It was, by then, clearly not a majority party, either by itself or possibly even when joined together with alliance partners.

While this was never publicly expressed in the debate, it is likely that public support was an important factor shaping the ANC's perception of the relative 'balance of forces'. Those favouring power-sharing could claim that the longer the ANC held out for complete triumph and majority rule, the greater the chance that their popular support might continue to erode and, once in government, they would not have a governing majority. Therefore, better to get an agreement and as much power as possible now, rather than wait and probably settle for less political power later on. Better to give the NP a power-sharing arrangement with sunset agreements than settle for a parliamentary coalition with the NP as a legitimate partner.

The result was the February 1993 deal between the ANC and NP on multi-party rule by June of that year, and elections by early 1994. These would select an interim parliament comprising all parties with 3 per cent of the vote. Parliament would in turn elect a president, who would choose a proportional cabinet (from all parties with 5-10 per cent) to rule for five years under an interim constitution.[51] The assembly would also write the final constitution operating on a two-thirds rule, but it would be limited by principles agreed to at the newly created Multi-Party Negotiating Forum. However, as a result of different dynamics brought on by the emergence and re-emergence of political parties to the Right, this basic agreement was to change.

Thunder on the Right

Inkatha. One thing not seen in the 1994 campaign was the long-anticipated electoral alliance between the NP and the IFP. Yet was this alliance as 'natural' as it originally seemed? Inkatha has always tried to portray itself as one of the 'big three' political forces in the country. Since the beginning of negotiations, however, the IFP has had great difficulty maintaining this image, ever since initial 1990 and 1991 surveys purported to show the IFP with only about 1 or 2 percent of support nationally. Such polls have both dented the IFP's image as a national political force, and limited its perceived value to the NP as a possible alliance partner.

When initial 'talks about talks' began, in fact, the government and ANC quickly moved to bilateral arrangements excluding the IFP. And while pre-CODESA talks accorded the IFP 'big three' status, the table at CODESA was clearly two- rather than three-sided. As Friedman notes, the ANC had no interest in making the IFP a main player, and the NP wanted to avoid alliance formations at the time (CODESA insiders reported that the NP was influenced by polls suggesting that it could win more black votes than the IFP). In key working groups, NP and ANC negotiators often left the room together to thrash out disagreements. In other groups, the IFP maintained that their proposals were simply not taken seriously.[52]

There was an increase in NP–IFP co-operation in April 1992: the government supported the inclusion of the Zulu king at CODESA and began taking more positions in common with the IFP. One reason was that Gerrit Viljoen had withdrawn from the talks and was replaced by someone more sympathetic to the IFP; another reason was evolving similarities on issues like federalism and the constitutional assembly.[53] A third likely reason was that recent HSRC surveys, using more comprehensive sampling methods to canvass rural KwaZulu, had begun to uncover significant increases in IFP support.

As we saw earlier, the NP had always attached great importance to its ability to attract significant black support. And, as we have seen, early optimism in this regard limited the value to the NP of an alliance with the IFP. However, NP success in the black community never materialised, and it gradually lost most of the initial support it had. Yet, by late 1992, deteriorating IFP relations with the negotiations process meant that the NP faced a stark choice between securing a quick agreement with the ANC, and building an electoral alliance with Inkatha, at the same time delaying an alliance with the ANC in order to dissipate its support levels. Subsequent conflict over this choice nearly split the cabinet.

On one hand, a younger faction (led by government negotiators Meyer, Leon Wessels and Dawie de Villiers) was very sceptical, on the basis of opinion polls, of the feasibility of such an alliance. Instead, they favoured obtaining the earliest possible agreement on power-sharing with the ANC in order to salvage whatever NP influence they could. On the other hand, a group of 'old guard' ministers, led by Foreign Minister Pik Botha (and including Tertius Delport, Hernus Kriel, Kobie Coetsee and George Bartlett), clung to the hope of forming a winning alliance with the IFP and other homeland parties.[54] Such a strategy, however, implied a much slower transition in order to dissipate ANC support and shore up NP support by restoring law and order.

However, the Meyer faction was able to force a policy decision to ditch the IFP as a serious negotiating partner in favour of concentrated bilateral relations with the ANC. Senior NP and government members who had previously seen the IFP as an important partner began to dismiss it as a serious political force.[55] Yet open hostility broke out in the cabinet, as well as in the party caucus, as the older faction objected to the September Record of Understanding and the government's apparent abandonment of Inkatha, which had now pulled out of negotiations. But Meyer privately argued that the government had no faith in an alliance with Buthelezi. The conflict became so intense that, by early 1993, key ministers and negotiators Meyer and Delport were hardly on speaking terms.[56]

In December 1992, Meyer publicly admitted that IFP–NP relations were worse than those between the NP and ANC, and warned that if the IFP or others chose not 'to be part of the solution', the government would press ahead without them.[57] In February 1993, the NP finally declared that it would 'follow its own clear path' in the election.[58]

Yet the hand of the conservative cabinet group was strengthened in March as polls began to indicate that the NP was losing significant numbers of white voters to Inkatha. Along with the recent defection of MP Jurie Mentz to the IFP, this set off a wave of panic within the party. Some officials even feared that it meant the possible loss of the entire party in Natal.[59] Three months later, Johan Scheepers, a Deputy Minister, resigned, in part because he believed that the NP was unable to attract sufficient black support. And soon after the setting of the 27 April election date, the press was rife with reports of 'panic' throughout the caucus among members who now were conceding that the NP had no hope of penetrating black areas.[60]

In June a new Research Surveys poll indicated more massive haemorrhaging to the Right from the party's white support base. When this was discussed in cabinet, NP 'hawks' looked desperately for anything which might turn the situation around. The Minister of Law and Order, Hernus Kriel, tried one solution and unilaterally ordered a series of arrests of key PAC officials supposedly implicated in recent attacks by its armed wing, APLA, on white farmers.[61] The raids were a public relations disaster: none of the charges stuck and Kriel was dressed down by the MPF on national television. Yet such was the state of party morale that Kriel's actions actually received enthusiatic acclaim from NP back-benchers in ensuing caucus meetings and parliamentary debates.

In late July, however, as a result of defections of party officials and white voters to the IFP, pressure from the Natal wing of the NP caucus, and an upsurge in ANC–IFP violence on the Reef and in Natal which demonstrated IFP muscle and ability to disrupt elections, the government actually launched a major effort to woo Inkatha back into the process. The conservative cabinet faction persuaded De Klerk to take Inkatha seriously again. The President began to declare repeatedly that the IFP could not be left out of the process.[62] This lasted for only a short time, however. While early August 1993 saw a wave of rhetoric from De Klerk and the NP about possibly postponing elections, De Klerk once again decided, in September, to press ahead with the agreed-upon timetable.[63] Whereas NP strategists, in early 1993, had been predicting gaining around 25 per cent of the vote while simultaneously holding the ANC under 50 per cent, by September polls showed the NP diving to near 10 per cent and the ANC well over 60 per cent. The party began to grow increasingly apprehensive and uncertain.[64]

Strange Bedfellows

Yet while the NP differed about what to do with the IFP, the IFP had moved in very different directions. After the 1992 Record of Understanding, it withdrew from all talks with the government, and then turned towards the Right and formed a conservative negotiating bloc with the governments of Ciskei and Bophuthatswana, the CP and the Afrikaner Volksunie, called the Concerned South Africans Group (COSAG). While this group did not constitute much of a threat to NP support beyond what the IFP already offered, it did plant the seeds for future troubles. These seeds sprouted in October 1993 when COSAG combined with the Afrikaner Volksfront under General Constand Viljoen to form the Freedom Alliance (FA), a group of black and white political parties united solely by their opposition to the constitutional process.

Within a month, the media carried several polls demonstrating growing strength for the FA, even suggesting it might overtake the NP in support.[65] This sent shivers through the government. Mandela mischievously speculated about appointing Buthelezi or Ferdi Hartzenberg as Deputy President, possibly to the exclusion of De Klerk, and threatening to shut the NP out of the cabinet if it failed to get 5 per cent.[66] The situation appeared so serious that, in a remarkable plea, ANC MP Jan van Eck called for the NP to play its role as a credible anti-ANC party in order to staunch the flow of white supporters to the Right.[67]

When Hartzenberg proclaimed in parliament that the FA was now the second-largest political grouping in the country, many alliance members, sensing the opportunity, urged the alliance to rethink its boycott. Thus, the FA entered last-minute negotiations in an attempt to maximise its chances by obtaining the double ballot, as well as to entrench further regional powers. These apparently endless talks drove on throughout December 1993 and extended into the 1994 campaign.

One reason for this deadlock may have been the realisation by many in the NP that attempts to bring the FA back into the process could be self-defeating. The dilemma was that a boycott would assure the NP of second place and a larger share of the total vote (and thus more parliamentary seats); yet it would also mean that the ANC would gain a larger share, and thus probably win over two-thirds of the vote. Yet FA participation could shove the NP into third place, and deprive De Klerk of a deputy presidency.[68]

Yet although the FA might have attracted support in some polls, its lack of common political interests could not credibly hold it together for very long. It began to come apart as various ANC–government concessions tugged and pulled at different parts of the alliance: greater provincial powers were offered, then the double ballot, then a *volksraad*, and possibly even some vague form of self-determination. Gradually, the bloc became unglued: first, Ciskei; then Viljoen in a breakaway party called the Freedom Front. Finally, after staring at a State of Emergency in Natal, Buthelezi blinked and Inkatha came back into the election in the very last week of the campaign.

NP Meltdown

Regardless of the less-than majestic ending for the FA, the coincidence of its brief rise with the year-long decline in NP support left an indelible imprint on the interim constitution. Panicked government negotiators hurried to secure a final agreement before the NP disintegrated. (By late September, NP support was widely reported at an all-time low of 12 per cent nationally – down by almost 50 per cent since the beginning of the year.) Not coincidentally, this year-long slide, but especially the September nadir, prompted some significant NP negotiating concessions by the time of the final agreement in November.

In fact, the government's performance in November came under intense criticism and bred bitter dissension and second-guessing among negotiators and cabinet ministers. When asked about these concessions, one government negotiator said that the NP was bargaining from such a weakened position that it could achieve no more. Another defensively added that their job was to 'sell off the family silver gracefully.'[69]

Among the NP's most important concessions in the final draft were the quiet abandonment of the NP's long-time demand that power-sharing be made a constitutional principle; its failure to obtain any super-majority threshold for cabinet decision-making (almost totally emasculating the entire purpose of a proportional cabinet); its acceptance of a deputy presidency that would only be consulted on matters of cabinet policy, but would have no veto or specific duties; its acceptance that provincial functions and powers could be overriden by central government; its agreement that provinces would have no exclusive powers and must obtain the consent of the national parliament in order to raise taxes; its unwitting agreement that the President be allowed to appoint a majority of the constitutional court; its acceptance of a deadlock-breaking mechanism of 60 per cent in a referendum; and its acceptance of 5 per cent rather than 10 per cent as a threshold for cabinet membership.[70]

In return, the government did get a few benefits, such as the inclusion of regionalism in the constitutional principles, the requirement of a two-thirds Senate majority to change regional boundaries and powers, and the requirement of a 60 per cent majority in the Senate to implement deadlock-breaking mechanisms.[71] However, these pale in comparison with its concessions.

In the final analysis, the most important NP concessions came not as a result of the ANC's mobilisation of popular power, but rather as a result of the NP's own inability to attract new supporters and its inability to hold those that it had, especially during its decline in the polls. It was this dynamic that sent real shockwaves and tremors through the government and led to a series of concessions designed to bring about elections as quickly as possible and to obtain enough positions in the new government, before the party entirely imploded.

Notes

1. John Rawls, *A Theory of Justice* (Cambridge: Harvard University Press, 1971).
2. Donald Horowitz, *A Democratic South Africa? Constitutional Engineering In A Divided Society* (Cape Town: Oxford University Press, 1991), pp. 265-269.
3. It is here that we see the special political impact of opinion polling. Not only does it alter political behaviour by providing new information, but it also has an impact by providing possibly flawed information which actors act upon (because of its social scientific nature) as if it were valid. In this case, the apparent black support for De Klerk and the NP may have been illusory and an artefact of telephone polling which was tapping a highly skewed sample of black South Africans.
4. NP secretary-general Stoffel van der Merwe estimated that the NP could eventually garner as much as 40% of black support. See David Ottaway, *Chained Together: Mandela and De Klerk* (New York: Random House, 1994), p. 258.
5. See Steven Friedman, 'The National Party and 1991', *Monitor: The Journal of the Human Rights Trust,* December (1990) pp. 46-48; Mark Swilling, 'Political Transition, Development and the Role of Civil Society,' *Africa Insight,* 20 (1990), p. 153.
6. Friedman, 'The National Party and 1991', p. 48.

7. Viljoen quoted in Friedman, 'The National Party and 1991', p. 46.

8. *Transitions from Authoritarian Rule to Democracy: Tentative Conclusions About Uncertain Democracies* (Baltimore: Johns Hopkins University Press, 1986), p. 61 (quote on p. 59).

9. Official quoted in Steven Friedman, 'The Shaper of Things to Come: National Party Choices in the South African Transition', *Reseach Report* (Centre for Policy Studies: Johannesburg, 1992), p. 12.

10. See Colin Legum, 'SA on Course for a Collision', *The Star*, 23 June 1992, p. 18; Allister Sparks, 'ANC Forced into a Corner as De Klerk Plays for Time', *Cape Times* 2 July 1992, p. 4.

11. Jeremy Cronin, 'What Is De Klerk Up To', *Work in Progress*, 82 (1992) pp. 7-9.

12. Anthony Johnson, 'Impasse Gives ANC Extra Time to Get Its House in Order', *Cape Times*, 29 July 1992, p. 6. Johnson points out that, in the final analysis, the CODESA impasse appears to have actually given the ANC time to revitalise, as a series of scandals rocked the government and sent De Klerk's black support numbers downward.

13. For instance, De Klerk's November 1992 proposal for elections in March or April 1994 was dismissed as 'totally unacceptable' by the ANC, who said they wanted them a full year earlier (March 1993). Significantly, however, the ANC had already proposed elections in only about only 12 months' time (November 1993) as negotiator Jeremy Cronin admitted publicly that the ANC would not be ready to fight elections any sooner. Barry Streek, 'FW Sets Date', *Cape Times*, 27 November 1992, p. 1.

14. The government's insistence on linking the constitution-making body and the interim legislature appears to have been a prime cause of the deadlock. As the Democratic Party repeatedly pointed out, elections for the constitutional body could be held far sooner if they had been separated.

15. Mike Robertson and Edyth Bulbring, 'ANC Rejects FW's "Super Council",' *Sunday Times*, 26 April 1992, pp. 1-2; and Philip van Niekerk, 'No Aces Left Up FW's Sleeve', *Weekly Mail*, 7 May 1992, p. 21.

16. David Breier, 'A "Sting" In Nat Proposals?', *Weekend Argus*, 24-25 April 1993, p. 18.

17. John MacLennan, 'Forging Our Future', *Weekend Argus*, 24-25 April 1993, p. 18 (quote from here).

18. Allister Sparks, 'Once Date Set, Campaign Can Begin', *Cape Times*, 14 June 1993, p. 4.

19. Allister Sparks, 'Solution at World Trade Centre Will Silence Wild Voices', *Cape Times*, 13 May 1993, p. 6.

20. Sparks, 'Entering 1993 in a Spirit of Optimism.'

21. Kader Asmal, 'Electoral Systems: A Critical Survey', Paper presented at the In-House Seminar, African National Congress (Lusaka; Zambia, 1-4 March 1988), pp. 2, 14 (cited in Horowitz, *A Democratic South Africa*, p. 106).

22. Horowitz, *A Democratic South Africa*, p. 268.

23. Andrew Reynolds, *Voting for a New South Africa* (Cape Town: Maskew Miller Longman, 1993), p. 41.

24. Yet PR also has a very co-optive side to it, as revealed by Asmal's defence of it by quoting Lyndon Johnson: 'I would rather have the son-of-a-bitch who is inside pissing out than outside pissing in.' Quoted in Timothy Sisk, 'A New South African

Social Contract? Institutional Choice in a Divided Society' (Ph.D. dissertation: George Washington University, 1992), p. 361.

25.   As early as March 1990, Fatima Meer predicted (on the basis of contemporary surveys) that the ANC would 'be ascendant' in elections for a constituent assembly and 'would win a substantial percentage of the African vote, almost half the Indian and coloured vote, and a small percentage of the white vote.' And in August of that year, pollster Jannie Hofmeyr, based on July 1990 data, estimated that the ANC 'would yield *over* 50% support' in an election, and would also fight for the remaining 24% with no opinion. See Fatima Meer, 'Negotiating a Non-Racial Democracy', *The Nation*, 12 March 1990, p. 349; and Jannie Hofmeyr, 'How South African Would Vote', *Monitor: The Journal of the Human Rights Trust*, August (1990), p. 58 (emphasis added).

26.   Regarding the use of the Alternative Vote and the Single Transferable Vote for these purposes, see the arguments of both Horowitz *(A Democratic South Africa?)* and Arend Lijphart, 'Electoral Systems, Party Systems and Conflict Management in Segmented Societies', in *Critical Choices for South Africa*, ed. R. Schrire (Cape Town: Oxford University Press, 1990).

27.   See Reynolds, *Voting for a New South Africa*.

28.   Hermann Giliomee, 'Trends of Past Show Likely Path to Future', *Cape Times*, 27 January 1993.

29.   Sisk, 'A South African Social Contract?', pp. 358-361.

30.   See R. W. Johnson, 'PR at Work: A Case Study', *Die Suid-Afrikaan*, February/March (1993), pp. 20-21.

31.   Johnson, 'PR at Work.'

32.   Giliomee, 'Trends of Past'.

33.   Hermann Giliomee, 'Trends of Past', p. 6.

34   There was internal division over the nature of this interim authority, however, as some ANC strategists feared the effects of joint responsibility that would come with interim government would actually threaten their victory chances in the first election. Thus, they argued that the ANC should focus only on joint control over the security forces and SABC. Steven Friedman, 'Responsibility Comes with Power', *Weekly Mail*, 11 to 17 October 1991, p. 15.

35.   S. Friedman, ed., *The Long Journey* (Johannesburg, Ravan Press, 1993), p. 90.

36.   Government negotiators later admitted that they blundered badly by rejecting the ANC offer which had been made without obtaining a mandate from its structures. See David Breier, 'FW in Bid to Gain Ground', *Sunday Star*, 5 July 1992, p. 5.

37.   Friedman, *The Long Journey*, p. 74.

38.   Friedman, *The Long Journey*, p. 78.

39.   As indicated in an earlier note, poll results in South Africa have been extremely problematic. In this case, the HSRC data still suffered from the fact that it was not surveying in the 'independent' black homelands, which could be presumed to be ANC strongholds.

40.   Editorial, 'Codesa Rolls On', *Cape Times*, 17 May 1992, p. 24.

41.   As the black weekly, the *New Nation,* argued as mass action proceeded: 'there is a considerable amount of optimism that the [government] will have to acknowledge the vast amount of support for the ANC's position and give in to its demands.' See 'Don't Turn Off the Tap', *New Nation*, 14-22 August 1992, p. 12.

42.   There had been significant anger within COSATU, for example, over the ANC

concession on 75% for the Bill of Rights because it would allow the government to block demands for 'second generation' rights relating to housing, health and jobs. See Eddie Koch, 'Season of Discontent as Negotiations Falter', *Weekly Mail*, 22-28 May 1992, p. 2.

43. Richard Steyn and Shaun Johnson, 'Let's Talk: Mandela', *Argus*, 5 September 1992, p. 1; and 'Keys Jolts Mandela into New Peace Bid', *Cape Times*, 16 September 1992, p. 1.

44. Friedman, *The Long Journey*, p. 154.

45. The government also conceded that Senate seats should be allocated on a proportional base within each region, and it proposed a three year limit on transitional government. In addition, new Constitutional Minister, Roelf Meyer, indicated that the Senate and exact percentages would be negotiable in return for ANC concessions that regional officials should play a role in adopting the constitution.

46. Friedman, *The Long Journey*, pp. 160-163.

47. First Mandela quote from Allister Sparks, 'Majority Rule or Power-Sharing the Basic Issue'. Second quote from 'FW Briefs Leaders on Plans for Multi Party Talks', *Argus*, 5 November 1991, p. 1.

48. 'ANC Unveils Proposals to Clinch Negotiations', *Cape Times*, 4 November 1992, p. 8.

49. Jordan's paper was entitled 'Happy Trails to You, or Riding into the Sunset Together'.

50. Barry Streek, 'ANC Meets on Interim Plans', *Cape Times*, 23 November 1992, p. 6.

51. Interestingly, while they eventually compromised at 5%, the NP (supposedly the champion of minorities) proposed a 10% threshold, which might have cut out the IFP as well as all other parties; the ANC called for 5%. Friedman suggests that the NP wanted to limit power-sharing to two, at most three, parties. The ANC wanted to include as many parties as possible in order to dilute NP or IFP influence. See *The Long Journey*, p. 179.

52. Friedman, *The Long Journey*, pp. 58-59, 75 & 90.

53. Friedman, *The Long Journey*, pp. 74-75.

54. In June 1992 Botha told supporters: 'It is our purpose to become the majority party and I believe we need another 10 percent to add to the 10 percent we have already gained; we will then approach the 50 percent plus situation.' Botha quoted in Colin Legum, 'SA on Course for a Collision', *Star,* 23 June 1992, p. 18. In September 1992 he argued that the NP was only a million voters short of a majority. Predicated on a 70% turnout of the approximately 20 million eligible (14 million), the government already had the support of three million whites, 1.5 million coloureds, 500,000 Indians. If Inkatha could deliver its estimated one million supporters, the alliance would tally six million. Anthony Johnson, 'Pik: Nats Will Win Non-Racial Poll', *Cape Times*, 2 September 1992, p. 5.

55. David Breier, 'Nationalists Fail to Woo Inkatha Back to the Fold', *Weekend Argus*, 31 July-1 August 1993, p. 19.

56. Norman West and Mike Robertson, 'FW Whips Restive Nats into Line Amid Talk of Revolt', *Sunday Times*, 18 October 1992, p. 2; Anton Harber, 'The Future Hinges on the Likgotla's Success', *Weekly Mail*, 20-26 November 1992, p. 23; Edyth Bulbring, 'Strains Show in Cabinet', *Sunday Times*, 13 December 1992, p. 2.

57. Simon Barber, 'Transition Can Happen Without Inkatha, Meyer Tells Americans',

Cape Times, 22 December 1992, p. 6.

58. Anthony Johnson, 'NP Aims to Go it Alone In Election', *Cape Times*, 2 February 1993, p. 1.

59. Edyth Bulbring, 'MP Goes Astray, But NP Is Set to Be Top Dog in All Three Houses', *Sunday Times*, 31 January 1993, p. 2; 'Dizzy Ride on the Roller Coaster', *Guardian Weekly*, 19-25 March 1993, p. 11; and Chris Louw, 'Ally or Enemy? Inkatha Could Divide NP Unity?', *Weekly Mail*, 28 May to 3 June 1993, p. 23.

60. Edyth Bulbring, 'Minister Quits Nats in Despair', *Sunday Times*, 6 June 1993, p. 1; Anthony Johnson, 'MPs Poised to Quit Nats', *Cape Times*, 9 June 1993, p. 1; David Breier, 'Panic Among Nat MPs As All-Races Poll Nears,' *Weekend Argus*, 12-13 June 1993, p. 9; 'One Man Who Knows', *Sunday Times*, 13 June 1993, p. 20.

61. Allister Sparks, 'Once Date Is Set, Campaign Can Begin', *Cape Times*, 14 June 1993, p. 4; and Edyth Bulbring, 'A Tired But Determined President Waits for a "More Normal Picture"', *Sunday Times*, 13 June 1993, p. 21.

62. David Breier, 'Nationalists Fail to Woo Inkatha Back to the Fold', *Weekend Argus*, 31 July-1 August 1993, p. 19; Anthony Johnson, 'Wily IFP Is Taking Full Advantage of Headlong Rush to Transition', *Cape Times*, 18 August 1993, p. 6.

63. Anthony Johnson and Barry Streek, 'FW Warns of Power Through Gun Barrel', *Cape Times*, 13 August 1993, p. 4; James McClurg, 'April 27 Election Might Be Wishful Thinking', *Cape Times*, 13 August 1993, p. 6; David Breier, 'Wessels Suggests an Election Without "Spoilers,"' *Weekend Argus*, 21-22 August 1993, p. 20; 'Elections on Track – F. W', *Cape Times*, 10 September 1993, p. 1.

64. Anthony Johnson, 'Once-Feared NP Machine Becoming Distinctly Edgy', *Cape Times*, 22 September 1993, p. 8; Michael Morris, 'Nat Party Searches Its Soul', *Argus*, 15 October 1993, p. 8.

65. Here again, we see the curious effect of opinion polls. While politicians react to them like sheep, a more dispassionate review of CP and FA performance in the opinion polls would indicate that whites have generally used the polls like disgruntled voters use by-elections, to blow off steam about the government without actually changing the government.

66. Even in September, NP insiders were beginning to predict that the party would come in third behind the ANC alliance and a right-wing–Inkatha alliance. John MacLennan and David Breier, 'FW May Face Party Revolt', *Weekend Argus*, 11-12 September 1993, pp. 1, 3.

67. Jan Van Eck, 'We Need Bold Opposition', *Sunday Times*, 22 August 1993, p. 22.

68. David Breier, 'Nat Dilemma: Bring in Alliance and Lose at the Polls?', *Weekend Argus*, 27-28 November 1993, p. 22.

69. Edyth Bulbring, 'Nats Cave In to the ANC in Race to Beat the Clock', *Sunday Times*, 14 November 1993, p. 1.

70. Edyth Bulbring, 'Nats Cave In to the ANC in Race to Beat the Clock', *Sunday Times*, 14 November 1993, p. 1; Mike Robertson, 'The Art of Scoring Top Marks on Bottom Lines', *Sunday Times*, 21 November 1993, p. 5.

71. Bulbring, 'U-Turn As NP Backs Single Leader,' p. 2; Chris Louw, 'Government Changes Tune on Power-Sharing', *Weekly Mail*, 18-24 June 1993, p. 2; Bulbring, 'A Tired But Determined President'; 'NP Reneged on Undertaking', *Cape Times*, 2 July 1993, p. 4.

2

The African National Congress and Its Allies

TOM LODGE

For many voters, the 1994 poll may have been a liberation election, but at no stage did the ANC take victory for granted. From the beginning, the organisation's strategists recognised that it confronted an experienced and well-organised opponent with the capacity to make deep inroads into the ANC's potential support. This chapter will begin with a short narrative overview of the ANC's campaign before turning to more detailed analyses of its stategies, policy appeals and campaigning. A concluding section evaluates the ANC's performance nationally and in certain regions.

Overview

For the ANC, preparations for the 1994 election began early with the establishment in late 1992 of its own election commission headed by the former United Democratic Front activists Popo Molefe and Khetso Gordan. Planning received extra impetus in February 1993 when the ANC's National Executive accepted in principle the concept of a power-sharing government of national unity. That month a 'solidarity conference' of 900 foreign anti-apartheid activists listened to an ANC appeal for funds to fight the election, and a two-day Patriotic Front meeting held in Lenasia discussed the formation of a broad election alliance around the ANC.

At the beginning of April 1993, Popo Molefe announced a fund-raising target of R168 million. Of this, so far, the ANC had raised R5 million. Seventeen election workshops had been held to date, mainly in the PWV area. Strategy would be decided by a series of national and regional seminars, beginning in June. Meanwhile, the organisation would begin training branch-level election co-ordinators as well as three monitors for each of the projected 10,000 polling stations. In all, the

ANC would seek to train 180,000 people.[1]

By the end of May, the commission had produced a more detailed campaign plan which emphasised door-to-door canvassing; it made provision for volunteers to speak to each potential voter at least twice before the end of July. According to this plan, canvassers should emphasise voter education issues and basic ANC policy themes: security, jobs and freedom. They should make special efforts to reach women, squatters and rural people. ANC activists should be equipped with door-to-door handbooks and voter education manuals. Four phases of grassroots activity would culminate in Victory Week, in which volunteers would deliver supporters to the poll, ensure that all knew how to vote, and arrange security and monitoring.[2]

Progress on implementing this scheme was rather slower than envisaged. Plans for universal door-to-door canvassing proved much too ambitious. Even so, certain regions invested considerable effort in door-to-door visits. For example, the PWV regional election commission reported that its 750 volunteers had visited 5,000 houses, speaking with about 20,000 likely voters in Soshanguve, Katlehong, Soweto and, surprisingly, Randburg. The regional organisation aimed to reach all voters within its boundaries by 10 December.[3]

More refined planning was generated by an election strategy workshop held on 26–27 September and attended by 150 participants from the ANC's fourteen regions. Here it was resolved that the ANC would campaign at the head of an alliance consisting of itself, the Communist Party and COSATU together with individuals from Patriotic Front organisations. ANC symbols would predominate. This option 'avoided needing to work with unpopular organisations while maintaining a broad front'. In mobilising support, the ANC should recognise 'how complex the electorate is'. The workshop acknowledged 'that while it may appear objectively correct for African people to vote ANC, the subjective inclination may not be there'. In composing its parliamentary lists, national strategic interests must be balanced against those of ANC members. The ANC should project 'one strong central message' but 'with different emphases for different sections of the electorate'.[4] Again, the emphasis at this stage of planning was on localised face-to-face contact with voters. In the next two months the ANC trained 15,000 volunteers.[5]

By November, the ANC was ready to launch its public electioneering. This would fall into two phases, 'hearing' and 'telling'. Nelson Mandela and other members of a small group of leaders who would represent the ANC's 'public face' would arrive at public gatherings convened by local and regional ANC structures. Those attending would have been summoned by open letters in the press. Each meeting would attempt to attract a specific audience: workers, teachers, women, or squatters, for example. Leaders would listen to addresses from the audience and respond to questions; they would not begin by making a speech. These 'People's Forums' began on 6 November in Uitenhage. By the end of November, Mandela was attending up to three a day. The hearing phase was scheduled to end in mid-January. It would be succeeded by rallies, posters and media campaigning in which the ANC would project its policies.

Nominations for candidate lists supplied the next focus of activity. The complex process began at branch level. The Youth and Women's League generated additional lists of nominees, as did COSATU. These lists were published early in the new year before a nomination conference took place at which 500 delegates selected the 200 national list nominees. This list was then adjusted by the ANC National Executive to ensure high rankings on the list for women and representatives of COSATU and other organisations.

Through January, the ANC released a succession of detailed proposals for specific areas of policy – education, mining, police, health, and so forth – and on 21 January a conference was held to debate and adopt a seventh draft of a Reconstruction and Development Programme. Nearly two weeks later, on 2 February, the organisation launched its official campaign at the Nasrec Centre outside Soweto, publishing its manifesto 'A Better Life for All'. Seven million of these were printed for distribution. For the next two months, ANC campaigning would mainly take the form of outdoor advertising, newspaper broadsides, and 'roadshow' tours by national and regional leaders. The parties had agreed at CODESA to prohibit television advertising, and radio electioneering would begin only on 28 March. ANC strategists believed that the National Party would benefit disproportionately from using sponsored broadcasting. In fact, television news and current affairs coverage probably played a significant part in projecting the ANC's message, with extensive reportage of the main parties' campaigning as well as almost daily interviews and panel discussions on *Agenda*. The campaign reached its climax with a television debate between President De Klerk and Nelson Mandela, and huge celebratory rallies in the main centres.

Strategy

To plan its campaign, the ANC commissioned an extensive series of surveys. These began in late 1992 with focus group discussions of selected groups drawn from different categories of potential 'swing' voters. Subsequently a preliminary national survey based on a 2,000-strong sample was undertaken in March 1993 and a larger sample of 8,000 was polled in July to gain a more definitive picture of the electorate and to establish distinctions between the electorates in different regions. The surveys included 'deep rural' respondents, and coloureds, Indians and whites were intentionally over-represented. The surveys enabled the ANC from early on to recognise the existence even among the African electorate of quite large proportions of uncommitted voters as well as significant inclinations among Indians and coloureds to abstain from voting. Overall it found in the July sample that 54 per cent favoured the ANC and 23 per cent were uncommitted.

The surveys helped the ANC to construct a ranking of the most important issues for different sections of the electorate: for Africans and coloureds, unemployment, political violence and housing were the three most frequently cited problems. There were other key findings. Amongst Africans, weak support for the ANC tended to correlate with voters who were female, rural and less educated. Significant numbers of Indian and coloured respondents believed that an ANC government would bring mismanagement, associated the organisation with political violence, and were apprehensive about its links with the SACP. In mock ballots, the ANC found that 8 per cent of its potential supporters might spoil their votes. More reassuringly, 83 percent of its African supporters believed that the ballot would be secret. The regional samples alerted the ANC to its weakness in the Western Cape as well as to a high proportion of uncommitted voters in that region. It indicated that amongst coloureds ANC support tended to be male, educated, urban and white-collar. Its coloured regional and national leaders tended to be not known or not trusted among Western Cape respondents. The July survey suggested that the ANC had more than twice the support of Inkatha (42 per cent as opposed to 18 per cent) but that 33 per cent of the sample was undecided. As with coloured voters in the Western Cape, ANC support amongst Natal Africans tended to correlate with higher levels of education and residence in metropolitan areas. In general, this research revealed that apart from Mandela, ANC leaders were often comparatively unknown amongst certain groups and regions. Mandela's appeal tended to transcend the limits of party support.[6]

These surveys were very important in helping to convince ANC planners that a large electoral majority was by no means guaranteed, and that voters would have to be won over. They supplied indications of which groups should receive most attention and which issues should predominate in particular appeals. They suggested that as much as possible, Mandela should personify the ANC's campaign, as no other

ANC leaders had comparable stature among swing voters. They emphasised the importance of educating voters about general voting procedures and overcoming their fears. Early on, they drew attention to areas in which the ANC was weak. Finally, the surveys demonstrated that the ANC had negligible white support.

More generally, this intelligence prompted the ANC to fight the election as a contest about issues rather than merely as a 'freedom poll'. The possibility of losing support as a consequence of voters being unprepared or apprehensive helps to explain the organisation's emphasis on mobilising voters through face-to-face contact and reasoned persuasion. Here, in any case it enjoyed a huge advantage over all its rivals; no other party possessed such comparably extensive organisation. Door-to-door canvassing had the additional attraction of boosting the morale of activists, many of whom had become increasingly critical of the leadership during the long period of waiting for the conclusion of the CODESA negotiations. The importance of newspaper advertising in a competition in which television and radio could play only limited roles also helped to define the style of the ANC's public message.

The election commission succeeded in enlisting the services of two of the architects of Bill Clinton's victory in the American presidential election, Stanley Greenberg and Frank Greer. Before his career as an electoral pollster, Greenberg was an academic specialist on South Africa. He and Greer had also worked as advisers in elections in Nicaragua and Chile. Greenberg and Greer helped to set the high moral tone of the ANC's print campaign with its informative and factual content as well as the general eschewal of negative advertising. Greenberg contended that negative campaigning could backfire amongst an electorate which would grow increasingly hopeful as election day drew nearer.[7] Reassuring people about the future was more important than reminding them about the past. ANC planners knew from their surveys that the National Party had been surprisingly successful in presenting itself as a reformed multi-racial party. 'But we have to show that even under the new transformed FW, policies still discriminate,' argued Joel Netshitendze, editor of the ANC's journal, *Mayibuye*.[8] To achieve this, careful analysis of policy and performance was required, not archive pictures of massacres. A final consideration affecting the ANC's campaigning content and style was the need to counter the perception that the organisation's leaders were too inexperienced to govern competently. Detailed policy prescriptions communicated through quantities of text would aim to dispel such an impression.

Meanwhile, the people's forums and the nomination of lists would help to emphasise the ANC's accountability and the extent to which its policies and representatives were subject to popular sanction. The forum concept was directly borrowed from the Clinton campaign as a highly effective device to dramatise a process of popular consultation. In the forums, leaders would occupy one podium, and speakers from the audience would address them from another stage of equal height to accentuate the impression of egalitarian accessibility. The nomination procedure had comparable merits, though it caused some embarrassment to the ANC when provincial lists were prematurely published and subsequently discovered to include people who had not been consulted beforehand. After the lists conference, the first 85 names were left alone by the National Executive, reflecting as they did the activist vote. The next 35 positions were rearranged to make way for women lower down the list (women had been promised earlier one-third of the ANC's parliamentary representation) and personalities from the less-popular Patriotic Front organisations. This caused some rank-and-file displeasure, especially with the elevation of the former tricameral politician, J. N. Reddy, into a superior position on the list to most Natal Indian Congress veterans. On the whole, though, the composition of the list was not determined by leadership preferences; after the election this became quite evident when the ordering on the list was ignored in the selection of the cabinet.

Outside of the constituent organisations in the ANC alliance, campaigning was undertaken in the name of the ANC alone. Neither the Communist Party nor COSATU issued much separate publicity, nor did the ANC draw attention to its partners in its posters and advertisements. Though members of the Communist Party were quite well represented on the national list, and indeed became the focus of an important theme in National Party propaganda, the ANC neither stressed nor sought to downplay their inclusion. For most African voters, affiliation to the Communist Party was not an important issue, and there was nothing to be gained by adopting a defensive posture about the ANC's links with the Communist Party amongst those sections of the electorate that objected to them.

Policy

From the beginning of January, the ANC published a series of extremely detailed policy documents. The culmination of this process was the drafting of the Reconstruction and Development Programme, which eventually appeared in the form of a 150-page booklet. The programme spelled out a succession of measures to create jobs through public works, redistribute land, supply low-cost housing, and extend clean water supply and domestic electrification, develop primary health care, provide universal pensions, and institute ten years of free compulsory education. Economic sections of the programme were much less specific, though they suggested that an ANC government would seek to reduce the level of 'concentration of economic power' embodied in monopolistic companies, in order to allow a significant role for the public sector to correct 'regional, racial and gender and structural imbalances'.[9] It would also restructure industries to promote the export of manufactures, and reduce tariffs while minimising unemployment. The Programme also committed the ANC to a wide range of affirmative action measures in both the private and public sectors.

The Programme was the product of an extended debate within the ANC, and the vagueness of its economic prescriptions reflected the disagreement which exists within different sections of its policy-making establishment. Much of the Programme was written by economists and other specialists associated with COSATU, and their particular concerns had to be balanced with the perceived need to reassure local business elites and potential foreign investors. None of the specific provisions of the Reconstruction and Development Programme are by themselves very radical in character. The ANC's land reform scheme, for example, suggests a legalistic process of redistribution through a land claims court. Much of the actual change of ownership will come about through the freer operation of market forces in what is perceived to be relatively inefficient and heavily state-subsidised commercial agriculture. Not surprisingly, this sort of detail was rarely present in ANC campaigning literature and speeches. Anxious not to be outflanked by the PAC, which had made land reform its main platform plank, the ANC merely told its supporters that it had plans for the redistribution of one-third of the land. Similarly, a million homes in five years was a phrase that suggested a massive extension of the welfare state, but in fact the ANC's promise to provide low-cost housing did not imply the massive expansion of state housing; rather, public funds would be used to underwrite private loans to low-income buyers. In essence, the ANC's housing proposals were very similar to those advocated by the National Party's housing minister, Louis Schill, which was not surprising as both were drawn from National Housing Forum deliberations. Nor did the ANC's education proposals represent a sharp break with the past; indeed, on their publication a National Party spokesman suggested that they were broadly in line with the government's education renewal strategy.

The Programme in its final form was a modified version of a slightly more radical set of proposals. In its general argument and tone it reflected very considerable faith in the role the public sector could play in guiding and stimulating economic development. The Programme was cryptic about the financial cost of social reform, though just before the election Trevor Manuel, the ANC's economics spokesman, said that R39 billion would be a realistic estimate of the public finance required for the extension of welfare, infrastructure and services.[10] The Programme acknowledged that personal taxation was already high and implied that some of the additional costs could be met through the rationalisation and reallocation of existing government expenditure.

Translated into populist manifesto promises, in 'A Better Life for All', this programme committed the ANC to employment and training for an additional 2.5 million people in five years; government patronage of small businesses; promotion of workers' rights and trade unions; ending of VAT on basic foods and the reduction of income tax for low wage earners; rural development and land reform; a million homes with running water and flush toilets; and free infant health care and immunisation programmes. Increased public expenditure would be derived from rising revenues created by more jobs and higher incomes as well as by foreign aid and loans. The manifesto was upbeat about the positive response from the international community 'to our call for massive investments'.

Whatever their technical shortcomings, the ANC's policy proposals had the merit of being simple, vivid and seemingly plausible; enough detail was supplied about methods and means to make them appear fairly pragmatic to the audience to which they were directed. No other party provided a similarly specific set of prescriptions or a manifesto which was as carefully tailored to well-researched public perceptions. And backing up the clear pledges of the manifesto was a battery of highly technocratic policy studies.

Campaigning

After the official launch of the campaign in February 1994, newspaper advertising supplied the ANC with the main means of communicating its message to supporters and, aside from printing, probably accounted for the main part of its R150 million election budget.[11] The ANC entrusted the direction of its press offensive to a leading commercial agency, Hunt Lascaris, within the parameters of a four-phase campaign. This was intended to emphasise, in turn, popular consultation through the people's forums; 'our plan' or the basic features of Reconstruction and Development; contrasts between the ANC's proposals and the government's previous record of achievement; and finally, reassurance about the future. Advertisements took the form of full-page or double-page features in the main daily and Sunday papers.

Accordingly, a series of notices appeared in late November and early

December, announcing the forums. 'Please join me at the People's Forums' entreated a broadsheet in the *Star* on 23 November, 'Or write to me'. Over a picture of Nelson Mandela, a series of meetings was posted for teachers at the Johannesburg College of Education, health and education workers at Vista University in Soweto, hostel dwellers at Kaserne in Johannesburg, Gandhi Hall (misspelt 'Ghandi') in Lenasia, and homeless people at the Ivory Park squatter camp. The tone of the announcement was inviting and personal: 'Come and tell us what you want from a new government.' 'We'd like to hear your views before finalizing our reconstruction and development plan.' 'Let us know where you stand. Because, above all, the ANC stands for you.' 'Now that she has the right to vote, will she be free to use it?' asked another advertisement in the series focusing on the plight of people in Bophuthatswana – this time illustrated with a photograph of a young woman addressing a microphone. Another poster published on 28 November used the testimony of a hostel dweller, Mr Mguni: 'The hostel is a pigsty, unfit for humans. We are appealing to the new government to build us a decent place to live in where we can stay as families. I am 47 years old. I have been here for 27 years.' All these advertisements included a postage-paid coupon for mailing to the ANC, on which readers were invited to tell Mr Mandela about their 'biggest concerns' and to 'suggest what we should do'. The series depended for its visual impact on strong photographs, sombre colours, sober text, and screenprinted zig-zag borders supplying a folksy 'home-made' appearance, very different from commercial advertising.

The 'We have a plan' sequence opened with a double-page spread on 31 January, the two pages almost entirely covered with italic print carrying a slightly abbreviated version of the ANC manifesto under the heading: 'After years without rights, it's fair to ask what will your country do for you.' The subheadings emphasised the basic themes which would be picked up in open-air placard publicity: 'Working together for jobs, peace and freedom', 'Uplifting the quality of life', 'Opening the doors of learning', 'Health, caring for all'. Here, Mandela's portrait supplied the sole decoration. This was followed by single-page advertisements spelling out in point form the essential measures in each ANC programme: putting a stop to crime; building houses and improving services; uplifting the quality of life; and so on. Initially unadorned with pictures, the advertisements in their later versions incorporated arresting photographic images: a pencil battened down with nails, half of them bent back to signify the ANC's intention of 'making education free and equal for all'.

The flavour of the third 'contrast' phase was embodied in an advertisement published on 27 March. 'The NP's economic policy has left 5 million people without jobs,' proclaimed a banner at the top of the page. An asterisk referring the 5 million figure to the Central Statistical Services supplied an impression of conscientious accuracy. 'We cannot afford more of this' – in block capitals five centimetres high. Then the details in italics, with the ANC pledge for a public works programme at the bottom of the page, alongside a grainy black-and-white photograph of desperate-looking unemployed workers. 'And you have the cheek to call me the weaker sex' asserts a perkier instalment in the same series, featuring a self-confident and smart-looking black woman and detailing a daily routine of domestic tasks, commuting, working and childcare lasting from 4 in the morning until midnight. 'Women have been the glue that has kept this country together. And we believe it is time that this strength was recognised. In real terms,' reads the commentary at the bottom of the page.

ANC press advertising became less frequent in the final weeks before the election, perhaps because funds were running out, and therefore the newspaper campaign did not develop very extensively the final 're-assurance' phase. That theme was reflected in the ANC's placard display in April, which focused on a large colour photograph of a smiling Nelson Mandela, the first full-colour picture used in the campaign. 'Vote ANC on April 27', a *Sunday Times* posted urged on 24 April, 'and win a better life for all'. The advertisement reproduced a ballot form and was printed in green, black and red, again in contrast to the monochrome which had characterised most of the ANC's press features.

In addition to the planned and phased thematic advertising, the ANC also used press notices to announce the composition of its national and regional lists (it was the only party to do this) and to respond to particular developments and to National Party propaganda. 'Should anyone walk away from the elections?' headed up an announcement on 18 February of the ANC's negotiating proposals directed at the boycotting parties. 'According to the NP you played no part in changing South Africa' challenged a caption beneath a picture of a crowd of demonstrators on 1 February. In a similar vein, a double-page spread took the Nationalists to task for their depiction of history. A cartoon pictured Mandela in boxing gear (recalling a much-reproduced youthful portrait) standing by a huge pair of toppled boots, labelled 'NP Apartheid'. 'I did it! I did it!' shouts a gleeful representation of De Klerk outside the ring. Underneath, the text runs: 'Judging from recent claims, the so-called "New National Party" is looking remarkably similar to the old one. In their lastest version of history they are the heroes that changed South Africa ... Next thing they'll be telling us Apartheid never existed. The lesson of history is clear: those who deny the past, may never be trusted with the future.'

On the whole, though, ANC messages had little to say about history; the modern National Party was their main concern, not its pre-De Klerk version. Generally, ANC print propaganda ignored the smaller parties (though on platforms ANC spokesmen would sometimes make gracious references to the Pan Africanist Congress as a fellow liberation movement). In the last days of the campaign, however, one national advertisement confronted the fresh challenge of Inkatha. Two columns under the headings 'Jobs, housing, education, peace and security' contrasted poverty, unemployment and oppression in IFP–NP ruled KwaZulu–Natal with the ANC's proposals for social and political reform.

A considerable variety of flyers and leaflets intended for distributing during rallies and door-to-door canvassing supplemented the advertising. These were printed in English, Afrikaans and a range of African languages. They popularised the chief campaigning slogan – 'Now is the time' – and reflected the mood of each phase of the campaign. Stickers promoted the ANC's logo and Mandela's image, both vital symbols for the ANC among illiterate voters, and both, of course, to appear on the ballot forms. Special leaflets were produced for particular groups: schoolchildren, students, industrial workers and the unemployed. In addition, different regions produced their own propaganda and published advertisements reflecting concerns which were pertinent locally. These regional intiatives were especially conspicuous in the Western Cape. Certain more prosperous branches produced their own publicity. The ANC's Lenasia branch, for example, distributed a newsletter which carefully directed itself at the preoccupations of a middle-class minority community. The April issue included messages of support from local Indian notables and featured Indian National Executive members' views on crime, religion, affirmative action and property rights. A message from Nelson Mandela recalled that 1994 was the hundredth anniversary 'of the establishment of the Indian Congress by Mahatma Gandhi' and reminded readers about the history of 'joint struggles between the Indian community and the African people'. A poster and a flyer also stressed African–Indian co-operation in an unusually fierce attack on the 'National Party's dark history'. 'Remember them?' asked a heading above five portraits of Malan, Verwoerd, Vorster, Botha and De Klerk.

This last item was uncharacteristic. Usually, printed ANC appeals avoided openly emotive language and often tended to understate their case. The restrained graphics, careful logic and general seriousness of the ANC's propaganda successfully projected an impression of moral responsibility, social compassion and intellectual sophistication. Part of the message was directed at the reassurance and disarming of potential opponents, as much as at conversion and retention of supporters. For though this was not a theme given explicit expression in published propaganda, ANC leaders were careful in their public speeches and television appearances to address white fears generally and elite concerns particularly. ANC publicity was characteristically socially discerning in its messages directed at particular communities, though on the whole it heeded its election planners' injunction that it should avoid 'the danger of balancing tactics, e.g. using militant tactics to win over one section [which] might alienate another sector'.[12]

The control and restraint characteristic of most of the printed publicity was offset by the informal and exuberant manner of the ANC's roadshow and rally events. Mandela set the tone, donning an astonishing variety of colourful shirts and appropriate hats, and apologising to crowds for his occasional appearance in a formal suit. Speeches at rallies tended to be short and were punctuated by music and performance. A report of a visit by Cyril Ramaphosa to the University of the North captures the tone:

> Ramaphosa enters on the back of a bakkie, drums rolling round and round the bowl of the stadium and intermingling with a solid unbroken roar of greeting and calypso rhythms. If this stadium has seen shows of defiance and resistance, this occasion is a carnival. An aspirant people's poet booms: 'We have reached the crossroads of freedom.'[13]

Not that all campaigning was cast in the form of entertainment. A soberly suited Mandela (no apologies this time) visited the Johannesburg Stock Exchange to deliver reassuring platitudes about the ANC's economic plans. They were based on 'market principles' and offered 'better management of the country's resources and more effective use of its savings'. They contained 'absolutely not a single sentence about nationalisation'. (Here Mandela was using politician's licence; in fact, Reconstruction and Development refers to nationalisation as a possible option to be considered by a future government.) Other speeches were as carefully nuanced in their appeals to particular audiences. At a huge rally in Durban in October 1993, which began with the Kushisha Impepho ceremony to call down the blessings of the ancestors on the 60,000-strong multitude, and after ninety minutes of prayer, song and dance, Mandela appeared in royal leopard-skin regalia. His address was in English and Zulu and largely comprised a roll-call of the tribes, chiefs and kings who had fought colonialism and apartheid. Mandela, on the whole stilted and ill at ease on television, was at his best in a crowd, as this description of one of the early people's forums indicates:

At Kaserne hostel, he danced with supporters toyi-toying in greeting. There the whole frantic cavalcade fell into context. With Johannesburg as a backdrop, about 500 people sat in a broad semicircle before their leaders in the age-old African way. The people spoke. They wanted jobs, houses and security. The junior chiefs tried to temper expectations with pragmatism. But when Mr Mandela spoke the people listened, he was the reason they were sitting out in the chill. Their faith was total. With 'the President' at the helm they could reach the promised land.

ANC speeches were less inhibited than the campaign literature in attacking the National Party and President De Klerk, though General Bantu Holomisa's bizarre claim that the porridge available at National Party meetings was laced with invisible ink to prevent people from voting was untypical.[14] Holomisa also alleged that National Party officials would stuff ballot boxes: 'they are going to get hold of ballot papers and inflate the votes for the NP by putting crosses next to that bald-headed man.'[15] Mandela himself did not encourage such fears; if people were offered money or mealie pap at National Party meetings, they should accept them as their due and vote ANC all the same. At times, though, his criticism of De Klerk was harsh enough, mocking the State President's claim to have ended apartheid and recalling what Mandela perceived to be the various breaches of trust in their personal relationship. Even so, this kind of rhetoric was usually held in check, moderated by spontaneous expressions of warmth, as when he reached out to hold De Klerk's hand at the end of their television debate. He was also sharply censorious of the times when his own supporters exceeded the 'ethos of robust campaigning', as for example when they stoned De Klerk at a roadside gathering. He telephoned the State President to promise that he would discourage such behaviour in future, one of a succession of telephone conversations between the two men that helped to defuse tension between them as well as establishing joint approaches to such issues as the Bophuthatswana insurrection and the negotiations with the KwaZulu authorities.

Such civility, though, did not characterise street-level campaigning. ANC supporters were notoriously intolerant of the efforts by the National Party and Democratic Party to establish followings in black townships (though the ANC and the NP managed to share an office building in Soweto quite happily). Nor was this intolerance confined to their adversaries. In Natal, local-level ANC leadership around Durban would not permit voter education by independent agencies, complained Paddy Kearney of the Democracy Forum; only voter education conducted by the ANC was acceptable.[16] Viewed from the top, the ANC campaign exuded benign intentions, rational discourse and festive high spirits; in the day-to-day experience of township neighbourhoods, it had an uglier underside.

Results

Sixty-two per cent of the national vote represented a respectable victory for the ANC, though it fell short of the vote which would have enabled ANC MPs to draft the final constitution by themselves. At the time of writing, no detailed results have been released by the IEC, only the national and regional totals; hence only the most basic commentary can be offered. In general, the ANC's performance confirmed the accuracy of most pre-election opinion polling. Early polling suggested that the ANC had a percentage share of the national vote in the mid-fifties but pointed to quite large proportions of undecided voters. Polls conducted late in the campaign indicated that with the swing voters the ANC was losing ground to the National Party. A marketing research survey in February put the ANC's share at 59–64 per cent and the National Party's at 16–21 per cent; these ranges reflected the ways in which the inclinations of undecided voters could be estimated.[17] Interestingly, the HSRC polls, often accused by ANC spokesmen of favouring the government, were usually over-generous to the ANC.

In most of the predominantly rural provinces – Northern and Eastern Transvaal, North West, Eastern Cape and the Free State – in which the ANC's vote ranged between 75 and 92 per cent, its share corresponded with the African proportion of the regional populations. In the PWV area, the ANC's share of 57.6 per cent was distinctly less than the 69 per cent represented by the African proportion of the population. With the traditionally white parties receiving 36 per cent of the vote, Democratic and National Party efforts to win black votes may have yielded slight dividends. Whites represent 26 per cent of the regional population, though Inkatha's 4 per cent probably accounted for most of the African votes that did not go to the ANC.

Only in the Western and Northern Cape does it seem certain that the ANC collected significant numbers of non-African votes. In the Western Cape, the ANC's 33 per cent share of the vote was well in excess of the 19 per cent proportion that Africans comprised within the regional demography. In the Northern Cape the ANC gained over 200,000 votes, about double the number of African voters. Early district returns reported on television suggested that the organisation in this province did well among impoverished farmworker communities.

Polls were confounded by Natal results, affected obviously by the belief that Inkatha would boycott the election. Even so, a Markinor poll, which suggested in March that the ANC would gain just under half the votes in the province, indicated that the organisation lost ground substantially in the course of April. Its final share of a third of the regional vote does not suggest that it was supported by the majority of Indians but rather that the figure accounted for the minority of Africans who did not opt for Inkatha. On the whole, then, the ANC's support was African.

With regional voter turnouts ranging between 81 and 92 per cent, high by most comparative criteria, it seems likely that the ANC was not disadvantaged by any popular reluctance to vote. Voter education either paid off or was unnecessary; just under 200,000 ballots were spoilt in the 19,726,579 votes cast, amounting to about one per cent.

Might the ANC have done better if it had campaigned more effectively in the two regions in which it was defeated, Western Cape and Natal? In the Western Cape, the ANC was caught between two popular constituencies with different perceptions and priorities, between a largely artisan coloured population concerned about job security (according to an SABC–Markinor poll, a rising anxiety during early 1994) and allocation of resources, and the desperately poor 400,000 or so Africans, many unemployed and living in squatter shacks. Working-class coloured voters were especially susceptible to National Party 'black propaganda' that ANC affirmative action would benefit Africans only. These fears were reinforced by new 'Xhosa-speaking' hiring policies implemented by private-sector enterprises in Cape Town as well as the illegal occupation by African squatters of new municipal houses designated for coloured tenants. A scurrilous National Party comic which claimed that the ANC favoured extending the vote to 'murderers, arsonists, extortionists, all criminals in fact' exploited popular hysteria generated by a sequence of serial murders on the Cape Flats. What is more, early ANC public discourse did nothing to dispel the image of an organisation of violent militancy: after Chris Hani's death, Winnie Mandela appeared in uMkhonto combat fatigues at a rally in Khayelitsha to urge the ANC youth to 'take the streets by storm and remain there until the fascist government was removed'. 'We want a revolution and we do not apologise to anyone,' Peter Mokaba exhorted at the same event.[18]

Until late 1993, the regional organisation was dominated by a strongly 'Africanist' leadership, headed by the militaristic Tony Yengeni. This replaced the local UDF hierarchy, which had been strongly rooted in coloured suburbs around Cape Town. The defection to the Democratic Party of Joe Marks, a former Vice-President of the UDF and a popular community leader on the Cape Flats, signalled a broader disenchantment among coloured activists. Marks cited as his reason for resigning from the ANC its shabby treatment of the Cape Housing Action Committee after CAHAC had voted to stay out of the ANC-affiliated South African National Civic Organisation.[19]

ANC national leadership efforts at damage control were ineffectual. Mandela's insistence that Allan Boesak should lead the regional ANC was probably miscalculated. A series of sexual scandals, a subsequent divorce, and reports of high living helped to discredit Boesak among his earlier supporters. A National Party accusation that Boesak had managed to spend R275,000 on a new house (cited from a court affidavit) successfully underlined the social distance between Boesak and the constituency he was supposed to represent.[20] Local ANC counter-propaganda was similarly unedifying: Dr Boesak told public meetings that R70 billion had disappeared into the pockets of cabinet ministers and politicians.[21] An ANC poster characterised the three black candidates on the ANC's regional list as three dogs straining at the leash held by Hernus Kriel, the National Party's premier-designate. Local ANC politicians cajoled and threatened their coloured audiences, accusing them of ingratitude and racism. Franklin Sonn attempted to manipulate coloured fears about housing when he said: 'We must not make the same mistake as the brown community in Namibia. When they asked for houses, Nujoma asked: For whom did they vote?'[22] In much the same manner, Allan Boesak suggested on the eve of the election that a regional victory for the National Party would compel the government to remove parliament from Cape Town. Desperate to contest National Party exploitation of coloured apprehensions, ANC activists circulated a leaflet in coloured townships recalling Marike de Klerk's remark that coloureds were 'left-overs' and 'non-people'.[23] 'Your vote is secret, but not before God. Don't vote National Party' commanded another ANC flyer, one of a series featuring coloured notables calling for an ANC vote. In the Western Cape many of the principles of the ANC's campaigning elsewhere were abandoned; here the stress was on fears and anxieties, not hopes and aspirations. And again and again, the ANC's discourse underlined its cultural condescension towards the people it was supposed to attract by referring to them as 'so-called' coloureds.[24] Things might have been different: in the 1980s the United Democratic Front had popular affiliates in coloured communities, and in mid-1993 a major proportion of coloured voters seemed from polls to be uncommitted in their affiliations.

In Natal, the IFP may have benefited from apparently widespread electoral fraud in rural districts, though this is unlikely to have accounted for all of its large margin of victory over the ANC. The regional ANC organisation was in a poor state, divided between three regional hierarchies sometimes at loggerheads with each other. In the Natal Midlands, in which the ANC might have expected to do well, the regional chairman, Harry Gwala, philosophically ill-disposed to power-sharing, committed little energy to the campaign. Outside of Kwa-Mashu, the ANC could not mount door-to-door canvassing because of the risk of attack from Inkatha partisans. Inkatha's association with the cause of the Zulu royal house was beginning to have a decisive impact on rural Zulu voters in February, an SABC–Markinor poll discerned. But not all local ANC leaders were enthusiastic about the efforts of their premier-designate, Jacob Zuma, to outbid Inkatha's ethnic appeal.

In Natal, though, the ANC's campaign was probably thwarted by factors beyond the control of leadership. Fear of continuing civil conflict may have prompted many voters to interpret an Inkatha vote as a vote for appeasement and peace. Inkatha's independent ideological appeal was certainly underestimated by most specialists, as was the probable size of the rural electorate in its stronghold north of the Tugela River.

Conclusion

This survey of the ANC's first electoral crusade is necessarily provisional and incomplete. Sustained analysis of its support base must await the release of local voting statistics. Much of the foregoing description of ANC campaigning has been confined to its formal and official discourses, and it depends heavily upon the impressions created by printed texts. These may have been very different from the political messages broadcast by local activists. How the ANC's appeals were understood and interpreted by voters is another vital question which this chapter has not considered. Though the ANC conscientiously fought the contest as an 'issue' election, many of its supporters may have simply opted for freedom and dignity. As one black ANC adherent told a journalist in Cape Town: 'This election is between blacks and whites, it is about colour, not issues.'[25] And in so many respects this was a freedom poll, not least because of the ANC's moral legitimacy among many electors as a liberation movement and because of the massive financial support it could raise from foreign sympathisers. Even so, the achievement represented by the ANC's campaign is quite formidable. In one year it constructed a sophisticated electoral machine, and in doing so, though it has yet to admit it, it made a successful transition from liberation movement to political party.

Notes

1. *Star*, 7 April 1993.
2. ANC, 'Election Campaign Plan', May 1993.
3. *Star*, 30 October 1993.
4. ANC, 'Election Campaign Plan', June 1993–April 1994.
5. *Sunday Times*, 5 December 1993.
6. Research Initiatives, 'The First Election: Baseline Survey Report', October 1993.
7. *Weekly Mail*, 25 February 1994.
8. Ibid., 15 April 1994.
9. ANC, *The Reconstruction and Development Programme* (Johannesburg: Umanyano Publications, 1994), p. 82.
10. *Star*, 13 April 1994.
11. Ibid., 6 November 1993.
12. ANC, 'Report', Elections Strategy Workshop, 25–27 September 1993, p. 22.
13. *Star*, 23 April 1994.
14. Ibid., 11 April 1994.
15. Ibid., 30 March 1994.
16. *Weekly Mail*, 31 March 1994.
17. *Star*, 31 March 1994.
18. Ibid., 18 March 1993.
19. *Sunday Times*, 28 March 1993.
20. Ibid., 19 February 1994.
21. Ibid., 10 April 1994.
22. *Star*, 15 April 1994.
23. *Weekly Mail*, 8 April 1994.
24. *Star*, 11 May 1994.
25. *Sowetan*, 26 April 1994.

3

The National Party's Campaign for a Liberation Election

HERMANN GILIOMEE

The National Party started its election campaign with conflicting images of the party and its performance in the constitutional negotiations. One, expressed by the ANC and the English language press, saw the NP as outfoxed and outlasted by the ANC in the prolonged negotiations. In the end, the NP became 'yet another of history's halfhearted reformers which was consumed by the forces it set loose.'[1] This view also suggested that the NP had succumbed to the temptations of the new system: the pensions of the current members of parliament and of civil servants were guaranteed; the change to a PR (proportional representation) list electoral system enabled most members of the NP caucus to return to parliament; and De Klerk and some senior members of his cabinet were assured of seats in a new cabinet.

The other image was that projected by the party leadership itself. This cast the NP in the role of a party which was the main architect of the new system. In a private letter to NP branches across the country, F. W. de Klerk observed that the constitutional foundation for a new and better South Africa has been laid, and added: 'To a large extent the NP has taken the lead in this. We have attained the constitutional goals we have set for ourselves in 1991. We have carried out the mandate which the electorate ... gave us in the 1992 referendum.'[2]

This chapter will first examine some of the developments which gave rise to these different images, before turning to an analysis of the NP's election campaign.

* * *

It has been one of the unique features of the South African political system that the NP leadership since the early 1970s has been able to protect its support base despite fundamental changes to the policies to

which it had committed itself. When the government started to negotiate with the ANC and other liberation organisations, the question was often posed whether the NP would retain the trust of its constituency and thus help to ensure a stable passage to an inclusive democracy.

A comparison with the Ulster Unionists in Northern Ireland is instructive. Here the working class retained its class cohesion and independent leadership. As a result it was able to block the reforms which the British government, in alliance with the Unionist moderate leadership, tried to introduce. In South Africa, by contrast, the Afrikaner and the larger white working class was smashed by the Rand strike of 1922 and subsequently co-opted within a bureaucratic structure of industrial relations. Becoming greatly dependent on the South African state for protection, the working class, like the marginal farmers and lower-level civil servants, lacked the leadership and the organisational means to block the reforms of apartheid which undermined their position of privilege.

The political demobilisation of the working class and lower middle class provided the NP leadership with large scope for political manoeuvre. When the reforms started in the early 1970s, the core element of the Afrikaner nationalist ideology was that of a group unified in its common ethno-national identity and obedience to its political and cultural leaders. The views of Afrikaner reformist politicians were complemented by the energetic input of academics, church ministers, professional people and businessmen. As a recent comparative study shows, there was no real parallel to this in the Ulster case. The contrast can be highlighted by viewing two influential organisations, the Afrikaner Broederbond and the Orange Order, in juxtaposition with each other. The Broederbond as an upper-class organisation retained widespread respectability in Afrikaner society. By contrast, Ulster's Orange Order is a predominantly lower-class organisation which many professional and intellectual Protestants associate with bigotry and violence.[3]

The latitude given by Afrikaners to their political leaders was tellingly illustrated by a survey conducted during the mid-1970s. It found that 60 per cent of a sample of Afrikaners interviewed would support the political leadership even if it acted in ways they did not understand or approve.[4] The split within the NP in February 1982, which saw 18 members of the caucus break away on 'power-sharing' with coloureds and Indians to form the Conservative Party, narrowed the NP's Afrikaner base considerably. Support for the CP among Afrikaners rose from 19 per cent in 1983 to 41 per cent in 1992.

The NP nevertheless remained able to defend its reformist pro-gramme. Reforms drew English-speaking whites to the party, and they were backed by the Democratic Party and its predecessors, enjoying 15 to 20 per cent of the white electorate's support. It was this alliance of reformist whites across party divisions that ensured a two-thirds victory in the referendum of March 1992, which tested white support for the constitutional negotiations.

The lack of serious class tensions within white society corresponding with party divisions was another reason why the NP could protect its reforms and push ahead with negotiating an inclusive democratic system. Itself middle class in composition, the CP leadership pitched its appeal to all income groups in the white electorate. By 1992 the socio-economic profiles of the NP and CP did not differ substantially. The NP drew slightly more than average of the high-income Afrikaners and slightly below the average of the low- and middle-income Afrikaners, while the opposite was true of the CP.[5] If there was a dog that did not bark in white politics in the 1980s and early 1990s, it was the absence of a significant class among whites mobilising on its own against the reforms.

The NP leadership nevertheless took great pains to defend itself from charges that it did not act in accordance with its mandate. Virtually the entire defence was built up around the person and leadership of F. W. de Klerk. When he was elected as NP leader early in 1989, few members of the NP caucus had a stronger claim than he to being a party functionary with no separate personal or factional agendas. He was in fact the ultimate centrist. In a biography written by his brother, he explained his role before becoming leader as follows: 'I saw my role in the party as the interpreter of the median of what the policy of the party was in each particular phase. Out of a sense of loyalty and as part of my own self-chosen role, I refused to engage in subtle word play to make a policy sound *verkramp* or *verlig* as it suited me or a particular audience.'[6]

An academic analysis of De Klerk's leadership style sketches the following picture: It is a consultative style maintaining an open door approach and valuing the opinion of colleagues and subordinates; a democratic style which strives to attain consensus through consultation; a style of team-work and team-building; a negotiating style which accentuates compromise and persuasion; a style characterised by in-formality, sincerity and integrity.[7]

After the NP congresses in 1986 accepted the principle of equal citizenship for all South Africans, the party contested the general elections of 1987 and 1989 on the platform of power-sharing with blacks. However, its plans for a new constitution were still squarely based on four racially ascribed groups. While this was the case and while it enforced a national State of Emergency and the proscription of the liberation organisations, the NP could find no negotiating partners of any substance. When De Klerk unbanned the ANC and other liberation organisations in February 1990, he also recognised the need to secure the interests of minority groups within a non-racial democracy.

The NP leadership considers its mandate for a consitutional settlement with the ANC to be derived from its policy statement of September 1991 entitled 'Grondwetlike Regering in 'n Deelnemende Demokrasie'. The key mechanism in this plan was a multi-party cabinet which would be compelled to execute the decisions of a presidential troika comprised of leaders of the three most important parties. In addition, each tier of government had to enjoy 'original and entrenched powers' with which the other tiers would not interfere.[8] The policy was, as an analyst described it, 'aimed very deliberately at equalising the power of the majority party and minority parties'.[9] The provincial congresses of the NP approved the policy document, but from this point on the party leadership moved steadily further away from the negotiating position the party structures had approved.

Without securing prior approval from the caucus, De Klerk in December 1991 announced a fundamental shift in the NP's negotiating strategy. Previously he had rejected an elected constituent assembly in favour of a new constitution negotiated by the (unelected) representatives of all the political parties with proven support. Now he accepted an elected constituent assembly provided it also served as an interim government for at least five years.[10]

Secondly, De Klerk had promised a white referendum if the NP in the negotiations was compelled to deviate substantially from its constitutional proposals. The referendum of March 1992 only asked for endorsement of the process of negotiation at a stage well before serious constitutional negotiations had begun. The fact that the NP leadership refused to hold either a whites-only referendum or a whites-only election made it possible for the negotiations to be consummated in a settlement, but it also led to whites seriously questioning the legitimacy of the NP's actions.

Thirdly, the constitution adopted in December 1992 appeared to be a serious deviation from the party's mandate. The presidential troika had disappeared, and in its place came a President elected by the majority party and two Deputy Presidents elected by parties which drew more than 20 per cent of the vote; with them the President only needs to consult. The multi-party cabinet is not constrained by a minority veto but is only required to take decisions with a view to both the spirit of national unity and the need for effective government. The constitution provides for no entrenched or original powers for the provinces but makes it possible for central government to subordinate the provincial assemblies through the power it holds to set national standards. In one of its full-page advertisements published just before the referendum, the NP asked people who were *against* majority rule to vote yes (i.e. for constitutional negotiations). But majority rule within a Westminster system of government was what the constitution provided.

While until the end of 1992 De Klerk had emphasised the constraints under which a future majority party would be compelled to operate, he began to sound a new note early in 1993. He said that party leaders participating in a government of national unity had to work out jointly a programme but he significantly also added that the NP did not want to frustrate majorities. As he phrased it: 'I don't think that a party with 5 per cent of the vote can say: "I am as strong as a party with 45 per cent of the vote."'[11] What happened was that De Klerk and his chief negotiators accepted the logical implications of majority rule and placed their hopes for preventing abuses of power on making the constitution (instead of parliament) sovereign, introducing a Constitutional Court and devolving some power to the provinces.

The reasons for this shift were never properly explained to the white electorate. In fact, the party leadership displayed serious inconsistencies in advancing reasons for negotiations with the ANC. As late as September 1989, De Klerk warned those wanting to negotiate with the ANC that they 'played into the hands of forces who are geared towards destabilising South Africa and destroying the good order'.[12] The collapse of the Soviet Union enabled De Klerk to justify negotiations with the ANC by claiming that it was no longer as serious a danger as it had been when it was an 'agent of Soviet imperialism'. Yet the NP leadership until polling day in April 1994 continued to warn that the ANC, in particular the communist faction within it, was a dangerous and irresponsible party which should not be allowed to become the majority party.

The NP also vacillated on the issue whether internal resistance and foreign pressure had compelled it to settle with the ANC. In the course of the 1980s NP leaders consistently denied that sanctions were having any influence on government policy shifts. Yet during the campaign for a yes vote in the referendum of March 1992, several NP leaders sang a quite different tune. The Minister of Justice, Kobie Coetsee, for instance declared that the country had been bled white by sanctions. Two years later, in February 1994, addressing a meeting of young black executives, De Klerk painted a different picture. It was not mass action, sanctions or the violence of the 1980s which had compelled the NP to change, he declared, but economic forces and in particular the steady advance of blacks onto the higher levels of the job ladder.[13] Yet in the same month he gave an interview to the London *Times* in which he said that but for the ditching of apartheid the country would have been plunged into a 'devastating revolution'. He added: ' If we had not done what we did before the end of 1990 South Africa would have been in a state of absolute turmoil, much worse than now predicted by pessimists. We would not have had 15,000 to 25,000 on protest marches. We would have had half a million and a million, as happened in Eastern Europe.'[14]

There was, of course, a case which the NP leadership could make to justify its shift. De Klerk is rumoured to have said on the eve of the unbanning of the ANC that his only bottom line in future negotiations would be preserving a well-functioning free enterprise system. The great advantage whites have in possessing capital and skills would ensure most of them a strategic role in the economy. De Klerk was also with reason confident that the NP and its allies would for some time enjoy the confidence of the bureaucracy, military and the business community, without whose support the majority party would find it difficult to move. Furthermore, he was optimistic that the country's dependence on foreign loans would be an adequate safeguard against the confiscation or nationalisation of property. When De Klerk said that he envisaged an NP 'hand on the tiller' for a long time to come, he had in mind a deracialised country in which the informal or private power of whites would be as effective a constraint on a future government as formal constitutional checks.[15]

This argument was nevertheless not convincingly made by the NP leadership during the time the negotiations took place. It gave rise to serious doubts among whites about the NP's performance in the negotiations. The white constituency was also dismayed by the continuing violence and strikes and the ANC's use of mass mobilisation after the CODESA negotiations had broken down in May 1992. As a result, the 'reform coalition' of NP and DP supporters which had made possible the resounding referendum victory lost ground. The NP support among whites dwindled from 56 per cent in July 1992 to 28 per cent in July 1993, rising again to 40 per cent in October–November 1993. Conservative Party support in the two years remained steady between 25 and 29 per cent but dropped to 18 per cent by the end of 1993. The biggest gain was in the uncertain/don't know/will not vote categories – up from 15 per cent early in 1992 to 31 per cent at the end of 1993. Given the fact that the ANC drew support from fewer than 5 per cent of whites, the NP's greatest challenge, as far as whites were concerned, was to persuade the undecided voters, and CP and DP supporters, to back it.

* * *

Most observers believed that as the party of apartheid, the NP's prospects for gaining support across racial lines were slim. Yet once negotiations for a post-apartheid democracy started, the NP suddenly found an unexpectedly large pool of potential coloured support. Apartheid never projected a final solution for coloured people, and many NP leaders, including even Hendrik Verwoerd, privately entertained the idea of one day incorporating coloureds into the white group as allies against the blacks. The 1982 NP split and the subsequent founding of the CP were due to irreconcilable differences over this issue. While the CP leader, Andries Treurnicht, objected to any dilution of political apartheid, the NP leadership took the view, as expressed by the editor of the party's propaganda sheet, that 'we at any price align the coloured people as a bloc of 2,5 million behind the whites to broaden our own power base and thus avoid turning them over to a black power situation'.[16]

The tricameral constitution of 1983, which excluded blacks but provided for limited power-sharing for coloureds and Indians, constituted a testing ground for conflicting views about coloured political consciousness. On the one hand there was the view of the Theron Commission, which investigated conditions among the coloured people in the early 1970s. It argued that there was only 'limited support' in this group for an alliance with blacks against 'considerable' support for one with whites. It was the view of the commission that 'the more advantaged coloureds are not disillusioned by politics but are simply uninterested' and that the socio-economic development of this community would have a peaceful rather than a politicising effect on them.[17] Successive NP governments subscribed to this view.

An opposite view held that coloureds had developed a powerful sense of relative deprivation which was radicalising the leadership of the community. This view strengthened in the first half of the 1980s as a result of the rise of the United Democratic Front in the Western Cape. Led by coloured activists, the UDF publicly propagated the Freedom Charter and appeared to have led a successful boycott of the elections to the coloured and Indian Houses of Parliament. The 1984–6 uprising, which saw clashes between the police and coloured demonstrators, strengthened the impression that important sections of the community were joining the liberation struggle.[18]

The image of a radicalised coloured community was never quite persuasive. It largely ignored the structural position of marginality in which the group finds itself. Worse off than whites but in a position of semi-privilege compared with Africans, most coloureds favour incremental changes which enable them to protect their position. Others display apathy bred by a sense that they were incapable of influencing the white–black struggle. A poll undertaken in the early 1980s to test support for the proposals which would be embodied in the tricameral parliament found that half the sample was uninformed about those proposals. Of the rest of the sample, 40 per cent indicated that the proposals held some benefit for the coloured people whereas 58 per cent believed that their chances of acquiring equal political rights with whites would be enhanced by them.[19]

The tricameral parliament was such a controversial political measure that dispassionate analyses have been rare.[20] This chapter can only touch on two points related to the controversy. Firstly, one must express doubts about the UDF claim that its boycott campaign was solely responsible for the low polls registered in the 1984 elections for the coloured and Indian Houses. A study conducted after the election among a sample of voters who had abstained found that more than half registered apathy or a sense of political impotence and disinterest. Ten years later, in April 1993, a study found the tendency towards withdrawal to be still strong. Asked whether they would participate in the election for an post-apartheid interim government, only 57 per cent of coloured people said they would take part, as against 78 per cent of whites and 81 per cent of blacks.

As the election date drew closer, coloureds showed little signs of enthusiasm. The October–November 1993 MPD poll found that only 16 per cent of coloureds thought they would be richer after the election, compared with 4 per cent of whites and 43 per cent of blacks. Finally an HSRC poll of February 1994 revealed that 35 per cent of coloureds (as against 20 per cent of whites and 70 per cent of blacks) were 'excited and happy' about the coming election, while the rest were either unhappy or worried and unexcited.[21]

There is also the question whether the tricameral parliament was merely a sham, as its adversaries claimed. The position was in fact rather complex. From the early 1970s the coloured community has been transformed from a largely destitute proletariat into a stabilised working and lower middle class. One of the main manifestations was a dramatic decline in the fertility rate, which plummeted from 6 children per woman in 1965–70 to 2.9 in the late 1980s. On the one hand the process was the product of economic growth and development but on the other hand the tricameral parliament did facilitate coloured advancement. More than 100,000 houses were built in the decade, of which 60,000 were in the Cape metropolitan area. Education improved significantly. The numbers of children in secondary school increased by a third, and the number of successful matriculants doubled. These changes were nevertheless too limited to produce a broad middle class. In 1988–9, 85 per cent of coloureds had a monthly income of less than R2,000, against 34 per cent in the case of whites and 97 per cent in the case of Africans.

Cultural differences have militated against a convergence between the coloured and African people on the lower income levels. While some attributed this cultural distance between coloured people and Africans solely to the divisive effects of apartheid, an opinion leader like Richard van der Ross takes a different view. As he expressed it during the election campaign: 'It is rather a feeling that there is not enough which is common between brown and black people. Although they share certain things there exists a great gap when it comes to culture, religion, language and attitudes towards family life. There is a measure of threat ... It is a fact that blacks are involved in much of the violence ...'[22]

For the NP it was difficult to turn this common cultural background to its own advantage while it still insisted on segregating the coloured people as a distinct category. Under P. W. Botha's leadership the underlying assumption was that the coloured people would accept segregation as a trade-off for the sectional advantage they enjoyed over blacks. Botha expressed this view in the (coloured) House of Representatives: 'Let me tell members something now: If it were not for [the] very Afrikaner and the National Party, the coloured population would not be in the privileged position it is in today.'[23] He only succeeded in eliciting a storm of protest.

Once the NP started to negotiate with the extra-parliamentary forces, it gave priority to the search for political allies. The leadership now promptly dropped the racial definition of the concept 'Afrikaner' and the emphasis on coloured distinctiveness. In 1991 its Transvaal leader, Barend du Plessis, in a parliamentary debate asked CP leader, Andries Treurnicht, why he did not consider the coloured members as Afrikaners. He added: 'They speak the way we do. They believe the way we do. They live the way we do. Why does he say they are not Afrikaners? He says he is not a racist. There is only one variable which remains and that is the colour of the skin: Is it correct that it is only the colour of the skin that remains?'[24]

Understandably the coloured people have not rushed to embrace the non-racial definition of Afrikanerhood. On the other hand there is also little support for the 'nation' or 'people' as defined by the ANC. Asked in a November 1993 MPD poll what was understood by liberation, only 12 per cent of coloureds and 13 per cent of whites (compared with 37 per cent of Africans) supported the idea that 'the people shall rule'.[25] A poll conducted at the same time revealed that 60 per cent of whites and 43 per cent of coloureds wanted to retain the existing national flag and anthems, whereas 71 per cent of blacks wanted them to change.

However, in a February 1994 MPD poll, coloureds were closer to blacks than whites in their response to the question: Can all South Africans become one united nation or are there different nations and national groups? In all, 61 per cent of blacks and 54 per cent of coloureds agreed, compared with only 25 per cent of whites.[26] Yet it is more than likely that most coloureds want this nation to be built around whites and coloureds rather than around the black majority.

The ANC from the start wanted to project an image of itself as a non-racial rather than a predominantly Africanist movement. Since it could draw on only a small stratum of white support, it considered it important to demonstrate broad-based coloured backing. In trying to win the coloured vote, the ANC was up against formidable difficulties, of which some were of its own making. The UDF's campaigns of the 1980s produced a mixed harvest. They propelled activists and opinion leaders like Trevor Manuel, Cheryl Carolus, Allan Boesak, Jakes Gerwel, Franklin Sonn and Randall van den Heever into the forefront of ANC ranks. At the same time, however, the leadership failed to build an effective political organisation which combined youth movements, trade unions and community-based or civic organisations. In Cape Town the trade unions remained weak, and civic organisations politically divided and ideologically split.

State suppression and a lack of political direction exacerbated these weaknesses. With students and youth taking the lead, the emphasis of the UDF campaign was on confrontation *per se* rather than organisation focused on local issues.[27] Consumer and school boycotts which were not properly thought through increased divisions. The attempts to rally Africans in a common struggle against the state foundered on the resistance of black leaders to what they considered as UDF meddling in township affairs.[28]

While Africans have been solidly mobilised behind the ANC through support organisations such as trade unions, civics and street committees, coloured politics are characterised by the absence of similar organisations wielding influence. In the case of trade unions, 42 per cent of Africans answered positively the question whether they would influence voters, against only 14 per cent of coloureds; for civics, the figures were 52 and 12 per cent; and for street committees, 46 and 11 per cent respectively.[29] Like whites, coloured people receive most of their political information from TV (58 per cent as against 34.5 per cent for Africans). Here the NP enjoyed a headstart over the ANC because of the favourable treatment it received until fairly recently on television. And as more than four-fifths of coloured people speak Afrikaans at home, NP-supporting newspapers like *Die Burger* and *Rapport* have wielded considerable influence. Of *Die*

Burger's 90,000 readers on weekdays, 30,000 to 35,000 are coloureds, and a quarter of *Rapport's* 400,000 readers buy the 'coloured' edition called *Metro*. The editor of *Metro,* Zelda Jongbloed, declares that over the past four years coloureds 'have made peace with themselves: they are content to be coloureds and Afrikaans'.[30]

In the first two years after the unbanning of the ANC and the other liberation organisations, coloured support for the NP remained high. In February 1992, 66 per cent supported the NP, 6 per cent the ANC, and 26 per cent were undecided. By April 1993, however, the NP was weakened by the growing perception that it was losing ground against the ANC. In this month a poll showed that 47 per cent of coloureds supported the NP, as against 19 per cent backing the ANC and 30 per cent undecided. Two years later, in a February 1994 poll the support bases were roughly similar. The NP was the choice of 42 per cent and the ANC of 17 per cent; 38 per cent were undecided or refused to divulge their voting intentions.[31]

That the NP did not weaken further was mainly due to two reasons. Firstly, De Klerk remained a popular leader. In the February 1994 poll, 53 per cent of coloured respondents supported De Klerk, whereas 42 per cent endorsed the party. Secondly, the ANC policy proposals failed to persuade coloureds that the ANC would rule more effectively than the NP. By the end of 1993, a MPD poll showed coloured respondents indicating by majorities of two to one and three to one that the NP would be more effective in enforcing law and order, create a climate of peace and reconciliation, make the economy grow, and promote education and health care.

Finally, after opening its membership to other races, the NP managed to enlist large numbers of coloured members. In March 1994 the Cape leader of the NP estimated that 45 per cent of the Western Cape party's membership were coloured.[32] For the party the greatest problem had become not so much to win over coloured supporters but to get all its potential supporters out to vote. There was the apathy factor to consider and also the fact that only a fifth of coloureds had voted before. Facing the same difficulties, the ANC had to contend with an additional problem: their success in the struggle turned on mobilisation against the state and its structures; the election, by contrast, depended to a large extent on political organisation in a community which put an emphasis on orderly change. In this the NP, with its vast experience of fighting elections, had a headstart.

The NP's hopes for attracting black support rested largely on the viability of the structures for black self-administration erected under the apartheid system. It was always an article of faith among the NP leadership that non-Xhosa homeland leaders would never embrace the ANC on account of the predominance of Xhosas in the leadership of the movement. It also hoped that the black local authorities introduced in 1982 would become the core around which a supportive black middle class would develop. These assumptions proved to be unrealistic. With the exception of Chief Buthelezi, none of the homeland leaders had a mass base of their own, and they were easily co-opted by the ANC. Corrupt or inefficient and hamstrung by a lack of resources, the black city councillors proved to be of little political value to the NP. The NP's concessions to the ANC in the negotiations alienated its only significant black ally, Inkatha. As the perception grew that the ANC was making great strides towards liberation, blacks flocked *en masse* to the movement. While the NP still had 8 per cent of blacks supporting it in mid-1992, this figure had dropped to below 1 per cent a year later.

*   *   *

'South Africa is changing. We have done it.' (NP poster)

The agenda of the NP's electoral strategy was spelled out at its federal congress which met on 2 February 1994 in Pretoria. High on the agenda was the need to combat defeatism, an aspect to which both De Klerk and Olaus van Zyl, Executive Director of the NP's Federal Office, devoted considerable attention in their communication to NP branches dated 22 December 1993. To bolster hopes, Van Zyl pointed out the following:
 —It was 'realistic of the NP to get 60 per cent of the whites, 70 per cent of the coloureds and 60 per cent of the Indian vote'.[33]
 —The potential for drawing black support existed. The party's own polls showed that 15 per cent of black voters regarded the NP as their first or second choice. More than 60 per cent of black respondents had 'no negative feelings' towards the NP. Indeed, 28 per cent of blacks 'felt good' about the NP.
 —Only 24 per cent of black respondents realised that the NP had changed over the past five years. NP support could grow once this information was communicated. The NP should also target the more than 50 per cent of black voters who indicated that they did not expect to be better off under an ANC government.
 —There were more than 30 per cent of blacks or 6 million voters still uncertain about which party to support. The NP's aim must be to win at least half of them over.[34]
 At the NP's federal congress, Van Zyl spelled out the different steps of

the party's campaign strategy. Firstly, the message had to be hammered home that freedom and the end of apartheid had already been achieved. The second step was to ensure fair and free elections through spreading the message that the ballot would be secret. The third and fourth steps were to present the 'new' NP's philosophy and policy programme and to depict the ANC as a dangerous party. The choice for the voters would be between 'the new NP versus the old ANC'.[35]

The NP insisted that it could only be judged in terms of the five years of the De Klerk administration. However, 46 years of uninterrupted NP rule made it difficult to sustain this claim. De Klerk has been a cabinet minister since 1978, and although he did not handle controversial portfolios, he was known to have pushed hard in the mid-1980s to increase the 'own affairs' dimension of the tricameral parliament.

The NP responded to the accusations of its opponents by making three points. Firstly, it claimed that the dramatic changes which South Africa had undergone since 1990 were all the work of the NP. At the NP's federal congress De Klerk asked all candidates to carry forth the message that the NP had already destroyed apartheid and liberated the country.[36] Secondly, the party marketed F. W. de Klerk as the leader who had the courage to turn the country away from the abyss, who had the honesty to abolish apartheid, and who had the formula for making peace in South Africa.[37]

Thirdly, it constantly proclaimed the idea that the election was not about the past but about the future. In a full-page advertisement published in December 1993, the words of De Klerk in his Nobel Prize acceptance speech were cited: 'The coming election will not be about the past. It will not be about apartheid or the armed struggle. It will be about future peace and stability, about progress and prosperity, about nation-building.'[38]

Before the campaign started De Klerk and the NP at large were all too inclined to parry demands for an apology for apartheid with the words that if South Africans dwelled on 'the real or imagined sins of the past' they would never be able to find one another in the present.[39] In an apology, issued more than a year before the campaign started, De Klerk merely acknowledged that the Afrikaners had 'clung too long to a dream of separate nation-states'. 'For that', he continued, 'we are sorry.'[40] Once the campaign began, De Klerk took a different line. Reporting on his tour at the end of February of coloured communities in the Western Cape, Anthony Johnson of the *Cape Times* wrote: 'In a bid to move past NP baggage from the centre of the election debate the NP leader routinely made fulsome apologies to his predominantly coloured audiences for the "heartache" caused by the NP's apartheid policies and urged voters to think about the future under a "new NP".[41]

Many blacks refused to dismiss these apologies as an election ploy. Commenting on the NP's federal congress of 2 February, John Perlman of the *Star* noted that the NP's willingness to say sorry for the past served to count for a great deal with many of its recruits from the black townships.[42]

But coupled with these apologies for apartheid was the NP's insistence that it deserved the credit for its abolition. When Nelson Mandela visited Robben Island on 2 February 1994 to light a 'flame of freedom', a full-page advertisement proclaimed 'Today Mr. Nelson Mandela honours President De Klerk'. It went on to list the 'achievements' (unbanning the ANC, negotiating a new constitution, and proposing fair and free elections, etc.) which had all been 'set in motion' by De Klerk's speech of 2 February 1990.[43] The ANC was understandably outraged by these claims. But if many blacks took issue with the NP, the message went down well in the coloured and Indian communities. In Natal, 27 per cent of Indians put the NP first in a simple choice poll, but in a simulated ballot exercise its support jumped to 63 per cent. In fact, a MPD analysis of the poll stated: 'it makes sense to see the Natal NP as predominantly an Indian party.'[44] Coloured voters outside ANC ranks appeared to accept fully the NP's apology.

The NP federal congress held in Johannesburg in February was an occasion to demonstrate the party's new image. Most observers were impressed. Instead of the all-white party faithfully singing Afrikaans songs like 'Sarie Marais', the two thousand delegates from all population groups chanted 'Viva FW' and swayed in unison to the strains of the workers' song, 'Tshotsholoza'.[45]

By contrast, the lists of NP candidates failed to capture the imagination. Of its candidates for the National Assembly 60 per cent were white.[46] One reason was that the party decided to dispense with a high-profile national list. Instead it submitted in each region one list for the national and one for the provincial assembly. More important, however, was the fact that no non-white political leader of any significance was prepared to stand for the NP, at least not in the first post-apartheid election. In defence, party leaders claimed that this was due to intimidation and that the composition of the lists was subject to a democratic process which limited window-dressing. A more credible explanation would have been that the party was still paying the price for its apartheid past and for rewarding old-guard loyalists.

Like most other parties, the NP went to commendable lengths to enhance fairness, openness and grassroots input in the selection of candidates.[47] The method followed in the case of candidates for the

Western Cape parliament is worth citing. Some 900 delegates from rural branches in the region met in Worcester to vote for 14 candidates. At the same time representatives of the NP in the metropolitan areas of the region met in Stellenbosch to vote for 20 candidates. The two lists were then merged by the party's provincial executive, which added an additional 8 names. The final lists then went to the NP's federal council. Because the NP was the favourite to win the contest in the Western Cape, this province attracted the most attention. Here 57 per cent of the electorate was coloured and a further 23 per cent African. Of the top ten candidates on the NP lists for the National Assembly and Western Cape provincial legislature, two and three respectively were not white. However, office-bearers pointed out that if the party won 55 per cent of the votes in the province, as it was confident of doing, a third of the successful candidates would be non-white. In Natal the position was worse. Of the top 27 candidates for the National Assembly, only 6 came from the strategically important Indian community, of which more than half backed the NP.

In general, the press agreed that the party's attempt to change its image was largely successful. The correspondent of the *New York Times*, Bill Keller, wrote that the party won over votes by its willingness to reject apartheid in order to renew itself. It compelled the ANC to adopt a similar strategy by also admitting past errors.[48]

* * *

'The State President in the person of Mr. F. W. de Klerk is without a doubt the NP's most important asset. As a matter of fact, we would argue that he is one of the most important assets of South Africa as a whole.' (Chris Fismer, co-ordinator of the NP's presidential campaign)

Along with presenting the image of the NP as a party which had fundamentally changed itself, NP strategists gave priority to marketing De Klerk as the leader best equipped to deal with the problems and challenges of post-apartheid South Africa. To deal with the task of image-making, the NP contracted the British firm Lowe Bell, which saw Margaret Thatcher through three election victories, and the advertising firm Saatchi and Saatchi. The financial resources of the party for its entire campaign, including the presidential part, were probably in the region of R30–40 million. According to NP estimates this was only a quarter to a third of the funds available to the ANC, even if salaries of NP parliamentarians were taken into account.[49]

At the NP's federal congress in February, Chris Fismer outlined the programme which De Klerk would follow on his 'roadshow', which took up most of his time in the first part of the campaign. He was to visit all nine provinces, meet as many people as possible, and create 'maximum opportunity' for the media to cover the President's visits. Fismer enthusiastically described some of the earlier campaigning: 'Every good speech is followed by still better speeches, he shakes hands with thousands of hands of as many admirers while his perennial smile conquers people for the NP.'[54] By means of the 'road shows', the NP hoped to demonstrate that it was a party which had supporters in every community and income group – that it was in fact the 'most representative party of the broad South African society'.[50] De Klerk completed his roadshows by the end of March. In April he addressed meetings and rallies in most of the important parts of the country.

Through the roadshows the NP gave proof that it had absorbed the lessons of the past few years. It avoided the traditional town-hall meetings with the attendant risks of heckling and teargas. Meetings were mostly unannounced blitzes where hands were shaken before the cameras. Mindful of the fact that the President was considerably more popular than the party, the NP tried to turn this to its advantage. Everywhere De Klerk introduced himself with the words 'I am not here as the President. I am here as leader of the NP.'[51] Addressing the crowds, De Klerk would present the NP as the fresh party and the ANC as the stale party carrying the excess baggage of Winnie Mandela, Peter Mokaba and COSATU.[52] In the Western Transvaal tour, De Klerk addressed 11, 000 people in three days.

His tours through coloured communities on the West Coast and through coloured townships in Cape Town were considered a resounding success. The pro-NP *Burger* called the Cape Flats tour a triumph which exceeded the boldest expectations. The *Cape Times* commented more soberly but still positively: 'The National Party leader was enthusiastically welcomed at all stops on his road show, encountering only pockets of resistance from ANC protesters.'[53] In the tour of the West Coast, his constant message was: 'The ANC is bad news for the country. The NP builds schools; the ANC disrupts schooling. The NP builds houses; the ANC breaks houses down. The NP stands for peace and reconciliation; the ANC intimidates people. The NP builds hospitals; the ANC's supporters toyi-toyi in hospital corridors while people die inside.'[54]

The NP-supporting press lauded De Klerk's roadshows but did not hold back on criticism. The correspondent of the newspaper *Beeld* wrote after his tour to the Western Transvaal and Northern Cape that, in contrast to similar ANC meetings, there had been little spontaneity in De

Klerk's encounters with blacks. In the case of farm workers, the question arose whether they came voluntarily or at the request of their employers. Piet Muller wrote in *Rapport* that the organisers had much to learn, adding that aides of a politician like Kennedy 'would never have allowed their boss to stop at a farm and address a group of exhausted, sour and overworked farm labourers', as had happened on a particular occasion.[55]

At most meetings, however, De Klerk handled critical crowds well, often counter-attacking when challenged by protesters. When in the Eastern Transvaal he was asked what the NP had done for black education, he enquired: Who introduced school boycotts? Who used children and teachers for years as political instruments? Who burnt down schools and destroyed textbooks?[56]

De Klerk had to contend with strong personal attacks on him by Mandela, who called him a 'coward', 'weakling' and 'unstable person' and accused him of being the 'evil mastermind' behind the black-on-black violence or turning a blind eye to the conflict so as to scare blacks away from the polling booths. De Klerk did not respond in kind. The furthest he would go was to describe Mandela as an 'old bull' who was living in the past, and to call himself a young bull, in addressing black audiences. But De Klerk's cabinet colleagues did lash back. They asserted that Mandela sang a different tune to different audiences, pleading for reconciliation when addressing moderate audiences but making dangerous threats when speaking to militants and radicals.[57]

While the foreign press labelled De Klerk's roadshows aimed at attracting rural black support 'mission impossible', he won critical acclaim from some of the most prestigious foreign newspapers. The *New York Times* reporter declared that in the task of addressing such meetings, Mandela was put in the shade by De Klerk, who often turned opposition into positive opportunities. The paper added that he conducted the campaign with all the resources of an 'energetic, risk-taking, resourceful and highly adaptable' politician. Where Mandela often came across stiffly, De Klerk could put fire into the same speech which he made ten times a day, touching the emotions of his audience.[58]

The NP was pleased with the effects of De Klerk's roadshows. When the last of the mini-trips were undertaken towards the end of March, more than half a million people were directly exposed to De Klerk; peak-time television provided extensive coverage. Blacks gave him a mixed reception, but he encountered increasingly enthusiastic coloured and Indian crowds.[59] These successes had to be balanced against the fact that the NP, like the DP, found it virtually impossible to embark on campaigning in the townships. With NP or DP supporters branded as traitors and party meetings very likely to be disrupted, the parties resorted to telephone canvassing where possible. In this climate of fear and violence organisers described the election as 'free and fair in theory only'. In the Eastern Cape the party frankly admitted that it was 'too dangerous to campaign in the black townships'.[60] The Independent Electoral Commission declared a week before polling day that the NP and DP had 'no access' to African township and shack areas in the Western Cape.[61] Even in the relatively peaceful Orange Free State, the large township of Botshabelo and Thabong outside Welkom were virtually inaccessible to these parties.[62]

* * *

'The ANC want to take South Africa back to the dark ages. It is a dangerous party which cannot be trusted and which had to be put in its place on election day.' (F. W. de Klerk, at NP federal congress, February 1994)

The NP realised that bringing the message 'We have changed' and marketing De Klerk as the great conciliator were not enough to break out of the bracket of 14–18 per cent overall support which opinion polls gave it. To expand its base, NP propaganda developed the dual theme that the ANC was a dangerous party with unrealistic policies which would wreck the economy, whereas the NP offered administrative experience and economic approaches that elsewhere in the world have brought prosperity and stability.

In the attempt to brand the ANC as dangerous, the NP made great play of the proportion of communists in senior ANC ranks. The ANC–SACP Alliance tried to counter by putting its figures on the table. According to Jeremy Cronin, an SACP office-bearer, 7 of the top 20, 16 of the top 50, and 34 of the total of 200 ANC candidates on the national list were members of its party, who would all be bound by ANC policies and discipline. But the NP leadership relentlessly attacked the ANC's list and claimed that the SACP statement was a deliberate lie. According to its own investigation, 25 of the top 50 ANC candidates were communists. In an advertisement it depicted the communists as the wolf and the ANC as the sheep in the Alliance.

The NP strongly criticised the ANC's Reconstruction and Development Programme. This programme set out the number of houses the ANC wished to build, provide with electricity and running water, and the number of jobs it wanted to create over the next five years, but did not specify the cost of the programme. Cabinet ministers called it a dangerous document – a 'menu without prices'. The NP-aligned press published an assessment of the ANC policy by the *Times* which called it a populist programme that would distort and set back the economy.[63] De Klerk told a meeting of black executives that the NP had the same goals as those envisaged in the ANC programme but that the NP wanted to avoid funding it in such a way that it would result in runaway inflation and unaffordable deficits.[64]

The NP was at pains to stress that it was as eager as the ANC to provide jobs, houses and services to the people. It pointed out that the government could have built many more houses had the ANC not brought programmes to a standstill over the past five to seven years in order to deny the NP credit for development. When in October 1993 black squatters occupied houses built for coloured people in Cape Town and for Indians in Durban, the NP was quick to make political capital out of the events. In Cape Town it placed a full-page press advertisement under the heading 'Your house is not safe under the ANC', followed by the assertion, 'The ANC is not yet part of the government and already its supporters are taking houses which belong to legitimate owners.' The advertisement concluded with the assurance: 'The NP stands for house ownership for everyone.'[65] It warned about the threat to people's most prized possession, their house, then identified the ANC as source of that threat, and ended by offering a solution to the problem: vote NP.[66] The pro-ANC weekly *South* conceded that the advertisement was a 'cunningly constructed piece of propaganda'.

In its own election manifesto, the NP committed itself to reconciliation through the creation of jobs, an aggressive home-building programme, and providing health care for all. The key to this was stimulating economic growth by lowering taxes, encouraging free enterprise, and reducing state intervention. In its manifesto the NP declared that the house-building programme must be driven by private enterprise; jobs had to be created through free enterprise, a market economy, and foreign investment. Peace and stability had to be achieved by a sound federal constitution, the rule of law, and community policing. An NP government, the manifesto emphasised, would follow the economic policies of the successful countries of Europe, America and the Far East.[67]

This became the dominant theme of the NP's campaign message. The economic policy of the ANC and SACP would bring the country to its knees, but the NP had the experience and ability to create order and economic prosperity out of chaos. In an advertisement the NP boldly proclaimed: 'The ANC makes promises; only the NP can deliver.' It went on to contrast the NP, which had built the richest economy in Africa, and the ANC, which has 'yet to run a township successfully, let alone a country'.[68]

The NP also exploited the disruption by ANC-supporters of NP and DP meetings. It alleged that Mandela had lost control over his followers, who ignored his requests not to disrupt meetings. If Mandela already was unable to control them, the NP asked, what would happen when he came to power?

But the NP's concerns went beyond comrades disrupting meetings. It accused the ANC of having many followers in its ranks willing to use violence to root out opposition. Hernus Kriel linked the violence and crime which has recently rocketed in South Africa directly to an ANC attempt 'to eliminate all opposition'. In an exchange with Allan Boesak, he charged: 'They [the ANC] have done nothing, except blame everybody else, to stem the killing.'[69] On another occasion he exclaimed that the ANC preached democracy but its members were not democrats. They had instituted no-go areas and consumer boycotts; they had introduced kangaroo courts and necklace murders to South Africa; they had brought the curse of the AK47 into the country.[70] The Cape leader, Dawie de Villiers, contrasted the disruptive behaviour of ANC supporters with that of the NP, which in 'the spirit of true freedom and democracy displays a spirit of reconciliation and tolerance'.[71] The NP constantly prided itself on its 'code of conduct' for its followers, which ruled out breaking up opposition meetings or manhandling vocal ANC supporters at NP meetings. The allegations of complicity by senior police officers in third force activities seriously undermined this message of the NP.

Hoping to ride to victory on the coloured vote in both the Western and the Northern Cape, the NP paid great attention to the aspirations and fears of this community. Most of its meetings in the first three months of the campaign were held before largely coloured audiences. The political fall-out from the occupation of coloured houses in October 1993 probably helped the NP greatly to reverse the decline it had experienced in coloured support. The next major issue was Mandela's remark in late January that coloureds and Indians who voted NP would 'betray' the revolution. Marthinus van Schalkwyk, the NP's media director, slammed this as a 'subtle threat' from a party which was in practice a black organisation that favoured Xhosa-speakers.[72]

The other constituency on which the NP concentrated was whites who felt that the NP had conceded too much in the negotiations and was now incapable of holding the ANC in check. The NP's task was made difficult by statements of prominent ANC spokespeople who presented the negotiations as an unqualified ANC triumph. Mohammed Valli Moosa called the constitution the 'terms of surrender of an undemocratic regime'.[73] Tokyo Sexwale declared that De Klerk would enjoy no power when he became Deputy President after the election.[74] Although it did not have a strong case, the NP issued a special supplement carried by the *Sunday Times* in which it argued that the most important aspects of its own constitutional proposals had been accepted. It went on to say that while the constitution ensured that power would be shared and minorities would be protected, it could not work properly without a strong NP presence on all levels of government.

In addressing the white Right, De Klerk repeatedly declared that there would never be a return to apartheid in even one inch of the country. A white *volkstaat* was quite unrealistic and white right-wing violence a 'dead-end'.[75] With polls showing the majority of right-wing supporters eager to vote, the NP dared Ferdi Hartzenberg and Constand Viljoen to allow their people to vote.

The fiasco of right-wing intervention in the Bophuthatswana turmoil in the middle of March and Viljoen's subsequent decision to lead a section of the right-wing in the election had a mixed impact on the NP campaign. On the one hand participation in the election by Viljoen's Freedom Front served to legitimise the government's decision to negotiate a democratic constitution. On the other hand the Front had the potential of drawing 400,000 votes away from the NP. The NP has nevertheless decided to persevere with its policy of concentrating on its battle against the ANC, and spend little time and money on fighting smaller parties.[76]

* * *

During the final month of the campaign, the NP devoted considerable resources to the Western Cape, the one province it looked poised to win. De Klerk wound up his election campaign in the Good Hope Centre in Cape Town, where he addressed a wildly enthusiastic audience of more than 10,000, of whom the great majority was coloured. The NP canvassers concentrated almost all their energies on coloured voters. According to accounts, party canvassers virtually ignored white voters on the assumption that the majority would in any event vote NP. White party organisers calculated that their party also needed to attract 60,000–80,000 African votes to score a victory in the province; but as we have seen, the party found it almost impossible to gain entry into the African townships and squatter camps.

The NP's coloured support remained steady throughout the campaign. The ANC and DP accused the NP of mobilising this support through fuelling anti-African feelings among coloured people. There is certainly some truth in this. A tribunal of the Independent Electoral Commission (IEC) ordered the NP to recall 80,000 copies of a photo-magazine which it issued as propaganda. In this, Uitsmyt, the dog of a coloured family, suggests that under the ANC one can expect to hear the slogan 'Kill a coloured, kill a farmer'.[77] A coloured woman is depicted as being prevented by black youths from attending church. Under the NP, she says, she could always rely on freedom of worship.

But simply to dismiss this development as the manipulation of racial fears is to ignore its larger significance. The NP did particularly well among minority groups because it was exceptionally attentive to the need of many voters in these groups to have their ethnic or communal identities confirmed. The ANC, by contrast, wanted such identities to be relegated to the private sphere and held up an ill-defined non-racial identity as substitute. In the Western Cape the NP greatly benefited from the fact that coloured people, as well as whites, through the years have seen themselves as having a prior claim to the province. With the NP attracting far more coloured people than whites to its meetings, the party could project itself as a brown party geared towards protecting brown interests and values. Anwar Ismail, one of the most effective coloured organisers in the NP, expressed this view as follows: 'We [the coloured people] are the majority here and we shall determine the course of the election. We speak Afrikaans, we live as conservatives, attend church and raise our children on traditional values. Hence we are National [Party]. The Xhosas of Transkei and the ANC are the real settlers here. The ANC with its black profile and Communist cloak repels us.'[78]

The NP managed to solidify its support for several reasons. Firstly, Hernus Kriel, candidate for premier of the province, and outgoing Minister of Police, had the image of a strong man not soft on crime. He committed himself repeatedly to providing greater personal security in the region.[79]

In the second place, the NP benefited from coloured fears about housing and jobs. The ANC had no way of countering negative propaganda after the occupation by African squatters of houses built for coloured people. ANC organisers admitted that this issue continued to hurt it throughout the campaign. Coloured voters also feared that under the ANC, both the government and private sector employers would give preference to Africans. Fuelling those fears were 'affirmative action' job advertisements which appeared in Cape Town newspapers. In a departure from the previous 'whites-only' style, a new code indicated the current preference – 'Xhosa speakers'.[80] Although ANC-supporting trade unions issued advertisements that 'everyone who has suffered under the apartheid regime, including coloured workers, will benefit from affirmative action',[81] the NP looked a more credible champion of coloured (and white) workers than the ANC.

Thirdly, the NP profited from the inept way in which the ANC started its campaign when it still believed that its appeal to non-racialism was sufficiently strong to ignore the different political cultures of Africans and non-Africans in the region. Franklin Sonn, an Afrikaans-speaking community leader, entered the campaign in its final phase but the damage was already done. The NP could label the ANC as an organisation for Xhosas and communists. In the end the NP's campaign to capture the coloured vote was astonishingly effective. On the basis of the MPD's February poll of Western Cape voters, it was calculated that two-thirds of the coloured people would vote for the NP as compared with the quarter who would put their cross next to the ANC.

The Indian community in Natal was also attracted to the NP on account of its unequivocal championing of the free market and property rights. When multi-party negotiations started in the beginning of 1992, the NP was the choice of 52 per cent of Indian voters as against 8 per cent who opted for the ANC. By July 1993 NP support had dropped to 39 per cent and ANC backing had climbed to 17 per cent, with nearly 40 per cent undecided. When the campaign started at the end of 1993, an MPD poll showed that the NP had large potential support. In all, 63 per cent of Indians gave the NP as their first choice, whereas 27 per cent singled out the ANC. Despite the prominence of Indians in the ANC campaign, the NP managed to win 60 per cent of Indian votes in the election.

The final six weeks of the campaign were crucial for the NP to persuade wavering whites, coloureds and Indians to rally behind it. The mood in these communities remained sombre. The MPD poll taken in February showed that twice as many whites felt worried and unhappy about the election as those who felt excited and happy; among Indians and coloureds the sentiments were not much more positive. Whites were nevertheless more committed to voting than any other group.[82] The NP managed to improve its support moderately in the last stages of the campaign. The MPD's February poll showed the party had 16.9 per cent support in the electorate compared with the 20.4 per cent which it received in the election. Many undecided voters in the non-African communities were probably influenced positively by the televised debate between Pik Botha and Thabo Mbeki and that between F. W. de Klerk and Nelson Mandela. While Botha concentrated on the significant number of communists in ANC leadership ranks, De Klerk gave an accomplished performance in which he argued that a party that could counterbalance the ANC was essential for making the constitution work and protecting minority groups. Against the ANC's 2–3 per cent, the NP is estimated to have won two–thirds of the white vote in the election –

up 10 per cent from the support it had received from whites in the 1989 election.

In contrast to its relative success among minority communities, the NP campaign failed to make any impact on African voters. The NP never managed to recover the 6–8 per cent support it drew from Africans between July 1992 and February 1993. It is estimated that the DP and NP together did not attract more than 2 per cent of African support in the election. Or to put it differently, in all the provinces except Natal the ANC won more than 90 per cent of the African vote.

The almost complete lack of African support came as a painful surprise. In the final days of the campaign, NP spokespeople had publicly expressed great hopes. They thought an NP-led alliance could win the PWV province, that the NP could attract a third of the votes in the Eastern Cape, and that the party country-wide could come close to a 30 per cent support level.

Why were these estimates so far off the mark? Most important, they failed to understand the extent to which *uhuru* feelings had gripped almost all Africans. Analysts R. W. Johnson and Lawrence Schlemmer described these as 'a dense concentration of practical wishes and desires – for peace, better housing, education, health, more jobs and so-so strong ... that it simply overwhelms any separate consideration of these issues as such'.[83] Almost all Africans who could vote turned up to reward the ANC for its historic role in the struggle for liberation. The NP had no counter to the ANC in an election which was for all practical purposes a racial census. Compounding its problems was the fact that the NP could gain no effective access to blacks living in the townships and the homelands.

But even if it had been possible for the NP to establish a presence in African areas, it would have been confronted with insuperable obstacles. Most Africans receive their political information from organisations like trade unions, civics and street committees dominated by ANC-aligned activists. Even those Africans outside this sphere of influence would have been persuaded with difficulty to vote against the ANC. According to a nation-wide survey, more than half of all Africans said that they lived in an area effectively dominated by a single party, while a fifth (as against only a hundredth of coloureds) answered positively to the question whether they were under any pressure to vote for a party they did not particularly support. A quarter said that neighbours were tough on people not supporting the 'right' party.[84] Sensing this, some NP strategists scaled down their expectations. This election, they said, was simply about positioning the party for the 1999 election, which would hopefully not be contested in an *uhuru* context. As De Klerk phrased it after the election results were announced: 'This was the first and the last liberation election. The next one would be a normal one in which all South Africans would look after their own interests when they vote.'[85]

* * *

Between the white election of 1989 and the general election of 1994 the NP underwent one of the most radical transformations any political party has yet experienced. It abandoned final control over the political destiny of whites for the uncertainties of securing white and other minority interests in an open, black–dominated political system. The negotiations caused a split between the NP and Inkatha, its largest African ally, and caused its endorsement level in polls to drop to 11 per cent by mid–1993.

The NP nevertheless managed to climb out of this deep trough. The election campaign helped the NP to expand its white support base and to win a large, new following in the coloured and Indian communities. Although its poor performance among Africans in the election came as a painful surprise, this blow was softened by the fact that the NP won two-thirds of the votes of the white, Indian and coloured communities. After the election De Klerk depicted the NP as the most representative party in the country, one whose goal was to win the next election.[86] Commenting on his own prospects, he said that if the NP did not make mistakes in the next five years he could possibly become President again.[87] This could be dismissed as bravado typical of politicians but it also reflects the NP's determination to project the transition as a process in which the NP would continue to play a major, if not dominant, role. It is this determination which enabled it in the campaign to transform itself so successfully into a non-racial party – one which articulates the values of property rights, family life and individual achievement and which can present itself credibly as the main champion of the non-African communities.

Notes

1. Cited by *Die Burger*, 15 February 1994, p.9.
2. (NP Head Office) Letter, De Klerk to NP branches, 22 December 1993.
3. For an illuminating study see A. Johnston, 'Covenanted Peoples: The Ulster Unionist and Afrikaner Nationalist Coalitions in Growth, Maturity and Decay', Ph.D. dissertation, University of Natal, 1993.
4. Theodore Hanf et al., *Südafrika: Friedlicher Wandel?* (Munich: Kaiser, 1978), pp. 421–22.
5. Hermann Giliomee, '"Broedertwis": Intra-Afrikaner Conflicts in the Transition from Apartheid', in Norman Etherington, ed., *Peace and Violence in the New South Africa* (London: Hans Zell, 1992), p. 175.

6. Willem de Klerk, *F. W. de Klerk: Die Man en sy Tyd* (Cape Town: Tafelberg, 1991), p. 26.

7. Hennie Kotze and Deon Geldenhuys, in *Leadership*, 9 (July 1990), pp. 12-28.

8. 'Grondwetlike Regering in 'n Deelnemende Demokrasie'

9. Lawrence Schlemmer, 'National Party Constitutional Proposals', *South Africa International*, 22 (1991), p. 66.

10. Johannes Rantete and Hermann Giliomee, 'Transition to Democracy through Transaction?: Bilateral Negotiations between the ANC and NP in South Africa', *African Affairs*, 91 (1992), pp. 515-42.

11. Transcript of a television interview conducted by David Frost, 14 February 1993.

12. De Klerk, *F. W. de Klerk*, pp. 62-3.

13. *Business Day*, 10 February 1994, p. 1.

14. *London Times* cited by *Weekend Argus*, 26/27 February 1994, p. 6.

15. Michael MacDonald and Wilmot James, 'The Hand on the Tiller: The Politics of State and Class in South Africa', *Journal of Modern African Studies* (March 1993), pp. 387-405.

16. Giliomee, 'Broedertwis', p. 353.

17. RSA, RP 38/1976, Report of the Commission of Inquiry into Matters relating to the Coloured Population Group, par. 20.43–20.85.

18. Johann Groenewald, 'Relative Deprivation: A Component of Transformed Political Awareness in Cape Town, 1976–1983', *Politikon*, 15, 2 (1988), pp. 31-48.

19. Richard van der Ross, *The Rise and Decline of Apartheid: A Study of Political Movements among the Coloured People of South Africa, 1880–1985* (Cape Town: Tafelberg, 1986), p. 353.

20. See Gerd Behrens, '"The Other Two Houses": The First Five Years of the Houses of Representatives and Delegates', University of Cape Town doctoral dissertation, 1989.

21. HSRC Report S-150, 'Kleurlinge se Persepsies van die Eerste Verkiesing vir die Huis van Verteenwoordigers op 22 Augustus 1984'; HSRC Omnibus Poll, April 1993; MPD 'Launching Democracy – I', p. 99; HSRC Omnibus Poll, February 1994.

22. *Die Burger*, 22 February 1994, p. 13.

23. Hermann Giliomee, 'The Leader and the Citizenry', in Robert Schrire, ed., *Leadership in the Apartheid State: From Malan to De Klerk* (Cape Town: Oxford University Press, 1994), pp. 130-31.

24. Giliomee, "Broedertwis", pp. 362-3.

25. Institute of Multi-Party Democracy, 'Launching Democracy: Technical Report', December 1993, p. 153.

26. Institute for Multi-Party Democracy, 'Launching Democracy II', February 1994, p. 145.

27. Colin Bundy, '"Action, Comrades, Action!": The Politics of Youth–Student Resistance in the Western Cape, 1985', in Wilmot James and Mary Simons, ed., *The Angry Divide: Social and Economic History of the Western Cape* (Cape Town: David Philip, 1989), pp. 206-17.

28. For an astute analysis, see Jeremy Seekings, 'The United Democratic Front in Cape Town, 1983–1986', UCT Centre for African Studies seminar paper, October 1992.

29. MPD, 'Launching Democracy – I', p. 87.

30. Interview with Zelda Jongbloed, 15 March 1994.

31.   Lawrence Schlemmer, 'Pre-Election Polls', *Indicator SA*, II, 1
        (Summer 1993), p. 8; MPD, 'Launching Democracy – II', p. 189.
32.   Interview with Dawie de Villiers, 7 March 1994.
33.   *International Herald Tribune,* 10 January 1994, p. 4.
34.   NP Head Office Bulletin, A 32/93 dated 22 December 1993; *Rapport,* 23 January
        1994, p. 2.
35.   Facsimile copy of speech by Olaus van Zyl to NP federal congress, 3 February 1994.
36.   *Die Burger,* February 1994, p. 1.
37.   Facsimile copy of speech by Chris Fismer at the NP federal congress,
        3 February 1994.
38.   *Sunday Times,* 12 December 1993, p. 20.
39.   *The Argus,* 27 April 1991.
40.   *Die Burger,* 10 October 1992.
41.   *Cape Times,* 23 February 1994, p. 16.
42.   *The Star International Weekly* , 3–9 February 1994, p. 2.
43.   *The Argus,* 2 February 1994, p. 13.
44.   *Cape Times,* 16 January 1994, p. 4; MPD, 'Launching Democracy – I'
        (Western Cape Report), p. 41.
45.   *Cape Times,* 9 February 1994, p. 6; *The Star International Weekly*, 3–9 February 1994,
        p. 2.
46.   *Weekend Argus,* 16/17 April 1994, p. 18.
47.   *Cape Times,* 26 January 1994, p. 8.
48.   Cited in *Die Burger,* 10 January 1994, p. 2.
49.   Interview with Olaus van Zyl, 10 February 1994; *Sunday Times,* 20 February 1994,
        p. 25.
50.   Interview with C. Fismer, *Rapport,* 30 January 1994, p. 23.
51.   *Sunday Times,* 23 January 1994, p. 4.
52.   *The Star International Weekly,* 20–26 January 1994.
53.   *Cape Times,* 26 February 1994, p. 1.
54.   *Die Burger,* 21 February 1994, p. 8.
55.   Cited by *Cape Times,* 4 February 1994, p. 6.
56.   Speech by Fismer, 3 February 1994.
57.   *Die Burger,* 7 February 1994, p. 2.
58.   Cited in *Die Burger,* 5 March 1994, p. 8.
59.   *Rapport,* 20 March 1994, p. 11; *Rapport,* 13 February 1994, p. 23.
60.   *The Star International Weekly,* 17–23 March 1994, p. 9.
61.   *Cape Times,* 22 April 1994, p. 9.
62.   *Rapport,* 27 March 1994.
63.   *Die Burger,* 27 January 1994, p. 16.
64.   *Business Day,* 10 February 1994, p. 16.
65.   *Die Burger,* 20 October 1993, p. 8.
66.   *South,* 5–9 November 1993.
67.   *Sunday Times,* 30 January 1994, p. 1.
68.   *Sunday Times,* 20 February 1994, p. 10.
69.   *South,* 11–15 February 1994, p. 7.
70.   *Die Burger,* 9 March 1994, p. 11.
71.   *Die Burger,* 24 February 1994, p. 2.
72.   *Die Burger,* 1 February 1994, p. 1.

73. *The Argus*, 8 February 1994.
74. *Die Burger*, 9 March 1994, p. 2.
75. *Die Burger*, 15 March 1994, p. 2.
76. *Rapport*, 20 March 1994.
77. *Sunday Times*, 27 March 1994.
78. *Rapport*, 20 March 1994, p. 13.
79. *Die Burger*, 23 March 1994, p. 17.
80. *Sunday Times*, 3 April 1994, p. 21.
81. *The Argus*, 12 April 1994, p. 11.
82. MPD, 'Launching Democracy – Fifth Report'.
83. MPD, 'Launching Democracy – Fifth Report'.
84. Lawrence Schlemmer, 'Demokrasie Nie Sonder Pyn te Kry', *Rapport*, 17 April 1994; MPD, 'Launching Democracy – Fifth Report'.
85. *Rapport*, 8 May 1994, p. 21.
86. *Rapport*, 8 May 1994, p. 11.
87. *Rapport*, 8 May 1994, p. 21.

4

The Inkatha Freedom Party

GEORGINA HAMILTON
AND GERHARD MARÉ

By mid-February 1994, foreboding shrouded KwaZulu–Natal. With the precipitate decision that the IFP would not participate in the election, KwaZulu Chief Minister, Mangosuthu Buthelezi, launched the prospect of his own and his party's electoral vitiation and political demise and of intensified civil war in the province. A thousand questions were asked as to his and his king's motivation for such brinkmanship. Variously it was thought that he was crazy, sick, desperate, or even a principled broker of federalism – a lone voice against the cobbled constitution for the new South Africa and a repetition of centralised control from Pretoria.

The great divide between the burgeoning civil society of the urban and peri-urban areas of KwaZulu–Natal and the chief-bound rural areas was never more stark than in the three months preceding the election. It was as if a cage had been constructed around KwaZulu and all other IFP strongholds in Natal. Disbelief and a degree of panic took hold of the region. People who were working towards an effective election were stunned at the possibility that it might not happen at all and that, if it did happen without the IFP's participation, the province was likely to be bathed in blood.

The election over, there is considerable suspicion of the brokered results and sadness that the astounding fortitude of first-time voters, who braved heat and distance and inordinate delays to make their individual mark, should be rewarded with a result that has as much to do with horse-trading as the casting of ballots. The region has been held to ransom twice in only a few months. First, a king's ransom. At the behest of Buthelezi and the IFP, the Zulu king, Goodwill Zwelithini, made an untimely call for the secession of KwaZulu–Natal from South Africa and supported the non-participation of the IFP in the elections. Perhaps most damaging was his continued identification of his monarchic responsibility with the IFP's political projects, thus excluding non-IFP Zulu-speakers from their heritage and exacerbating already appalling civil strife.

The second ransom was the election result. If it was not substantially rigged by both of the main contenders in KwaZulu–Natal, the IFP and the ANC, it is hard, even considering a grossly bungled electoral process, to understand why the final tally should have been arranged behind closed doors by the two parties. Furthermore it seems that the arrangements were not made at the regional level but, as usual, by national leadership.

In Natal itself, the king's intervention in politics seemed to many to be something new. In this chapter we suggest that the frantic and dangerous maneouvrings of Buthelezi, the king, and the IFP in the months preceding the election were neither as irrational nor as unheralded as sometimes perceived. Nor indeed was the king's politicking particularly out of character. In order to make sense of the past four months and the present, it is necessary to mention the history of interaction between the king and Buthelezi over the past 25 years, and the way Buthelezi and the Inkatha movement (latterly the IFP) have used ethnicity and regionalism to further their political projects.

Following a brief look at the region's history, as it involves these issues, we will review the way in which the KwaZulu government, the IFP, the king, and Buthelezi have engaged in, spoiled or boycotted multi-party negotiations since they began in 1991.

In describing or analysing the elections in KwaZulu–Natal, an overemphasis on the dealings of the IFP is inevitable because the IFP, the king, and Buthelezi determined the parameters in which a regional tragedy was enacted nationally. In terms of negotiation and concession the ANC played a largely reactive role to IFP initiatives. On the ground in KwaZulu–Natal, and in the townships of the PWV triangle, the issue of culpability for violence may be thrashed out for years or possibly subsumed by a spirit of reconciliation. It is not within our scope to comment about who did what to whom. Nor is it possible at this early stage to garner a sense of how electoral activity was structured by political parties in rural areas and remote localities. Nevertheless, the historical overview of the past two decades will attempt to offer some interpretation of the development of opposition in the province to bantustan governance and of the severe constraints that this posed.

Some reflection on the electoral process is possible from our own experience and from press reports. Thus we will offer an impressionistic and rather anecdotal account of the election days themselves, and finally look at the way in which the election results may offer insights about the future of the KwaZulu–Natal region and the country as a whole.

Historical Overview

King Goodwill Zwelithini's demand for a constitutionally entrenched and autonomous Zulu nation, made with great clarity at the beginning of 1994, has as much to do with events in the past two decades as with his claimed inheritance of Shaka's mantle. King Goodwill issued an extreme political demand for the recognition of an independent Zulu kingdom, based on pre-capitalist and colonial historical justification, and encompassing the whole of the region of KwaZulu–Natal. This call was directly linked by Buthelezi to the IFP's inability to negotiate a truly federal principle to bind the constitution–makers.

Reflecting on competing historical claims as to the territorial extent of a Zulu kingdom, historian Jeff Guy wrote in the *Sunday Tribune* (20 February 1994):

> Zulu nationalists will emphasise the expansionist military aspects. Those supporting a more broadly based South Africanism will emphasise the restricted side of Zulu rule, and the divisions within the kingdom. In fact it is my feeling that these complex, but emotionally charged, historical debates are being raised at this moment not to make the past clearer, but to make the present more obscure.

The obscure present begins to reveal its peculiar nature if we look at the relationship between the king and Buthelezi as it influenced the thrust of Inkatha's plans.

The 'prime ministerial' relationship of the Buthelezi clan to the Zulu royal house dates back to the role played by Buthelezi's forebear, Nqengelele, under Shaka's rule. 'Prominence in Zulu affairs' was accorded to the Buthelezi chiefdom when Nqengelele's son, Mnyamana, was prime minister to nineteenth-century Zulu king, Cetshwayo.

Almost a century later, in 1968, the contemporary Buthelezi was elbowed out of Zulu royal affairs after the death of Cyprian, father of the present king, Goodwill, whom he had served for sixteen years. In 1969 Prince Israel Mcwayizeni became regent until Prince Goodwill should come of age and marry. A rift developed between Buthelezi and Prince Israel who apparently wished to ask from the South African Government for a Territorial Authority for the Zulus. Buthelezi claimed that he did not want such an entity to be initiated from within the royal family or by Prince Israel Mcwayizeni. This was the beginning of a rift between Buthelezi and the Zulu royal family that played itself out over the next decade.

Ironically, it was the creation of the Zulu Territorial Authority, that first building-block of the KwaZulu bantustan, that enabled Buthelezi to reassume a central political role. He was elected by Zulu 'traditional leaders' to lead it and the subsequent KwaZulu Legislative Assembly (KLA) from 1972. Apartheid saved the chief from possible obscurity and did so in a way that minimised the power of the Zulu royal family. Buthelezi's tactics rested on occupying a commanding position in KwaZulu that could not be challenged by an alternative position such as that of the Zulu monarchy.

In the early years of bantustan-building, powerful forces in the South African state and within Zulu society tried to set up a system of government for KwaZulu that paralleled Swaziland's executive monarchy. These forces included disgruntled traders threatened by the close links that Buthelezi had built with white business, black apostles of apartheid, a brand of 'Zulu traditionalists', and South African security police agents. The South African state aimed to diminish the power of a rebellious Buthelezi over the bantustan, which contained the largest ethnic group in South Africa. Buthelezi's resistance to taking full independence as an ethnic satellite state was a thorn in South Africa's side.

Buthelezi, on the other hand, initially tried to delay the installation of Goodwill Zwelithini as king of the Zulus. Throughout the struggle that developed between Buthelezi and the king over the next eight years, the former was supported by bantustan politicians, many of whom were ex-members of the ANC in Natal, and by economic interests that saw advantage in a less executive role for the king. They argued that the king and his advisers were violating custom by attempting to adopt a political role. Buthelezi defeated King Goodwill Zwelithini politically by having his executive capacity written out of the KwaZulu constitution, which was formulated in 1972. However, it took a further oath by the king in 1976, and a continuing struggle to the end of the decade, to ensure the king's humiliation. Finally in 1980 strict protocol silenced the king effectively, and in 1981 the imposition of a fine added teeth to the constitutional clause that kept the king out of 'politics'.

Running alongside these power battles was the growing influence of Inkatha. Buthelezi's political skill is nowhere better manifest than in his creation of Inkatha, the National Cultural Liberation Movement. How better to distance himself from the taint of the bantustan than by pursuing populist mobilisation around Inkatha and drawing on the legitimating symbolism of the ANC. Yet Inkatha was deeply bedded in the KwaZulu Legislative Assembly, hardly separable from it, and thus had a bureaucratic and governmental network through which to influence, mobilise and control people, both those actually living in KwaZulu and those in Natal who were grafted into KwaZulu through

Tribal Authority structures. Nationally and internationally, powerful people, especially in business and government, were readily susceptible to the claim of Inkatha to be a flowering of popular will and relieved to ignore the coercive imprint of its bantustan roots.

The issues that have become flashpoints in politics nationally since 1973 are exactly those that came under Inkatha's control as governing party within a bantustan. By the late 1970s when KwaZulu moved into the final phases of self-government, housing, education, policing and township administration became points of struggle within KwaZulu. In policing and education, Inkatha moved swiftly to initiate and reinforce its own interpretation of the world and to identify its enemies.

Violence flared up regularly from the mid-1980s. Many Africans, who did not align themselves with Inkatha even though they were Zulu-speaking and may have been loyal to a variety of shared cultural practices, found themselves having to deal with oppressors on two fronts: the South African government, which in its mission to fight off 'the total onslaught' found a willing ally in Inkatha, and KwaZulu leaders, whose mission was to politicise and unify Zulu ethnicity around their own goals.

From the formation in 1975 of the Cultural Liberation Movement, Inkatha leaders appealed to an ethnically exclusive constituency, despite an ambiguous link to national politics. Initially, in fact, membership of Inkatha was limited to Zulus. This was at odds with the early mobilising claim that Inkatha was the resurrected ANC of the 'founding fathers'.

During the 1980s Inkatha moved from concentrating on developing a power base focused primarily on KwaZulu, to consolidating power in the region as a whole. The Buthelezi Commission, which conducted research on the interrelationship of the economy and the people of Natal and KwaZulu, was an early manifestation of the attempt to consolidate regional power. This was followed by the constitutional negotiations of the KwaZulu–Natal Indaba, a process which, though it happened regionally, foreshadowed the negotiations followed some six years later at CODESA and the MPF. In addition there was, during the 1980s, the actual setting in place of regional administrative and service structures such as the Joint Executive Authority and the Joint Services Boards.

The thrust toward regional consolidation also rested firmly on the legitimacy that King Goodwill gave to it and to Buthelezi as 'traditional prime minister to the Zulu nation'. The legitimacy was based on continuities, however vaguely defined in terms of territory or constituency, of a 'Zulu nation' that laid claim to the region, and that had its own 'traditional' power structures. 'Tradition', in the Inkatha sense, had always meant loyalty to chiefs, to Buthelezi himself, and to the king.

Zwelithini's role, once he was firmly in the Inkatha fold, was to define who could be admitted to membership of the 'Zulu nation', to determine the conditions of such membership, and to identify those to be demonised as traitors or as ethnic foreigners. This was achieved through carefully staged public appearances and speeches.

Effectively relegated to a symbolic role, it was not until 1982, when the South African government tried to cede a large portion of northern KwaZulu, called Ingwavuma, to Swaziland, that King Goodwill Zwelithini was brought prominently into public life. For the first time in his ten-year reign, he shared the political platform with Buthelezi. Unsurprisingly, it was a moment when a greater nationalism than that afforded by the KwaZulu bantustan was needed to counter the hardy tradition of the independent Swazi monarchy.

In 1986 the king made two other well-publicised appearances which bolstered Inkatha's ethnic revivalism. At one, he announced the formation of the United Workers Union of South Africa (UWUSA) as a counter to COSATU, and called for 'Zulu' attendance. The second appearance was a Soweto Day 'Address to the Zulu nation' at Nongoma. There the king called for the purging from Zulu communities of the presence of the UDF, the ANC and COSATU. He also appealed for a restoration of 'Zuluness' to avert the 'alien values' that had entered 'the largest population group in the whole country'.

In terms of the world-view defined by the king, Buthelezi and Inkatha, organisations like the United Democratic Front, COSATU and the ANC were portrayed as bodies led by non-Zulus; indeed, by people of 'alien values'. All organisations that had a national thrust and following were located outside the ethnic fold, despite the fact that they had a predominance of Zulu-speaking members or followers in KwaZulu and Natal. From Inkatha's position it was necessary to exclude such organisations as they ran counter to a specifically regional ethnic mobilisation and to its other regional projects.

Negotiations in the 1990s
When F. W. de Klerk made his landmark speech in February 1990, his government had resumed negotiations with Inkatha over the Indaba constitution of 1986. Events, however, had rapidly shifted to the national level and such divisive regional options as the Indaba were quickly moved to the backburner. The release of Mandela in the same month relegated Buthelezi to third place in the national leadership stakes. In addition, the signing of two Minutes between the government and the ANC (the Groote Schuur Minute, facilitating the release of political prisoners, and the Pretoria Minute, in which the ANC renounced armed

struggle) gave an indication that these two parties were to define the issues and, later, the outcomes as well.

Buthelezi saw that Inkatha had to make another move to claim a role in national politics. By mid-February 1990 he called for the movement to transform itself into a political party. In July 1990 it became the Inkatha Freedom Party (IFP). Buthelezi said at the launch that 'no power on earth will stop us being a powerful force at the negotiating table'. He added that while he held out a hand of friendship to Mandela he would not allow the ANC's policies to be 'rammed down Inkatha's throat'. At the symbolic level the IFP changed its colours from the black, green and gold of the ANC by adding red and white.

Although the Pretoria Minute of August 1990 ensured that the armed struggle ended, and with it the formal operations of the state's security establishment against the ANC, there was an immediate escalation of violence between ANC and Inkatha members on the East Rand. This followed a massive stayaway of workers in July, organised by the ANC and COSATU to promote peace in Natal and KwaZulu. Violence in the region continued, however, throughout the period of negotiations, despite peace agreements reached by Mandela and Buthelezi at leader-ship level, and by several communities at grassroots level, and despite the signing of a regional peace accord.

By June 1991 nearly all apartheid legislation had been removed, except for the Republic's constitution, and the laws ensuring the existence of the bantustans. Because the coup leaders, Ramushwana and Holomisa, who came to power in Venda and the Transkei respectively both supported the ANC, that organisation did not call for the abolition of the bantustan system, but concentrated its demands for reincorpora-tion on certain of these apartheid creations, especially Bophuthatswana and KwaZulu. Buthelezi, with some justification, pointed out the inconsistency in the ANC demand, and claimed that it was aimed at KwaZulu because of the non-compliance of the 'Zulu nation' with ANC prescriptions in negotiations.

When the first multi-party talks, the Convention for a Democratic South Africa (CODESA), started in December 1991, most existing political parties were present, as were the ten 'homeland' administrations. A 'Patriotic Front' was launched in February 1992, which excluded the IFP, even though it included the coloured Labour Party and some bantustan leaders. The Patriotic Front, under the leadership of the ANC, was intended to draw other anti-apartheid groups into a negotiating alliance. It never functioned effectively.

The launch of CODESA 2 in May 1992 saw the unfolding of the next stage in the strategy employed by Buthelezi for the duration of negotiations. He refused to take part, as King Goodwill was not allowed to represent the 'Zulu nation' as a full member at the talks. Buthelezi, from then on, presented his demands largely from a position based on 'traditional' legitimation: that of the king, the KLA as government of the 'Zulu nation', the 'nation' itself, and himself as 'traditional' prime minister. It seemed that what Buthelezi was hoping to gain from this strategy was the creation of structures and a political power-base that did not owe much to the democratic process which the country as a whole was engaged in. It was a strategy that might provide him with a 'sanctuary' if the IFP lost the regional elections badly.

A second demand that Buthelezi and the IFP made was for a 'single-stage' process in drawing up the new constitution. Their argument was that all the parties at the talks, and possibly even some others, should draw up a constitution for South Africa and that elections should then be held to confirm it. The counter-argument was that some of the participating parties had a dubious measure of support and, under an interim constitution, support should be tested before major parties drew up the new constitution.

In a way, the core constitutional 'principles' that were agreed upon before the April 1994 elections already limit the constituent assembly. In addition Buthelezi managed to gain additional principles while staying out of the direct process. These included the acceptance of a monarchy, the kingdom of KwaZulu–Natal, and the principle of what Buthelezi calls 'asymmetry', which would allow different regions to have specific constitutions to meet their needs, rather than a single model imposed by the central government.

Despite Buthelezi's absence, the IFP did participate in CODESA 2 with a negotiating team led by Dr Frank Mdlalose, now IFP premier in the new province of KwaZulu–Natal. These talks were, however, of short duration as the ANC withdrew after the Boipatong massacre on the East Rand, and launched a 'rolling mass action' campaign. The withdrawal was used by Buthelezi several times to argue that the ANC were the wreckers of negotiations and that they had employed confrontational strategies.

In September, after the Bisho shootings when an ANC-led march on the Ciskei homeland was fired upon, the government and the ANC signed a Record of Understanding. This was to enable the release of political prisoners, to ban the carrying of 'traditional weapons', and to allow the fencing of hostels. It is obvious that two of these issues related directly to the IFP. Most of Inkatha's Transvaal supporters live in the migrant labour hostels, and the carrying of 'traditional weapons' had been, and remained, a non-negotiable issue for Inkatha's leadership.

What the IFP resented most was that they saw at work in the Record a negotiating process that excluded all parties, other than the government and the ANC, except in a rubber-stamping role. Inkatha participated in the formation of the Concerned South Africans Group (COSAG) in October 1992, specifically to protest against the bilateral agreements. By October 1993 this group of right-wing organisations became the Freedom Alliance, comprising the Afrikaner Volksfront, the IFP, and the administrations of the Ciskei, Bophuthatswana and KwaZulu. The Front was based on a manifesto that accepted the 'right to self-determination of peoples of southern Africa', limited central state power, and asked that people living within regions should determine their own boundaries.

The KLA tried to strengthen its hand in the negotiations by releasing its own constitution for the region, in December 1992. That it should originate nominally from the KLA and not the IFP was an attempt to give credibility to the existence of a political entity (the KLA) in the region other than the IFP. We have already argued that Buthelezi had moved outside of the IFP in the demands he was making on the negotiators. Instead, he was positioning himself as the protector of the interests of the Zulu nation. The IFP, as a national party, it was argued, could no longer do this.

In April 1993 a new Multi-Party Negotiating Forum was established, now including the Conservative Party, the PAC, and 'traditional leaders', and the IFP returned to the process. IFP participation was of short duration. They left after the ruling on the procedure of 'sufficient consensus' went against them in June, the month when the date for the first democratic elections was set.

What must be kept in mind the whole time when examining the IFP's refusal to 'participate' is that neither the IFP nor Buthelezi, wearing his hat as traditional prime minister to the Zulu king, ever left negotiations. They continued to demand concessions, and to enter into bilateral talks until the last moment. This ensured that their names and demands remained in the newspapers, and that their followers remained at a feverish pitch of politicisation. Rallies were held, both by the king and by the IFP, marches took place, and TV coverage continued.

A few weeks before 27 April 1994, Inkatha even went so far as to put up 'election' posters with the cryptic message, under a large photo of Buthelezi, for people to vote 'When the time comes'. The ANC aimed a considerable part of its regional strategy at assuring voters that they respected the king as much as anyone else, but that he should stay out of the political arena, in much the same way as Inkatha had forced him into a 'non-political' role before using him to give legitimacy to its own project and leadership.

Buthelezi had successfully shifted the focus of negotiations to an apparently separate field which raised the status of the king in the region. The government and the ANC took this seriously and attempted to meet with the king several times, the last time being the gathering at Skukuza in the Kruger National Park in early April. At that meeting the ANC offered the king a fairly comprehensive package, which he turned down. The offer acknowledged the existence of a 'kingdom' in the region, but then awarded the king symbolic rights only.

There was one last chance, it appeared, before talks would finally break down and the horror of an election in KwaZulu–Natal without the IFP would be upon South Africa. This last chance was the mediation process agreed upon by the IFP and the ANC at a meeting in Durban on 1 March 1994. However, the delaying tactics that the IFP seemed intent on employing during the mediation process were scuppered when the ANC's Cyril Ramaphosa refused to have the election date itself made one of the mediation issues. The ANC's insistence, or at least the insistence of Ramaphosa, could be seen as a way for the ANC to get out of a mess of their own making. When they agreed to the mediation process, the ANC became a partner in a deal that could not but have delayed the election date if actually entered into. In the event, what the mediation amounted to was a costly exercise; one of many. The mediators gathered, only to be sent home.

That the IFP agreed to participate a mere week before the election date is now history. There is still considerable speculation as to what caused the apparent swing, and whether Buthelezi and the forces around him actually accepted less than was offered at Skukuza. There was, however, more to the deal than simply capitulation by Buthelezi. He managed to gain agreement that the mediation process would be continued after the elections, building on the concession already made that the king would have a kingdom, albeit with undefined powers.

A massive newspaper advertising campaign took place during that last week. The IFP benefited, one imagines, from the novelty of IFP election advertising at such a late stage. Other parties' advertisements were by now at best familiar, but mostly repetitive and dull. The IFP even used a photo of the king, saluting Buthelezi, leaving little doubt as to where Goodwill stood in the campaign. The ANC rather weakly protested, once more, that the IFP was dragging the king into politics.

Electoral Process

For KwaZulu–Natal the overwhelming concern, from January 1994 until the election itself, was the IFP's decision not to participate in the election. When non-participation meant that voter educators were seen as partisan, even deserving of death by staunch followers of the IFP, the province was plunged into despair.

Prior to the IFP's non-participation stance there was already a high level of tension and fear. The semantic arguments of newspaper editors and political commentators notwithstanding, political actors and many people caught unwittingly in a spiral of violence felt themselves to be in the middle of a war. In some areas and for some people this had begun as early as 1985. With varying intensity it left few parts of KwaZulu–Natal untouched. Even in the relatively safe and predominantly white city centres, crime increased, and many were gripped with fear that mass rallies and marches would spill over into political riot.

Beyond the city centres, in townships, squatter settlements and in the rural areas of KwaZulu–Natal, the threat and reality of violence were so dire that the main strategy of electoral workers and of the long-experienced Network of Independent Monitors, even prior to the IFP boycott, was to concentrate on minimising strife and death around political rallies and all forms of political activity.

To the credit of the politically engaged non-government sector of KwaZulu–Natal society, it needs to be said that their planning and intentions were admirable. From the early days of 1993, an umbrella organisation, the Natal Forum on Education for Democracy, co-ordinated the electoral education work of non-governmental organisations including the ecumenical Diakonia agency, Lawyers for Human Rights and numerous bodies with strong church and community contacts.

Just prior to the establishment of the Independent Electoral Commission (IEC), a new umbrella organisation, the KwaZulu–Natal Electoral Observer Network (KNEON), was established in co-operation with the Natal Forum on Education for Democracy and the IEC to facilitate the training and deployment of domestic observers. It intended to mobilise a volunteer non-partisan force of observers who, because of their local knowledge and concern to promote free and fair elections, would provide back-up for the paid IEC monitors. Observers were intended to be a non-interventionary presence, responsible for reporting both to KNEON and to the IEC on irregularities and disputes.

Much good intention was lost in the fray of the days immediately prior to and during the election. The deployment of observers was extremely uneven, and in some of the potentially most dangerous areas of Natal there were few domestic observers to be seen. IEC monitoring seemed equally uneven and disorganised. At best there was the generally plausible excuse that planning time was too short for both KNEON and the IEC. Without the resources of the government bureaucracy at their disposal, organisation did indeed falter. In Natal the faltering was compounded by the very late entry of the IFP into the elections.

Until a week before the elections any form of electoral activity in IFP strongholds was seen by IFP supporters as a partisan challenge The *Bulletin* produced by the Natal Forum on Education for Democracy had the following report (14-21 February 1994):

> In this climate, meeting the information needs of those who do wish to vote, setting up effective monitoring and observing operations to help ensure a free and fair election and assuring people of secrecy are near-impossible tasks. Voter education groups in Eshowe say the language of democracy has been poisoned by the elections conflict. 'Secret vote' has become a loaded term in areas where the traditional leadership says that there should be no secrets in open communities. For leaders who maintain that there is no reason to hide one's voting intentions, the fact that voter education is non-partisan makes it unacceptable!

In one district of KwaZulu that had become notorious for violence against voter educators, the election days were surprisingly free of strife. By 7 a.m. on 27 April, the time at which the voting stations were supposed to open, there were lengthy queues at most voting stations. Electoral officers were unpacking boxes of voting materials delivered hours or minutes before. However, the IEC monitors whose presence was required for the opening of voting stations were nowhere to be seen. They began to arrive at some stations as the morning wore on, but at other stations the presiding officers made the decision to go ahead without them in order to placate long queues of voters. In a few cases, instead of IEC monitors opening the stations, overseas or domestic observers supervised the opening formalities. This was not within the scope of observers' duties and in fact breached their code of conduct, but the day rapidly became one of creative invention.

In one case an Italian observer who came to South Africa under the aegis of a European parliamentary grouping spent the 27th more or less running a voting station. After the station had been in operation for an hour or so, it was clear to him that the electoral officers were uncertain of procedure and that voting was happening extremely slowly and chaotically. He suggested to the presiding officer that a bit of on-the-spot training might help. Thus the voting station was closed temporarily while the Italian parliamentarian ran a quick workshop for the electoral workers, involving role-playing and knowledge gleaned from observing elections in other parts of the world. After this, the efficiency of the station picked up.

An overall impression was that the voters in this district were magnificently patient and determined, and that the electoral staff did their best with limited back-up and, in some cases, very limited training. The voting days proceeded without significant strife despite enormous problems in both the administrative and monitoring wings of the IEC.

As it happened, a number of ballot boxes from this district were disputed during the counting of votes. It seems likely that the irregularities crept in during the transport of the boxes or, if they happened at the voting stations, may have been due to insufficient training as to the sealing and marking of boxes, rather than to political machination.

In other areas of KwaZulu–Natal there were reports of manipulation and intimidation. It was suggested that in some IFP strongholds people were swayed by chiefly dictates and were afraid to vote as they wished. On the other hand, the IFP feared the domination of the electoral process by its opponents and claimed that in large measure the IEC employed ANC supporters.

Voting and Results

The election results surprised many, if not all, observers. We have not found any polls or predictions that gave Inkatha most support in the region, never mind an absolute majority. In the end, after all the behind-the-scenes agreements at top-leadership level, Inkatha won 50.3 per cent of the votes that were counted in the region. (It seems from IEC head-office statements that votes that were blatantly outside even the relaxed rules employed by the IEC towards the end were not counted.) This gave the party 41 of the 81 provincial seats.

The ANC came second with 32.2 per cent of the votes (26 seats); the NP third with 11.2 per cent (9 seats). The only other parties to gain representation in the provincial assembly were the DP (2.2 per cent of the vote, 2 seats), the Minority Front (1.3 per cent and 1 seat), the PAC (0.7 per cent and 1 seat), and the African Christian Democratic Party (0.7 per cent and 1 seat).

A noteworthy feature of the results is that only the NP gained in votes cast in the province for national representation, as against votes cast for provincial representatives (15.8 per cent of votes counted, as against 11.2 per cent for the provincial assembly). Each of the other parties lost a percentage point to the NP in the vote for the National Assembly. This would seem to indicate a significant measure of voter choice in using the second ballot, based on the realisation that it made more sense to strengthen the NP in the National Assembly than to add a few votes to the parties who were weak at national level. The second ballot, while initially rejected by the government and the ANC on the grounds that it would be too complicated for voters, was a concession made to the IFP.

The fact that KwaZulu–Natal had the lowest percentage poll of all provinces (80 per cent) should not say much, other than maybe reflecting the larger number of votes not counted in the province. The percentage polls were probably exaggerated generally, as they were calculated on the admitted underestimation of voters in South Africa as a whole.

From the national results it is also obvious that the IFP had not been able to move beyond the region for its support in any meaningful way at all. The IFP gained 10.5 per cent of the national vote, giving it 43 seats in the National Assembly (this came from 2,058,000 votes, of which 1,844,070, or some 90 per cent, came from the KwaZulu–Natal province). These results indicate that despite its national thrust, supposedly separate from the claims made by the king and Buthelezi to represent the ethnic component of 'Zulu nationalism', the party has little hope of representation in the National Assembly on any basis other than its regional strength. Even the NP, seated most firmly in the Western Cape, has significant support in Northern Cape, the PWV, and even in KwaZulu–Natal.

The regional ANC, through the immediate voices of Natal Midlands firebrand Harry Gwala and southern Natal media spokesperson Dumisani Makhaye, rejected the results as not meeting the 'substantially free and fair' status that Judge Kriegler and the IEC were willing to give to the election. The ANC have, however, taken their seats in the provincial assembly and have contributed three ministers to the provincial government. How this matter resolves itself remains to be seen.

Conclusion

It is not clear how far the votes attributed to parties in this region are removed from the actual preferences and voices of those who were treated so badly by the election machinery and political parties, and who had borne the brunt of more than a decade of violent confrontation.

The published results were a product of a trade-off between the competing parties. Despite all attempts at creating transparency in the voting process, the trade-off that characterised the final moments of vote-counting in KwaZulu–Natal remains opaque. It is widely assumed that the ANC's reluctant acceptance of the results had to do with averting further violence in the region. The electorate is being asked to accept that disputes about irregular ballot boxes and allegations concerning the lack of security in the transporting of boxes and the issuing of temporary voter cards to under-age voters have been shelved, perhaps only temporarily, by both the ANC and the IFP in an attempt to normalise politics in the region.

It seems likely that national polls, conducted before the election, underestimated the strength of Inkatha support in the KwaZulu–Natal region. There are numerous reasons, including those intrinsic to market research, which might have led to polling inaccuracy: the inaccessibility of much of KwaZulu and the fear that ruled the region which made people likely to say what they thought pollsters wanted to hear or whatever made them feel safer. Despite the extraordinary irregularities, both alleged and observed, during the election days, there is much to suggest that the favourable IFP result was not as far off the mark as is claimed by ANC militants such as Harry Gwala.

The reasons for this are rooted in the history of the past 22 years in the province and in the whole history of segregation and apartheid. A possibility is that ANC penetration in the rural areas was minimal because of the very construction of the bantustans, and also because the alternative or opposing forces in the province remained reactive to or largely ignored KwaZulu-based political initiatives. In addition many opponents kowtowed to a sort of regional cabalism run by people who had national interests at heart; a proper construction of local interest groups would have led perhaps to better-mobilised opposition to Inkatha and latterly the IFP. In fairness, this occurred because opposition was continually hindered by the National Party government's support of KwaZulu and Buthelezi and plenty of tacit and explicit support of the IFP by regional, national and international business.

Though in many areas of KwaZulu–Natal the election resembled a sort of mass action around voting stations, there is hope that it is now possible for people to re-invoke the politics of interest, issue, constituency and locality rather than continue to be guided by the historical loyalties of the past.

5
The White Right
JOHANN VAN ROOYEN

General Constand Viljoen's arrival at the electoral offices in the World
Trade Centre outside Johannesburg shortly before midnight on 4 March
1994 was in marked contrast to his more dramatic appearance at the same
building nine months previously. Then he was surrounded by 3,000
marauding supporters of the Afrikaner Volksfront (AVF) who physically
took possession of the building in which the multi-party negotiations
were in progress, assaulted black delegates, and caused large-scale
disruption and damage to property. This time a demure Viljoen came
with more peaceful intentions, to register a hastily created party called
the Freedom Front (FF) in order to ensure right-wing participation in
the April election.

Viljoen's decision to participate in the election was a decisive turning-
point in the run-up to South Africa's first democratic election. With his
impressive military record he commanded the respect and loyalty not
only of the more threatening of the para-military forces of the Right
(including over fifty retired security force generals) but also of sections of
the South African Defence Force (SADF). Not only did Viljoen's
decision take the sting out of the right-wing threat to disrupt the
proceedings and launch an Afrikaner war of secession, but he instilled
into his disbelieving right-wing supporters the acceptance that the era of
Afrikaner and white rule had passed forever.

This chapter analyses the role of the white Right during the final
months of 342 years of white domination and 46 years of Afrikaner
hegemony, and in particular its efforts to cling to these part 'glories'
through its demand for Afrikaner self-determination in a *volkstaat*
(people's state). Although two distinct approaches were followed by the
Right to achieve this objective, namely participation in the democratic
process and extra-institutional pressure and resistance, this chapter focuses

primarily on the FF's participation in the election. However, it is necessary to commence the chapter by placing the partially completed evolution of right-wing policies – from self-inflicted isolation to active participation – into historical perspective.

An Historical Overview

Following a decade of limited National Party (NP) reforms and stagnation under P. W. Botha's leadership, the accession to power by F. W. de Klerk in 1989 resulted in a radical transformation of South African society. Within four years the fortunes of the right-wing – along with those of millions of black South Africans – had changed irrevocably, relegating its chief component, the Conservative Party (CP), from official opposition in parliament to that of an irrelevant, confused party tainted by racism and associated with a return to apartheid.

Halfway through the De Klerk era, the CP achieved its final political success by forcing the NP government, through a succession of convincing right-wing by-election victories between November 1989 and February 1993, to renew its mandate for reform in a final, whites-only plebiscite – the March 1992 referendum. Contrary to the expectations created by a swing of 14 per cent to the Right in the by-elections, the referendum confirmed the core of right-wing support at approximately one-third of the white electorate (875,000 votes) and finally laid to rest the image of the CP as a 'government-in-waiting'.

This watershed event in white politics finally destroyed the fragile unity of the CP, torn between its moderate and hard-line factions. Demoralised and weakened, having lost seven of its MPs to the centre because of its inability to adjust its apartheid policies to new realities, the CP was now largely forced into extra-parliamentary politics. Together with conservative black groups it formed the Freedom Alliance in 1992 (originally known as COSAG, the Concerned South Africans Group), crossing racial lines and linking up with the Inkatha Freedom Party (IFP) and an assortment of unsavoury homeland governments. The CP also took a leading role in the first successful attempt in the history of right-wing politics to create a united front, the AVF, in May 1993. And although the CP continued to play a leading, if obstructionist, role within this movement, it was now up to the leadership of Constand Viljoen, a former chief of the SADF, to lead the right-wing – with or without the CP's blessing – into the 'promised land'.

The recent origins of right-wing participation in the April 1994 election can therefore be traced back to the founding of the AVF in April 1993. This umbrella right-wing movement was founded amidst the violence and racial tension that erupted after the assassination of Chris

Hani in April 1993, and was a response to the leadership vacuum that emerged after the death of the leader of the CP, Andries Treurnicht.[1] The AVF incorporated 21 right-wing groups, and its goal was to unite and to mobilise the right-wing in order to pursue the goal of Afrikaner self-determination more effectively.

As some of the right-wing organisations had considerable ideological differences, keeping the alliance together and controlling the extremist elements, such as the AWB, proved to be Viljoen's first major task. In spite of Viljoen's military stature, this proved to be easier said than done, for it soon became clear that the AWB had its own agenda on violence and that it viewed the AVF merely as a convenient base from which to strike out at the transitional process.

A pragmatist at heart, Viljoen soon realised that the resistance strategies of the AVF, the neo-apartheid ideology of the CP and the extremism of the AWB, although marginally effective over the short term, would not ultimately ensure the creation of a *volkstaat*. He then considered the alternatives, including direct negotiations with the ANC and keeping an open mind on crucial issues such as the degree of Afrikaner sovereignty, the borders of the proposed *volkstaat* and participation in the elections. To this end the AVF submitted its proposals for the creation of a *volkstaat* to the technical committee of the multi-party negotiating forum in July 1993. The proposals demarcated an area for the *volkstaat* which comprised approximately 16.5 per cent of the country's surface, largely in the Transvaal and Free State; and with the help of very innovative cartography, it suggested that the area contained a majority of 2.3 million whites compared with 2.1 million blacks.

Not surprisingly, these proposals failed to make an impression on the chief negotiators in the forum; the constitutional formula agreed upon by this body in August 1993 made no reference to the AVF's proposals. Undaunted, the AVF submitted four principles underpinning its demand for a negotiated *volkstaat* in September 1993. These included a separate constitution devoid of discrimination, separate defence and police forces, the right to levy taxes, and the right to secede from South Africa in case of irreconcilable differences. Although Viljoen denied that these principles implied federalism – something the CP would not readily have agreed to – he conceded that they might contain elements of both federalism and confederalism.

With the demise of the moderate Afrikaner Volksunie (AVU) under the leadership of Andries Beyers late in 1993, renewed tension between the moderates and the hard-line faction within the AVF erupted. Once the voice of moderation and realism within the AVF had gone, Viljoen found himself isolated, and his willingness to negotiate and compromise came under increasing attack from the hard-liners in the AVF. By now the CP had realised how powerful Viljoen had become, and decided that the party had to curb his powers or risk losing its control of the right-wing. When he was forced by Hartzenberg in October 1993 to suspend his talks with the NP and the ANC, Viljoen had to decide whether to submit to the dictates of the hard-line faction or to split the AVF. As the most popular right-wing leader, he would most likely have succeeded at this point in taking with him a considerable number of moderate CP supporters. Viljoen, however, did not want to sacrifice the new-found Afrikaner unity, and believing that he could achieve more as part of the AVF, decided to bide his time.

His tactics worked, for in November 1993 the AVF presented a revised plan for a *volkstaat* based on a territory comprising only 14 per cent of South Africa's land mass, with limited autonomy for Afrikaners within that territory rather than full independence. However, the CP's influence was also visible in this proposal: it stipulated that blacks would have only limited voting rights, in so far as they would only be allowed to vote for the central government and not the regional government. This was to ensure that the regional government would be permanently controlled by Afrikaners.

Although the ANC rejected qualified voting rights for blacks within the *volkstaat* region, negotiations between the two organisations were now back on track. Both parties declared that they were moving closer to an agreement. Nelson Mandela opined that 'the more we talk to the right-wing, the closer we get to one another', while a joint ANC-AVF delegation left for Europe to study the local and regional government systems of Belgium and Switzerland.[2] By the end of November 1993 Viljoen had accepted that Afrikaner independence was out of the question. The ANC in turn allegedly considered offering to the AVF the Eastern Transvaal (with Pretoria as its capital) as the basis of its federal region within a united South Africa.[3] However, the mutual enthusiasm of the ANC and Viljoen was not shared by everyone – the CP leader, Ferdi Hartzenberg, contradicting Viljoen, announced that his party remained 'utterly committed' to confederalism, that is, an independent Afrikaner homeland.[4]

In spite of the recalcitrance of the hard-line component of the AVF, Viljoen decided to push ahead with negotiations with the NP and the ANC. His surprising UDI announcement late in November 1993, that the AVF was unilaterally going to establish a *volkstaat*, was clearly an attempt to pacify Hartzenberg, rather than an indication of a change in his approach. Viljoen's determined efforts nearly came to fruition on 20 December 1993 when he announced that he had reached an agreement with the NP and the ANC, and that the AVF would be entering the transitional process. However, under pressure from the hard-line faction and the AVF's partners in the Freedom Alliance, Viljoen was unable to sign the deal. Nevertheless, he emphasised that the provisional agreement which had been reached on regional autonomy and participation by the right-wing in the 1994 elections was not nullified by his failure to sign it, and that it would be signed at a later date. The unratified agreement reached between the ANC and the AVF stated that both organisations were determined that the aspirations of many Afrikaners to govern themselves in their own territory should be addressed. In addition, a joint working group had been set up to examine the financial and economic viability of a *volkstaat* and the civil rights of Afrikaners outside the *volkstaat*.

The working group was to report back before 24 January 1994, but in the meantime, Viljoen came under renewed attacks from the hard-line faction within the AVF, especially after Mandela insisted that he would never permit the creation of a *volkstaat*. On the insistence of Hartzenberg, the AVF again suspended its talks with the ANC. Presumably in rejecting the *volkstaat*, Mandela rejected a *volkstaat* as a sovereign entity apart from South Africa, for in Mandela's discussions with Viljoen, the former appeared more positive towards the idea of a federally based *volkstaat* with the same powers as the other nine provinces. Viljoen himself caused confusion in this respect. Since actively entering politics in 1993 he had remained ambiguous about the degree of sovereignty which he demanded for the *volkstaat*. Although he himself accepted that independence was not a realistic option, he failed, either wilfully (for political reasons) or through ignorance, to differentiate clearly between confederalism and federalism, between whether he saw the *volkstaat* as just another province of South Africa and whether he wanted greater, asymmetrical powers or even full sovereignty (in line with the CP's demands). Only in early April 1994 did he commit himself unequivocally to the fact that Afrikaner self-determination meant regional autonomy, when he said that the *volkstaat* would remain part of South Africa and that it was not an escape mechanism.[5]

Shortly before the 24 January 1994 deadline, negotiations once again resumed after concessions by the ANC. There were indications that progress was being made in the trilateral negotiations between the three parties.[6] In direct contrast to the ANC's optimism, the right-wing, as part of a ploy to pressurise the ANC into further concessions, opted to portray a scenario of doom: Viljoen grimly warned that 'limited violence' was an option to force a *volkstaat*, Terre'Blanche threatened he ANC with 'total war', and the CP announced plans to implement a 'transitional Afrikaner authority' before the end of January.[7] In addition, the Afrikaans newspaper *Rapport* (by now openly sympathetic towards the Right) published several articles during these critical times in which one of its chief journalists, Z. B. du Toit, the former editor of the CP mouthpiece, *Patriot,* cited 'unknown' or 'highly secret' right-wing sources as evidence of a plot by the Right to take over parts of the country and to launch a bloody civil war.[8]

When the January deadline passed without an agreement having being reached, the ANC offered to allow the right-wing to vote for the *volkstaat* but insisted that an ANC government would retain power to veto the outcome. However, having demanded a two-ballot electoral system and the right for each of the provinces to write its own constitution, both the AVF and the IFP rejected that ANC's counter-proposals as inadequate, and threatened to boycott the elections. By early February 1994, the ANC offered the members of the Freedom Alliance a concession on the two-ballot issue, but in turn demanded that the Alliance give assurances that it would be more flexible – also without success.

With no progress in sight and in view of rising levels of violence, the ANC and NP made a bold attempt to break the constitutional deadlock by offering the Freedom Alliance sweeping concessions in mid-February 1994. These included greater decentralisation of power to the nine provinces, and went a long way in addressing most of the demands of the members of the Freedom Alliance. In particular: a split ballot was proposed for national and provincial elections; provinces would receive more powers regarding their finances; provinces would have the power to determine their own legislative and executive structures; these powers would not be fundamentally altered by a new national constitution; provinces could determine their own names; and lastly, the principle of the right to self-determination would be included in the constitution. The reaction from the pro-participation faction of the AVF was one of guarded optimism, but the Hartzenberg group rejected the offer as inadequate, as it would not provide the AVF with a *volkstaat* before the elections. The IFP also rejected the offer and launched a renewed violent offensive against the ANC in Natal, while the AWB and other extremist right-wing groups temporarily laid siege to several towns and cities in the northern provinces.

The Hartzenberg faction's uncompromising stance and its threats of a 'Boere UDI' made Viljoen's position as the leader of the AVF increasingly difficult. Ostensibly, even his grassroots support appeared to have diminished; in January 1994 he was shouted down by the majority of 10,000 AVF members in Pretoria after having made a passionate plea for a strategic alternative to violence, through participation in the elections. Viljoen's already fragile position was further compromised by a public challenge from F. W. de Klerk, who called on Viljoen to have the courage of his convictions to lead the 'reasonable majority' within the AVF into the elections. Viljoen did not take kindly to De Klerk's invitation to split the AVF, and responded sharply by accusing De Klerk of running a 'one-man show' and of having lost control of the reform process and the support of the Afrikaner people.[9]

The Founding of the Freedom Front

However, De Klerk's comments, in addition to the constitutional concessions made by the ANC and NP, made an impression on Viljoen, for twenty minutes before the midnight deadline on 4 March 1994, he registered the FF for participation in the election. Viljoen took the unexpected step of choosing a different vehicle for registration purposes, because he knew that Hartzenberg and the AVF's 'executive council/ transitional parliament', the *volksraad*, would not approve of the registration, and had in fact, twice in recent months, firmly rejected participation in the elections. Within twenty-four hours the *volksraad* overwhelmingly rejected Viljoen's decision by 73 votes to 20 in a secret ballot and decided to allow the registration to lapse.[10]

The more extremist factions within the AVF accused Viljoen of treachery. But for the sake of unity Hartzenberg made a gesture by thanking Viljoen for his 'foresight' in effecting a provisional registration. He insisted, though, that the AVF would not give legitimacy to the new constitution by participating in the election. Viljoen indicated that he would accept the AVF's decision and would remain a member of the front, but it was clear that his position within the AVF had now become impossible. Now that he had created a political base for himself in the form of the FF, enjoying the support of at least six to ten CP MPs and the generals in the AVF, and was encouraged by growing grassroots support among right-wingers for participation in the election, it was only a matter of days before he would finally break with the AVF.

His opportunity came one week later during the second week of March, when the government of Bophuthatswana, a member of the Freedom Alliance, collapsed under pressure from striking civil servants and a mutinying security force. In a last-ditch effort to maintain a grip on power, its president, Lucas Mangope, asked for Viljoen's help. Viljoen mustered a force of between 3,000 and 5,000 under the command of a former SADF commander, Jan Breytenbach, and it was agreed that the force would be armed by loyal members of Bophuthatswana's security forces. On being informed of the imminent right-wing invasion of the homeland, Terre'Blanche mustered his own force of about 500 men in the Western Transvaal and met up with the AVF's main force at Bophuthatswana's airport. On arrival, Terre'Blanche's men were told that they were unwelcome and were asked by the (mainly white) commanders of the homeland's defence force to leave the territory. Although Terre'Blanche initially refused, the AWB eventually began withdrawing, but in the process AWB convoys drove through the homeland shooting and terrorising black civilians. The remainder of the AVF forces were escorted in an orderly fashion out of Bophuthatswana by SADF troops.

However, the damage inflicted upon the AVF and Viljoen's reputation by the marauding members of the AWB's troops was immeasurable. For a man who used to be in command of the SADF's highly disciplined troops in what was Africa's strongest defence force, being associated with the undisciplined mob of nine-to-five 'soldiers' of the AWB was the ultimate humiliation, and the last straw.[11]

Viljoen immediately resigned form the leadership of the AVF and submitted his list of candidates the same evening, hereby ensuring that his FF could enter the elections. He defended his decision as follows: 'We dare not ignore our options anymore. The changes to the constitution provided us with new options.'[12] Viljoen's departure, along with most of the generals, many grassroots party officials and seven MPs (later followed by two more), severely weakened the AVF.[13]

Terre'Blanche responded to Viljoen's decision by calling him a 'political Judas goat', a 'Brutus' and a 'government agent sent to split and lead the Afrikaners to slaughter'.[14] The CP futilely responded to Viljoen's actions by finally revealing its map of its own proposed *volkstaat* late in March 1994. The map indicated that the CP was no nearer to reality than three years previously when it had first accepted the idea of a smaller white homeland – the proposed *volkstaat* still covered almost two-thirds of South Africa's territory. In addition, blacks would have no citizenship rights and the territory would be independent.[15]

One of the former CP MPs who joined Viljoen's new party, Pieter Mulder, attempted to brush over the split in the AVF by arguing that the FF's participation in the election allowed the Afrikaner to follow a two-pronged strategy, one pertaining to extra-constitutional pressure and resistance, the other to constitutional participation in the new dispensation: 'The differences are not over the goal of a *volkstaat,* but over the methods [of how to achieve it].'[16] His carefully worded defence of Viljoen's decision was obviously an effort to pacify right-wing supporters who were still undecided about the issue of participation. Mulder also pointed out that participating in the election was a method of proving how many Afrikaners supported the idea of a *volkstaat*, as well as finding out where they were located so that the borders of a *volkstaat* could be more precisely determined.[17] Viljoen agreed that the ultimate goal of his party, and that of the AVF, was the same – the creation of a *volkstaat*. He even insisted that as far as he knew, he was still a member of the AVF and that the dual road taken by him and Hartzenberg could converge again after the elections. Hartzenberg's cool response was that those who participated in the elections would be expelled from the CP.[18]

Ensuring the FF's Participation

Although the FF launched its election campaign immediately after submitting its list of candidates in mid-March, Viljoen repeatedly warned that his participation in the elections was by no means guaranteed. He insisted that he required more assurances from the NP and ANC about the powers and nature of the proposed *volkstaat* before he would participate in the election. He received these assurances early in April 1994 when a draft accord was reached between the FF, ANC and NP, which was to be signed before the election. The accord made provision for the formation after the election of a statutory council, the *volkstaatsraad,* consisting of 20 members, and an advisory body of 25 members, elected by local (presumably *volkstaat*-supporting) communities in the nine existing provinces. These two bodies would investigate the possibility of creating a *volkstaat* and report back to the Constitutional Assembly, and in general would prepare the ground for Afrikaner self-determination in a *volkstaat*. Provisions of the draft accord revealed interesting new developments regarding the creation of a self-governing Afrikaner province.[19]

The official signing of the accord between the FF, ANC and NP was not without its own drama. The signing was postponed three times during April as the parties attempted to iron out remaining problems, but when the official ratification had not occurred three days before the start of the election, an impatient Viljoen accused the other two parties of deliberately causing delays to prevent it from being signed before the election. He threatened to withdraw from the election and indicated that he was 'prepared to go to war' if the accord was not signed within 24 hours. In fact, orders were send out countrywide to mobilise right-wing forces.[20] Viljoen's threats obviously made an impression, for the accord was formally signed the next morning – 23 April 1994 – by Viljoen, Thabo Mbeki of the ANC, and Roelf Meyer of the NP. The CP rejected the accord as useless and the AWB described it as a 'pathetic little sham masquerading as an historic agreement'.[21]

The Campaign

During the election campaign Viljoen suggested that at least one-third to one-half of Afrikaners would have to vote for the FF in order to prove that 'sufficient' support for a *volkstaat* existed.[22] This formed the essence of the FF's campaign and of its efforts to convince right-wing supporters to ignore Hartzenberg's calls for a boycott of the election. The FF was greatly encouraged by pre-election polls, which indicated that almost 70 per cent of the almost 900,000 traditional right-wing supporters would vote – those who voted for the CP in the 1989 general election and who voted 'no' in the referendum. In numerical terms this meant that over 600,000 rightwingers would cast their ballots, and Viljoen predicted that his party would receive the majority of these votes.

However, he was also relying on the large reservoir of disillusioned NP supporters who were unhappy with the outcome of the negotiations but could not bring themselves to vote for the racism and dead-end policies of the CP. The NP conceded that the FF's participation would rob them of 400,000 right-wing votes, which the NP could have received in the absence of a right-wing party, but vowed not to lose any of its own supporters to the FF as well. This battle for votes from each other's supporters formed an important part of both the NP's and the FF's campaigns: the NP attacked the FF on the grounds that the *volkstaat* was unrealistic and impractical, as 'Afrikaners did not form a majority in any part of the country', while the FF accused the NP of having caved in to the demands of the ANC and of having sold out the whites.[23] The FF summarised the difference between itself and the NP as follows: 'The FF stands for similar freedoms to the NP but offers the additional guarantee of self-determination. If the NP could not contain the ANC when in government, how will they do so as the opposition?'[24]

In addition to targeting the NP's supporters, the FF also focused upon the IFP's support base, at least until the latter's last-minute entry into the election. A poll published by the HSRC indicated that the FF enjoyed the support of 5.3 per cent of the electorate, making it the third most popular party out of 26 parties nationally.[25] The poll also suggested that the FF's support would decline by 15 per cent should the IFP participate, the implication being that the FF enjoyed considerable support among IFP supporters.[26] As the possibility of the IFP's participation in the elections appeared to become more remote during April, Viljoen took the opportunity to capitalise further on this potentially vast Zulu nationalist vote – a natural step, in light of the fact that he and Buthelezi had been close allies as part of the Freedom Front until recently. Viljoen began openly courting IFP votes by stating that the FF promoted self-determination for both Afrikaner and Zulu nationalists: 'The FF is strengthening the case of the Afrikaner by promoting the right to self-determination of the Zulu people together with that of the Afrikaner. Together the Afrikaner and Zulu are capable of much more.'[27]

Having received a considerable amount of state funding (approximately R400,000) in terms of the Electoral Act, the FF launched its first large-scale media blitz towards the end of March 1994. This consisted mostly of full- and half-page advertisements with large photographs of Viljoen and suitable captions, such as 'Cometh the hour ... Cometh the man!'[28] It was a clear indication that the FF was going to base its campaign primarily on Viljoen's popularity among Afrikaners and on the respect which he enjoyed across the political spectrum.

Another standard pillar of the election campaign was the emphasis on 'peace, prosperity, freedom and self-determination'; the fight against communism (and for 'Christian values') also featured prominently. The FF's media advertisements generally were quite dramatic and were intended to shock and scare voters with the *swart en rooi gevaar* tactics.[29] For example, one illustrated graphically an arm with protruding veins being readied for the siphoning of blood ('Prevent yourself bleeding to death financially'); another portrayed a judge's hammer slamming down ('How you can prevent being hammered by injustice'); yet another contained a picture of a titledeed being torn up ('How you can prevent your property and wealth from being redistributed').[30]

In addition to its printed media campaign, candidates of the FF – primarily Viljoen and the Mulder brothers – regularly participated in televised political debates. During these debates the FF's participants often targeted the NP rather than their 'true' opponents, the ANC. This can be explained in two ways: firstly, because old habits die hard – the NP has always been the CP's main political opponent within the narrow confines of tricameral politics; and secondly, because wavering NP supporters constituted a potentially larger source of right-wing voters than wavering ANC supporters. The FF also held numerous public meetings during the election campaign. These were generally well attended, with numbers ranging from between 600 at the first meeting in Potchefstroom to 1,200 in Vereeniging one week later, and up to 1,500 in Kraaifontein.

The FF election campaign effort was largely aimed at Afrikaners in the northern provinces, although its election manifesto gave a broader (white) definition: 'to promote the security, freedom and peaceful co-existence of the Afrikanervolk and those patriots who associate themselves therewith, in actively striving for the establishment of an own Volkstaat/Self-determination'. Viljoen was more candid, referring to a *volkstaat* for 'Boere Afrikaners' and defining these as 'white Afrikaner descendants of the Voortrekkers living in the Transvaal and Orange Free State'.[31] Once it had defined its supporters as such, it could be expected that the FF would have a difficult task in selling its message to those Afrikaners living outside of these areas, and to other right-wing whites. Nonetheless, the FF established regional offices in all nine provinces and drew up a list of candidates, including a prospective premier's candidate in each. In the Western Cape, the region geographically furthest away from the traditional *volkstaat* regions, the party fought its campaign with undiminished enthusiasm. Here its campaign was led by the fairly obscure Eleanor Lombard, who forcefully argued that supporters of the FF in the Western Cape would not physically have to move to the *volkstaat*, but should rather view the *volkstaat* as an 'insurance policy', as a place where Afrikaner culture would be protected and 'as a place to which one can always escape'.[32] As a consolation to his Afrikaner supporters in the Western Cape, Viljoen added that they could decide for themselves on the degree of self-determination they would prefer, possibly in conjunction with their coloured fellow-citizens. He also argued that Article 34 in the constitution made provision for self-determination for Afrikaners outside of the *volkstaat* through the creation of Afrikaner 'community councils' linked to the government of the *volkstaat*, as in the case of Belgium, and that any Afrikaner region could possibly be linked to the *volkstaat* through a canton system along the lines of the Swiss confederation.[33]

Throughout the FF's election campaign, the party emphasised that although it had (reluctantly) agreed to participate within the system, it still regarded the constitution as fatally flawed, and was only participating to prove support for a *volkstaat*: 'The interim constitution produced by them is flawed and unacceptable. Minorities should be better protected. Self-determination will bring peace.'[34] Viljoen reiterated his criticism of a 'flawed' and 'failed' constitutional process several times, sometimes in a manner which brought into question his understanding of democratic values: 'The constitutional process started in 1990 had failed because it had been poorly managed and dominated by the ANC and the NP. We now have a democracy of one man, one vote in a heterogeneous society and this brings us tyranny.'[35]

Moreover, to counter the impression that the FF had unconditionally participated in the election, the party repeatedly emphasised the point that voting in the election would indicate support for the idea of a *volkstaat*, if nothing else: 'It would serve the FF no purpose to participate unconditionally in the election. Our votes would only be overwhelmed by the ANC vote. The only option is to vote in the election, but to vote for a *volkstaat*. According to the constitution all votes for the FF will be regarded as votes for the *volkstaat*.'[36]

Support for the FF
Apart from its nine former CP MPs, eleven of the almost 80 right-wing-controlled local government councils, and up to 150 former CP organisers, were involved in or supported the FF's election campaign. The party had no overt support in the printed media, except for the editorial praise Viljoen had received across the spectrum for his decision to participate in the elections. However, the Afrikaans newspaper *Rapport* came very close to openly endorsing the FF through the tone of its articles dealing with the right-wing. *Rapport*'s gradual shift to the centre–right during the past two to three years under the influence of its editor, Izak de Villiers, became a *cause célèbre* among the right-wing and a source of irritation for the NP. The former chief secretary of the CP, former leader of the AVU and subsequently NP MP, Andries Beyers, even engaged *Rapport*'s editor in a public debate on this issue.[37]

The FF also received endorsements from a number of individuals. Following Viljoen's defence of the three police generals suspended by the government for allegedly providing the IFP clandestinely with weapons and fostering third force activities aimed at destabilising the transitional process, the FF received the public endorsement of more than fifty retired police and Defence Force generals, including a former police commissioner, General Mike Geldenhuys, and Leon Mellet, until recently the head of the public relations section of the police. Not all the support was equally welcome, such as the endorsement by the mass murderer, 'White Wolf' Barend Strydom. The FF rejected Strydom's unsolicited support as harmful to its image and claimed that it was an attempt by the extreme Right to discredit the party. The FF also received a surprising endorsement from a well-meaning Nelson Mandela, who described Viljoen as 'one of South Africa's greatest politicians'.[38] Although Mandela's commendation was a sign of the respect which Viljoen was commanding from across the political spectrum, it can safely be assumed that the FF regarded this as an unwelcome 'kiss of death'.

Right-wing Opposition to the FF's Campaign
The FF had to contend with a hostile rebel right-wing Afrikaans radio station, Radio Pretoria, and an increasingly agitated CP, AWB and what was left of the AVF. The CP viewed Viljoen's efforts to achieve a constitutional breakthrough with the ANC and NP as counter-productive to its own resistance campaign. In addition, Viljoen's *volkstaat* proposals did not meet the CP's requirements of complete

sovereignty. Its own proposals, however, had little to offer, being immersed in delusions of 'independence' through unilateral acts of secession. In late March 1994 the CP declared Pretoria the capital of the *Boere-Afrikaanse volksrepubliek* (people's republic), with Hartzenberg as 'president' and with its own transitional cabinet and constitution. The CP's plan for active resistance was largely focused on the less than 80 town councils under its control. None of the grandiose plans by the CP to use these councils to obstruct the transitional process became a reality. The lack of enthusiasm among the councils forced Hartzenberg to concede that the elections could be conducted in the municipal facilities of these towns.

As the election date rapidly came nearer and violence increased, Viljoen made one final effort to obtain a postponement to enable the IFP and CP to join the elections. After the IFP's decision to participate, Viljoen intensified his efforts to entice the CP and the AVF to drop their boycott of the election. Following further negotiations between him and Hartzenberg, the latter announced that the AVF would participate if the NP and the ANC constitutionally guaranteed the creation of a *volkstaat*, should the right-wing receive at least 800,000 votes. Both the ANC and the NP rejected Hartzenberg's proposal.

After the election Hartzenberg lamely argued that because of irregularities the election should be declared null and void. He further claimed that the CP's boycott stance had been vindicated and that the party would regard the new government as the 'illegal product of an invalid election'.[39]

Most of the 20-odd members of the AVF boycotted the election, but very little came of all the threats of war and disruption of the election. During the last five months prior to the election, a few minor incidents of violence occurred in which extremist groups were involved. The para-military Boere-Krisisaksie (BKA) raided an SADF arms depot in the Northern Transvaal town of Pietersburg in November 1993, and stole more than three tons of arms and ammunition. The Pretoria Boere Kommando Group (PBKG) achieved international attention in December 1993 for a highly publicised but totally futile occupation of an historic building dating from the Anglo-Boer War. As hundreds of right-wing families arrived on farms in the Western Transvaal during April 1994, the AWB declared the area to be 'safe' for its supporters and threatened to *donner* (thrash) the security forces if they 'touch one right-winger'.[40] After a spate of right-wing bombings aimed at buildings and railway lines during the first three months of 1994, a more lethal campaign of indiscriminately planted car bombs was launched by the AWB, taking the lives of 21 people and injuring 173 during the week of the election. Within days, 32 members of the extreme Right were arrested, mostly members of the AWB's elite Ystergarde (Iron Guards). In all, relatively little came of Terre'Blanche's threats of civil war and large-scale disruption of the elections.

Results

The final results gave the FF 424,555 votes nationally, or 2.2 per cent of the total vote, placing it fourth after the ANC, NP and IFP. The party received nine seats in the national parliament. It fared poorly at the national level, considering that it received 451,064 fewer votes than what the right-wing had received in the 1992 referendum.

Taking only white votes into account, and assuming that 86 per cent (or 2.9 million) of the total white electorate (3.4 million) actually voted, the FF received only 14 per cent of the white vote nationally – that is, less than half the right-wing vote in the 1992 referendum.[41] If it is assumed that the vast majority of the FF's votes came from Afrikaners and 86 per cent of eligible Afrikaners voted, the FF received only 27 per cent of Afrikaner votes nationally.

The FF fared considerably better at regional level, where it received a total of 639,643 votes in the nine provinces, and was the third strongest party in six of these. Viljoen's party also received a total of 14 seats in the nine provincial parliaments. The discrepancy between national and regional support for the FF clearly indicates that 215,088 regional supporters of the FF chose to vote for the NP or IFP nationally. Presumably this was because they thought that larger parties such as the NP or IFP would provide more effective opposition to the ANC.[42]

Considering white votes only, and assuming an 86 per cent white turnout, the FF received just over 20 per cent of the white regional vote, which is still considerably less than what the Right had received in 1992. It did, however, receive 41 per cent of the Afrikaner vote on regional level, which is just short of what its estimated Afrikaner support was in 1992. The FF achieved its best regional results in the PWV with 6.2 per cent of the vote (or 24 per cent of the white vote, considering an 86 per cent poll), and in the Northern Cape and Free State with 6 per cent of the vote in each.

To evaluate further the FF's performance in persuading right-wing voters to vote for it, the regional election results in 1994 can be compared with those of the 1992 referendum. Although the referendum regions differed considerably from the nine new provinces, four of these largely coincide. These are:

KwaZulu–Natal (the two 1992 referendum regions of Durban and Pietermaritzburg): 56,998 'no' votes in 1992 v. 28,625 votes for the FF in 1994;

Free State (the two 1992 referendum regions of Bloemfontein and Kroonstad): 92,296 'no' votes in 1992 v. 81,662 votes for the FF in 1994;

Eastern Cape (roughly the 1992 referendum regions of Port Elizabeth and East London): 48,407 'no' votes in 1992 v. 23,167 in 1994;

Northern Transvaal (the 1992 referendum region of Pietersburg): 49,820 'no' votes in 1992 v. 41,193 votes in 1994.

From these figures it is clear how well the FF succeeded in persuading the majority of 1992 right-wing voters in traditional right-wing regions, such as the Northern Transvaal and Free State, to vote for it (82 per cent and 88 per cent respectively).

Conclusion

Early in April 1994 Viljoen said that the reason he participated in the election was to prove Afrikaner support for a *volkstaat*. He further argued that substantial support for the idea would require the FF to obtain between one-third and one-half of the 1.8 million Afrikaner votes.[43] As the poll was 86 per cent, one can assume that he meant that the FF required one-third to one-half of 1.5 million Afrikaner votes cast. In this the FF failed if judged on a national level, where it received approximately 27 per cent of the Afrikaner vote.

Viljoen did, however, mention that he was primarily focusing on the provincial results, for these would enable him to prove the strength of support for his idea in the regions, and determine where the *volkstaat* should be located. In this he had greater success, for his party obtained the support of approximately 41 per cent of Afrikaners who voted regionally (639,643 votes for the FF out of an estimated 1,548,000 Afrikaner votes cast).[44]

As 73 per cent of the traditional hard Right core supported his party regionally, it can be said that Viljoen has effectively gained control over right-wing politics and that Hartzenberg has come to the end of his political career. The majority of the traditional Right had opted to let Viljoen negotiate for a *volkstaat* through the *volkstaatraad* and in the national and regional parliaments. If the results are any indication, such a province would have to be negotiated in those few electoral districts in which the FF's support is at its strongest, presumably in the areas in and around Pretoria and east and west of Johannesburg, in the Eastern Transvaal and the western district of the North West province.

Ultimately, however, these results have proven that an insignificant proportion of South Africa's total population, and less than half of all Afrikaners, support the idea of Afrikaner self-determination. In most democracies this would have meant the demise of the prospects of a *volkstaat*, but the ANC's recognition of the threat posed by scorned ethno-nationalism, and the mutual agreement between the major parties that Afrikaner self-determination could be effectively accommodated within the existing constitution, have left the back door open for the possible creation of a tenth province, the *volkstaat*. This was Viljoen's greatest contribution to the 1994 election: not only did he convince the ANC that the majority of right-wing Afrikaners wanted autonomy *within* a united South Africa, but he also convinced the bulk of the right-wing, which wanted nothing to do with South Africa's transition to non-racial democracy, of the need to participate in and accept the outcome of the democratic process.

Notes

1. Hartzenberg was not an inspiring leader and was regarded by many as too rigid and too caught up in the Verwoerdian time-warp.
2. *Rapport*, 5 December 1993.
3. *Rapport*, 21 November 1993.
4. *Cape Times*, 27 November 1993.
5. *Die Burger*, 9 April 1994.
6. *Cape Times*, 20 January 1994.
7. In January 1994 the AVF announced the names of the members of its 'transitional cabinet', which included Hartzenberg and Terre'Blanche.
8. *Rapport*, 23 January 1994; 20 February 1994.
9. *Rapport*, 23 January 1994; 20 February 1994.
9. *Rapport*, 27 February 1994.
10. *Sunday Times*, 6 March 1994.
11. South Africa produced seven nuclear bombs between the late 1970s and the late 1980, making it the world's seventh recognised nuclear power. F. W. de Klerk gave orders to have the bombs destroyed shortly after he came to power.
12. *Rapport*, 13 March 1994.
13. The capitulation of the Ciskei and the demise of Mangope also effectively meant the end of the Freedom Alliance.
14. *Sunday Times*, 13 March 1994; *Cape Times*, 24 April 1994.
15. *Rapport*, 27 March 1994.
16. FF, *Strategiese Alternatiewe vir Afrikaners* (April 1994).
17. *Rapport*, 20 March 1994
18. *Sunday Times*, 20 March 1994; *Rapport*, 20 March 1994.
19. *Cape Times*, 5 April 1994.
20. *Sunday Times*, 24 April 1994.
21. *Cape Times*, 25 April, 1994.
22. *Die Burger*, 9 April 1994.
23. *Rapport*, 17 April 1994.
24. *Rapport*, 24 April 1994.
25. *The Times*, 28 March 1994.
26. The FF's advertisement euphorically exclaimed: 'What a beginning! After only one week, already third out of 26 parties.' See *Rapport*, 27 March 1994.

27. *Rapport,* 10 April 1994.
28. *Sunday Times,* 20 March 1994.
29. The election tactics pertaining to the imaginary black and red peril, so successfully used by the 'old' NP, were used again by Hernus Kriel on behalf of the NP in the Western Cape during the election.
30. *Rapport,* 17 April 1994; *Sunday Times,* 17 April 1994; *Argus,* 21 April 1994.
31. *Cape Times,* 15 April 1994.
32. *Die Burger,* 15 April 1994.
33. *Rapport,* 17 April 1994.
34. *Sunday Times,* 20 March 1994.
35. *Argus,* 15 April 1994.
36. FF, *Strategiese Alternatiewe vir Afrikaners* (April 1994).
37. Beyers especially took exception to *Rapport*'s derogatory references to him as 'Moses' and *'Soetkys'*, referring no doubt to his roaming between parties.
38. *Cape Times,* 22 April 1994.
39. *Argus,* 30 April 1994.
40. *Cape Times,* 25 April 1994.
41. All racially based voter statistics in this section were obtained from the Central Statistical Services as cited in *Rapport,* 3 April 1994.
42. However, it is almost certain that the majority of this number would have voted for the IFP rather than the NP, considering the deep resentment that right-wingers harbour towards the NP and that the IFP enjoyed considerable support from the white Right – several former dissident CP MPs had joined the IFP, most prominently Koos van der Merwe, and the AVF had been in alliance with the IFP for more than a year. In the provincial election in KwaZulu–Natal for example, only 32 per cent of the 57,000 'no' voters in the 1992 referendum voted for the FF. It is likely that the rest might have voted for the IFP.
43. *Cape Times,* 9 April 1994.
44. However, this represents only 20 per cent of the white voters who had voted regionally and only 3.2 per cent of all South Africans who had voted regionally.

6
The Democratic Party

DAVID WELSH

For the Democratic Party the result of the election was an unmitigated disaster. The resignation of its leader, Dr Zach de Beer, on the day the election returns were finalised signified his personal sense of dismay at the scale of the defeat.

The DP traces its lineage back to the formation of the Progressive Party in 1959, after twelve United Party MPs had broken away in disgust at their party's refusal to repudiate unequivocally racial discrimination and embrace policies that accepted as their premise an evolutionary movement towards a democratic, non-discriminatory society. The Progressives were cautious liberals, and it was not until 1979 that they abandoned the idea of a qualified franchise and accepted universal adult suffrage.

Unlike the smaller Liberal Party (which had, in any case, been seriously weakened by the banning of many key members in terms of the old Suppression of Communism Act), the Progressive Party opted not to disband when the curiously named Prohibition of Political Interference Act made it an offence for parties to have racially mixed memberships. Indeed, it was the strong likelihood that the Progressives would win some of the parliamentary seats created, on a separate or communal basis, for coloured voters that had led the governing National Party, with the ready connivance of the United Party, to introduce the legislation.

For long years the Progressives languished in the political wilderness: between 1961 and 1974 they were represented solely by Helen Suzman, whereafter their representation rose slowly. The demise of the New Republic Party (the renamed United Party) in 1977 and subsequent opposition realignments during the 1980s saw the Progressive Party become, successively, the Progressive Reform Party, the Progressive Federal Party and, in 1989, the Democratic Party. The last name change reflected what was hoped to be a significant realignment in which dissident Afrikaners, like the ex-NP MP Wynand Malan, and the followers of the former South African Ambassador in Britain, Denis Worrall, joined forces with the original Progressives, who were still the dominant force in the PFP.

In the 1989 election the DP, led by a triumvirate leadership of De Beer, Malan and Worrall, won 33 seats in the (white) House of Assembly, which represented 21 per cent of the white vote. This amounted to a small expansion of the old PFP's support base in urban English-speaking middle class constituencies, but nothing like the breakthrough into Afrikaner support that Malan's and Worrall's joining forces seemed – at least to DP optimists – to herald. The DP picked up marginal support in the (coloured) House of Representatives and the (Indian) House of Delegates, but it campaigned only halfheartedly in the elections for these Houses since it was well known that few credible coloured or Indian politicians would offer themselves for election to the thoroughly discredited tricameral parliament.

The DP, accordingly, remained highly ambivalent about participating in elections to the coloured and Indian Houses, fearing that the taint of the tricameral parliament would rub off on it, notwithstanding the PFP's spirited (though unsuccessful) opposition in the referendum of 1983, in which the white electorate endorsed the tricameral constitution.

On the eve of the election of April 1994, the DP was represented by 27 MPs in the Assembly, 7 in Representatives (all of them ex-Labour Party members), and 3 in Delegates. Overwhelmingly it was a white-based party, but even its white support base looked a little wobbly: five DP MPs (none of them political heavyweights) left the DP to join the ANC, and thereafter sat as independents; and another, Mike Tarr, had joined the Inkatha Freedom Party.

The changes initiated by State President F. W. de Klerk's historic speech of 2 February 1990 were welcomed by the DP. It and its forerunners had long campaigned for exactly the kind of changes that De Klerk had made, and it welcomed the opportunity to participate in the negotiating process that eventually got under way in December 1991. At the Convention for a Democratic South Africa (CODESA) in 1991–2 and, thereafter, at the Multi-party Negotiating Forum in 1993–4, individual DP stalwarts like Ken Andrew, Colin Eglin and Tony Leon played a role whose significance was out of proportion to the party's strength in the (enlarged) electorate that would vote in April 1994. As brokers, mediators, catalysts and constitutional mechanics they earned the respect of their political rivals. Some interventions (notably Leon's agitation to dilute political influence in the appointment of judges on the Constitutional Court) significantly strengthened the interim constitution.

Substantially, the interim constitution was to the DP's liking. In many respects its and its predecessors' policies had pioneered the way for some of the constitution's important features: federalism (or, at least, some degree of federalism), proportional representation, a justiciable bill of rights, an independent judiciary, and a multi-party executive had all been elements of these policies. Perhaps the interim constitution was insufficiently federal for the DP's taste, but it could be said to have more federal potential than might appear from the text. The DP was also party to the pressure exerted on the ANC and the NP to change the original provision that a single ballot would determine both national and provincial representation: this was changed to allow the individual voter · two ballots, one national and the other provincial. This, argued the DP and other critics, was more democratic. It was also more likely to benefit smaller parties, especially if they were provincially based.

DP pressure, however, failed to secure another change that could have serious consequences for it and other small parties: section 43 of the constitution provides that an MP who ceases to be a member of the party · which nominated him or her as a member of the National Assembly shall be required to vacate his or her parliamentary seat. This is not only a profoundly undemocratic provision, but also one that will seriously inhibit any possible realignment of parties over the next five years. The list system of proportional representation already places considerable power in the hands of party leaders; section 43 massively enlarges that power to create within parties an 'Iron Law of Oligarchy' that would startle even Robert Michels. (It would also cause the maker of the great speech 'To the Electors of Bristol', Edmund Burke, to shudder.)

During the 1980s the PFP and, thereafter, the DP promoted what was called 'convergence', i.e. the role of catalyst in bringing ANC and NP thinking closer to each other. While it would be an exaggeration to claim that the DP was the main agent of the convergence that did, in fact, take place in the constitutional negotiations, DP negotiators can claim some credit if only as honest brokers. The constitution that finally emerged from the process was, arguably, closer to core DP views than was the NP's original constitutional programme of September 1991 or the ANC's Constitutional Guidelines of 1988 (which were, it is true, substantially amended later on).

From the DP's point of view, 'convergence' had played some role in the negotiating process; in the elections, however, the DP would ruefully have to acknowledge, 'convergence' was shown to have succeeded so well that it all but squeezed the DP out.

In facing up to the election the DP found its problem was twofold: firstly, as the first fully inclusive election it was inevitably going to be a 'liberation' or *uhuru* election with a vengeance. For new voters, casting their ballots would be an immense, cathartic experience. Secondly, given the apparent convergence of thinking around a constitution that was squarely liberal–democratic in character, the DP would struggle to find a distinctive niche for itself in the political marketplace. Constitutional issues could not be a major issue in the election campaign since all parties (with the exception of the Inkatha Freedom Party and the Freedom Front) had agreed to the terms of the interim constitution; economic issues would be more relevant, but here, too, parties agreed, for instance, that South Africa needed higher growth and that inequalities and the sheer lack of facilities that afflicted many blacks must be addressed as a matter of priority.

A substantial degree of consensus, indeed collusion (a word often used by DP speakers during the campaign), between the ANC and NP on major issues left only one area to be exploited for political capital: the past. The ANC belaboured the NP as the party of apartheid, while the NP drew upon its repertoire of communist-bashing, accusing the ANC of harbouring die-hard Marxist–Leninists in its midst. For all of this seemingly inflammatory rhetoric, the campaign conflict between the two bigger parties was surprisingly muted (lending some credibility to the DP's accusation of collusion).

As its strategic *point d'appui*, the DP opted to attack both the NP and the ANC on their records, principally in respect of human rights and of economic management (which, obviously, would be prospective in the ANC's case). As a strategy document put it in 1992,

> our sober assessment [is] that, despite the impressive performance of their respective leaders, neither the African National Congress nor the National Party has any deep-seated commitment to liberal democratic values or to market oriented economics. Both organizations are power-hungry, both have constituencies whose demands are more important to them than ideals or the broader interests of all South Africans, both have embarked on the first stages of what promises to be a destructive election campaign. Worse than this, both see advantages in mobilizing voters in terms of a 'them or us' campaign.

The strategy document went on to argue that if this bipolarity was played out and only two significant parties emerged, the old political divide would be created in a new form:

> It will essentially be a black vs white, haves vs have-nots political battle, characterised by intransigence, hostility and extremism. This

political battle will inevitably spill over into violence, with
potentially cataclysmic effects on our country, our economy and
... our people.[1]

It was necessary, the DP argued, to propagate liberal democratic values
among the new electorate. In subsequent publications the DP offered
itself as the nucleus of a new, democratic centre 'untainted by violence,
corruption, apartheid and socialism'.[2] Herein lay another DP hope,
modelled on the pivotal position played in successive German coalitions
by the (liberal) Free Democratic Party: that it could hold the balance of
power as a centrist party. The reasoning was that the ANC and its allies,
together with the 'far Left', might win a total of 50 per cent of the vote;
the NP, its allies and the 'far Right', 35 per cent; and the centre, with 15
per cent of the vote, would hold the balance of power. For itself, as the
catalytic core of the centre, the DP hoped for 10 per cent of the vote.

During the campaign the DP punted itself on its long and honourable
record in the field of human rights: 'Unlike the other parties the DP has
always stood for freedom for the individual, human dignity and the Rule
of Law.' It offered the voter protection from the abuse of power and
'effective opposition'. It attacked both the ANC and the NP, although
individual DP speakers singled out one or the other for more emphasis:
'The ANC is a mixture of moderates and radicals, and are divided as
regards their policies. They have no experience in the administration of a
country. The NP was lousy in government, they will be just as bad in
opposition.'[3]

To succeed even partially in its strategy the DP had to do two things:
to persuade voters that under PR no vote was wasted; and to acquire
even modest amounts of support from African, coloured and Indian
voters. The first issue had long plagued the DP and its predecessors. For
many years white opposition voters had continued in large numbers to
support the UP on grounds that to support the Progressives would 'split
the anti-Nat vote'. Even after the demise of the UP, the issue surfaced in
a different form, as droves of opposition voters supported the NP to
shore it up against a perceived threat from the Conservative Party.
Exactly this happened in the 1983 constitutional referendum and in the
1987 parliamentary elections.

In 1994, in the entirely different context of an inclusive election, the
issue would recur, this time as large numbers of 'old' and new (coloured
and Indian) voters, who might otherwise have been sympathetic to the
DP's policies, voted for F. W. de Klerk's NP as the best counterweight to
what was perceived as a rampant ANC. The message that no vote was
wasted under PR did not get through; nor did voters widely understand

that the stakes in this election had been significantly lowered by the principle of having multi-party executives at both national and provincial levels. In the PR systems of Western Europe it is relatively rare for a single party to win more than 50 per cent of the vote. Nevertheless, stable, effective and democratic government is the norm (despite what critics of PR aver). In the provincial elections, however, it was readily apparent that winning on the basis of plurality was insufficiently satisfying; topping the 50 per cent mark and thus winning an outright victory became an all-important symbolic goal.

The second issue proved even harder for the DP to surmount: just as it and its predecessors had struggled for decades to recruit significant Afrikaner support (with scant success, notwithstanding the mirage of an Afrikaner 'fourth force' in 1989), so the DP in the 1990s struggled in vain to break into the newly enfranchised communities. Prominent Africans, known to be staunchly committed to liberal democratic principles, were approached confidentially by the DP, but none was prepared publicly to support the DP, let alone become a DP candidate. One consequence of this was that the handful of Africans who appeared on the DP's national list were, in national terms, politically unknown.

In a sharp criticism of the DP's pretensions as the 'true liberal conscience', Paulus Zulu pointed out that ideological issues were of secondary importance, if they featured at all, to the millions of newly-enfranchised African voters for whom this was a 'liberation' election. Moreover:

> The DP has largely been a white party in spite of its protestations to the contrary. When the politics of non-participation was the principal strategy for the liberation movement, the DP happily participated in an all-white parliament and reaped the fruits of that participation for itself. Suddenly to expect the erstwhile disenfranchised voters to forget that easily is beyond imagination, if not political day-dreaming.[4]

Zulu's analysis, however, did not discount the appeal of liberal ideals to a growing African middle class, but he considered it irresponsible and arrogant of the DP to assume that it alone could carry the mantle of liberalism (which, incidentally, is not actually the DP's view).

Recruitment in African areas, both urban and rural, was made difficult, if not impossible, by the strength of predominantly African parties, who regarded the DP as interlopers on 'their' turf. Throughout the 1990s instances of intimidation and actual physical strong-arm action against known African DP supporters have mounted in number. During the election campaign in 1994, the DP was effectively precluded from any sustained campaigning or canvassing in any concentrated areas where Africans lived. In Soweto, for example, the chairman of the DP's branch was so threatened that his wife, in turn, threatened to leave him since he was endangering the family. Much of KwaZulu–Natal was a 'no-go' area because of the endemic violence. Similarly, much of the Eastern Cape province was impenetrable: Errol Moorcroft (now a DP Senator), who ran the DP's rural campaign in the Eastern Cape, informed the writer that credible death threats, in some cases purporting to come from APLA (the PAC's armed wing), had curtailed activities in the Port Alfred area. When DP organisers were told that if they set foot over the Kei River 'they would be killed', Moorcroft refused to send canvassers into the area. All in all, the DP was denied any real access to some two–thirds of the electorate – and much the same was true for the NP.

'For reasons of state' South Africans have been required to subscribe to the latest national myth, namely that the elections were 'substantially free and fair'. They were nothing of the kind, and hardly any of the sanctimonious foreign observers who fell about themselves to declare it so would for one moment have accepted the validity of an election subject to such flaws in their own countries.

It can, of course, be validly contended that even if the DP (or the NP) had had the access that was denied them, it would have made little or no difference to the outcome of the election. This is almost certainly true, but it does not meet the objection raised above, nor those, mentioned by several DP and PAC members, concerning irregularities in the counting process and the fact that in many polling and counting stations 80 per cent and more of the officials were ANC-aligned.

Fundamentally the DP's performance was disastrous because, to quote the well-known words of Donald L. Horowitz, 'This was no election – it was a census.'[5] Overwhelmingly, race was the basis of voter choice: only two or three per cent of white voters supported the ANC, and conversely a similar percentage of Africans supported the NP and the DP. Substantial majorities of coloured and Indian voters in the Western Cape and KwaZulu–Natal, respectively, supported the NP in the belief that it, rather than the DP, was the most effective counterweight to the ANC. These, too, in other words, were racially-based votes.

In many respects the DP's poor performance mirrors that of putatively multi-ethnic parties in other deeply divided societies. While Northern Ireland and South Africa are very different societies, they share in common a high degree of ascriptive voting. Given the differences of context and the nature of the conflict, it is nevertheless true that the DP's position resonates with that of Northern Ireland's Alliance Party, an intersectarian party which was 'distinguished for its good intentions rather than its achievements'.[6]

Genuinely non-racial parties have not prospered in deeply divided societies, and there seems little reason to anticipate that South Africa will prove different, at least in the short to medium term.

Criticism of Dr Zach de Beer's leadership surfaced in the DP during 1993, with some members maintaining that his style was insufficiently aggressive. De Beer has had a long political career, beginning in 1953 when he entered parliament – as its youngest member – for the United Party. He was one of the original Progressives who broke away in 1959, but lost his seat in 1961. De Beer has had distinguished careers in medicine and in business, but his interest in, and commitment to, the Progressive Party and its subsequent incarnations had never flagged. He assumed the leadership of the DP when the original tripartite leadership, consisting of himself, Wynand Malan and Denis Worrall, fell away.

At 65 De Beer had no doubt lost some of the fire that had once made him one of the finest orators (in both English and Afrikaans) in South African politics. He remained, however, one of the best TV performers in the country, even if he did not do himself justice in this medium during the 1994 campaign. Whatever the criticisms, it was clear during 1993 that no-one else could have led the DP without destructively divisive effects. He remained throughout urbane and courteous, and enjoyed the respect of his opponents for his hard business sense and his staunch commitment to democratic principles.

It was De Beer's misfortune, and that of the DP's, that the election rapidly assumed the character of a presidential race between Mandela and De Klerk. As leaders of the two biggest parties they attracted the lion's share of media attention, and the TV debate between them was the media event of the campaign. It squeezed the DP and other smaller parties to the margins, and even some outstanding debating performances by individual DP members (for example, Ken Andrew's dissection of the articulate Pallo Jordan of the ANC) and fair coverage of the charismatic, sharp-tongued Transvaal DP leader, Tony Leon, could not hide the truth: that the media did not find the DP especially newsworthy. A number of leading English-language newspapers (including the *Sunday Times, Sunday Tribune, Natal Mercury, Daily Dispatch, Business Day* and the *Financial Mail)* supported the DP but in several cases it was grudging support, even damning it with faint praise.

Proportional representation is supposed to help smaller parties, and in general it does so. As has been noted, however, the DP found it impossible to get across the message that under PR no vote is wasted. The introduction of the double ballot, for which the DP and other smaller parties had pressed, did apparently bring some marginal advantage to the DP at the provincial level. At national level the DP won only 338,526 votes, but at the provincial level it won 538,655 votes – a discrepancy of nearly 200,000 votes – which was significantly more than the 450,000 (white) votes it won in the 1989 parliamentary elections. Clearly, much of the discrepancy reflected the wish of voters to support De Klerk nationally, but the DP provincially. Thus far, there is little evidence to suggest that traditional white support, concentrated in the Johannesburg and Cape Town areas, deserted the DP *en masse*. For the DP the problem was that it failed to break through into the African, coloured and Indian voters. In the Western Cape, for instance, where the DP had some impressive coloured leaders on its list, including Professor Richard van der Ross, Chris April and Joe Marks (a former ANC stalwart), it won only about three per cent of the coloured vote; the figure for the Indian vote in KwaZulu–Natal was probably comparable; and for the African vote the figure was less than one per cent.

The DP and its predecessors have found it difficult to break out of the urban, English-speaking, white, middle-class confines of liberalism. The DP's cerebral approach to politics, with its carefully worked out, rational policies, lacks mass appeal in a political system where calls to racial and ethnic 'blood' (even if concealed in the rhetoric of non-racialism) are the stock-in-trade of politicians on the stump. Since the election, there has been considerable euphoria, welcoming the relative peacefulness of the elections and the graciousness of Nelson Mandela and his (genuine) commitment to reconciliation. The euphoria will soon wear off, and the tough issues that South Africa will have to face will stand out as sharply etched as before. It takes more than a peaceful election to erase the scars of a traumatic past.

For the DP the options have narrowed. Even with its small numbers (seven MPs and three senators), it will continue to play the watchdog role in a parliament in which open opposition will be muted by virtue of the major parties' membership of the government of national unity. No doubt, some of its able negotiators, like Colin Eglin, Ken Andrew and Tony Leon, will keep a watchful eye as the final constitution is forged.

Party affiliations will remain in the mould prescribed by the interim constitution, but beneath the surface of the ice-bound lake undercurrents will continue to swirl. It is premature to speak of realignments, but the possibilities exist, if not necessarily in the short term. There are significant numbers of ANC, NP and Inkatha members who do not differ very substantially on any ideological axis from the DP, but whether any catalyst can 'bring together those who belong together out of inner conviction' (to quote the famous words of D. F. Malan) is a question that cannot yet be answered.[7]

Notes

1. 'The Democratic Party Strategy' (1992), Introduction.
2. DP: *Invest DP for Power and Peace* (1993).
3. Ibid.
4. *Weekly Mail,* 18–24 February 1994.
5. Donald L. Horowitz, *Ethnic Groups in Conflict* (Berkeley: University of California, 1985), p. 86).
6. Patrick Buckland, *A History of Northern Ireland* (Dublin: Gill and Macmillan, 1981), p. 135.
7. The writer wishes to thank senior DP MPs for providing him with information for this chapter.

7

The PAC and AZAPO

SATHS COOPER

'A concoction of rumours' is how Johnson Mlambo, Deputy President of the Pan Africanist Congress of Azania (PAC), dismissed media reports (11 May 1994) of serious dissatisfaction within the PAC over the leadership's steering of the election campaign. But there has clearly been surprise, if not shock, in many circles at the dismal performance of the PAC. Most analysts did not expect such poor showings from a party that has a strong liberatory tradition.

Part of the reason for the PAC's inability to make a better showing at the polls was its leadership difficulties. At the best of times the PAC leadership displayed incoherence and lack of clear direction. Its lapse into rhetoric, more often wild and of the 'one bullet' and 'whites must leave' variety, and historically based claims of legitimacy, were the most common features of its campaigning in the run-up to the election. Clearly, though, this was insufficient to garner the required number of votes to retain the PAC's erstwhile status as a key player in national political life.

Immediately after the formal election results were publicly announced, dissension within the PAC began to resurface. The PAC was riddled with leadership problems from the time that Potlako Leballo assumed the reins of power soon after the PAC went into exile some 34 years ago. The PAC was never able to enjoy stability in its leadership after that time. There was a very short period when in the late 1980s Zephaniah Mothopeng, who had been released from prison on health grounds, managed to pull the various factions of the PAC together. His death resulted in the obscure ex-Robben Islander, Clarence Makwetu, being resurrected and brought from his farm in the Transkei to the national political stage, but he was singularly unable to make effective use of his new position. Mothopeng was one of the PAC's original founding leaders with Robert Sobukwe when the ANC's Orlando branch, suspended for its Africanist tendency, went on to become the nucleus of the PAC in 1959. With Mothopeng's death the PAC also began its demise as a central player in the transition to democracy.

Makwethu did not have an understanding of the modern media and was often caught out making ponderous responses which were not soundbyte friendly. When he did respond shortly, it was in a taciturn or monosyllabic fashion which tended to confound and turn off listeners or viewers. Benny Alexander and, to some extent, Patricia de Lille were the PAC's more effective public communicators. During the run-up to the election Alexander was not given any public role. Indeed, the 'campaign' of the PAC was stark by its absence. Their posters lauding the 'African Hope', Makwetu, only went up a few weeks before the actual election, and then too in relatively bad positions and in numbers that made no impact. The PAC message was not heard at all. It had no cogent election plank. When media opportunity presented itself, it was not effectively exploited. The abiding memory many potential voters had of the PAC was of its president making a public complaint about lack of funds, especially from the 'imperialists' and 'capitalists'. The abiding memory many existing voters had of the PAC was its apparent anti-whitism. Despite carefully intellectualised arguments about the definition of an African as a person owing allegiance to the soil rather than skin colour, nearly all whites fear the PAC.

When one is used to interaction within a close-knit circle of minds in general agreement, one can easily be seduced into believing that times are favourable to one's thinking and that those who don't agree suffer from lack of clarity in vision and understanding. One then runs the risk of remaining purist in thought and action without any effect. One can rest in the self-consolation that one has *the* policy, if only the world would take note and benefit! This in some measure is the malaise that afflicted both the PAC and the Azanian People's Organisation (AZAPO).

AZAPO has steadfastly refused to be drawn into the negotiation process, believing it to be flawed. It accordingly stayed out of the election, which it maintained was similarly flawed. What AZAPO did not take into account was the massive support that this first democratic election elicited from the vast majority of the populace.

AZAPO was caught in the rhetoric of the past and was therefore unable to come to terms with the reality of the change ushered in by F. W. de Klerk. Like the other far-Left organisation, the New Unity Movement, and its associate, the African People's Democratic Union of South Africa, AZAPO had great difficulty in accepting that the changes wrought and the nascent democracy ushered in were irrevocably part of the new landscape of the country. Their even greater difficulty was to accept that the masses have really come of age and are able to articulate effectively what they want outside of system propaganda. This realisation of the ability of the majority in South Africa to identify their own needs and aspirations was misunderstood by most commentators and do-gooders in South Africa, especially those who forecast massive voter illiteracy, mistaking lack of formal education for inability to choose and understand. Having *the* policy is of no avail if one hasn't the ability and capacity, perhaps even the inclination, to relate effectively to the masses.

The reliance on armed propaganda by the PAC, and more recently by AZAPO, worked to their disadvantage. The national mood was one of a serious desire for reconciliation and peace. The warmongers in our midst appealed to a very small percentage of the total population. By and large, South Africans are law-abiding people who desire conditions of stability and security so that they can get on with bettering their lot without let. The strong message coming from APLA (the PAC armed wing) and AZANLA (the Black Consciousness armed wing) was one of total rejection of the changed conditions; they also continued to prey on suspicions and mistrust of the past, and threatened attacks on unarmed civilians. The PAC's indecisiveness in dealing with the APLA threats, which the media instantly relayed to the public, caused the PAC leadership to be further undermined in the public mind. The PAC leadership tried to suggest that APLA had its own command structure outside of the PAC hierarchy when under media fire, and then claim APLA allegiance when it suited them, added to the PAC's diminution in support. Very few people in current-day South Africa wish to be led by leaders whose versions differ according to the occasion and who palpably don't have the ability to rein in errant members who give them a bad reputation.

It is significant that the PAC stayed out of the Transitional Executive Council and only joined it when the TEC's term of office was about to end, in order to secure the incorporation of APLA cadres into the new South African National Defence Force. It is also significant that the PAC was forced to suspend the armed struggle and become involved in the election after public rebukes from Tanzania and Zimbabwe. The head of APLA died in exile at about the same time. In a sense, the PAC went into the election without unanimous agreement for such a decision within its ranks and because it had to do so in order to retain Tanzanian and Zimbabwean backing and its own ailing support base at home.

The PAC's putative support bases nearly all failed to materialise, with the PAC only succeeding in gaining five seats in the National Assembly and a solitary seat each in the legislatures of the PWV, Eastern Cape and Natal. Their total voter support was 243,478 votes for the National Assembly, which accounted for 1.2 per cent of projected eligible voters. A discernible percentage of voters who supported them in the majority of provincial legislatures did not vote for them on the national ballot. Indeed, it seems as if many supporters of the PAC voted for the ANC in the belief that they had rather vote for a *winner* from the national liberation movement in this first democratic election so as to end white minority rule and change their quality of life. It may be that a small percentage of diehard PAC members, particularly from their youth formations, simply stayed away from voting because of their principled opposition to the negotiation process.

The PAC had the powerful and evocative issue of the land question which they failed to project effectively. They laboured under their own illusion that they would be the 'surprise' performer in the election, as the ZANU–PF had been in Zimbabwe. In this they were rudely surprised. This election was about ending minority white rule, about bringing peace and creating conditions for national reconciliation, stability and prosperity, and improving the quality of life of the majority. These issues were largely ignored by the PAC and AZAPO, which tended to stand more on principle and socialist rhetoric, putting themselves beyond the reach of the masses on whose behalf they purported to speak.

The failure in performance of the PAC and the obdurate refusal by AZAPO to participate in the country's first democratic election mean that the real loser will be the country's fledgling democracy, which vitally needs vigorous criticism, which the PAC and AZAPO had the promise of offering to both the compacts already reached and those likely to be reached by the two major players in government. The PAC and AZAPO need to reassess their positions immediately, pay urgent attention to the new reality for South African politics after the Cold War, and work to rekindling potential support if they are to retain any modicum of support in future, whether the current government succeeds or not.

8

The Mass Media
and the South African Election

DANIEL SILKE AND ROBERT SCHRIRE

Introduction

The remarkable changes characteristic of the 1994 South African general election provide the media analyst with a host of new images. Political freedom and tolerance, which had been fostered over the four year period since the release of Nelson Mandela in 1990, reached new heights during March and April of 1994, and the media were able to part take in a level of democratic expression unheard of before the transformation.

The divided nature of South African society has long been reflected in the popular mass media, but while freedom of expression was largely tolerated in the print media, albeit under severe restrictions, television and radio found themselves at the mercy of the regime of the day. During the election, the press, radio and television, and even the mass marketing and advertising campaigns of the participating political parties all contributed to an ideological liberalisation of the society. However, past loyalties did remain, and this chapter deals with the beginnings of a drift away from patronage to a more independent approach across the media spectrum.

The Press and the South African Election

Historically, the South African newspaper industry has been divided on linguistic grounds. The English press under the watchful eye of their parent bodies, Times Media Limited and the Argus groups, provided effective, watchdog opposition to the NP government despite the impact of severe reporting restrictions and penalties. Conversely, the Afrikaans-speaking press has almost exclusively supported the NP. Major dailies like *Die Burger* in Cape Town and *Beeld* in Johannesburg advanced the cause of Afrikaner nationalism and steadfastly supported all past NP administrations.

In line with the results, this was a media election campaign dominated by the two major political parties. Both the NP and ANC were adept in drawing attention to themselves as they capitalised on the asset of having the two most prominent South African political personalities within their midst. The ANC enjoyed the edge in being able to draw on massive crowds to create atmosphere, and Nelson Mandela's showman-like performances across the length and breadth of the country meant that the ANC were able to receive the lion's share of coverage from newspapers that were known to be favourably disposed to either the DP or NP. But the uniqueness of an NP campaign that targeted the once-oppressed black masses as potential voters was enough to provide pressmen with outstanding visual material. Pictures of President F. W. de Klerk draped in tribal blankets and Pik Botha dancing with rural black NP supporters were manna from heaven, especially for international journalists.

None of the small political parties could compete with the personalities of De Klerk and Mandela. Even within the Democratic Party-supporting English press, their own party of choice hardly made headlines. DP leader, Zach de Beer, personally failed to inspire, and other party candidates were sorely out of touch with their audience. This was reflected within the print media, which largely ignored DP public meetings and functions at the expense of the more exciting and impressive NP or ANC rallies.

However, despite the two-party nature of the campaign, the balance of 'editorial endorsements' failed to go to the main players. Having largely reduced the DP to an insignificant party throughout the two-month period, most of the English press continued to support the party in their endorsement editorials in the run-up to the election. This loyalty shown towards the South African liberal opposition had often placed the English press in an awkward position. For, even though endorsements from leading newspapers were theoretically bound to have a spin-off effect in promoting liberal democracy, editorial endorsements and political bias had never really resulted in great successes at the polls for the DP or its predecessors. Indeed, much of the English-language press (with the exception of the conservative *Citizen*) was consistently out of touch with its readership. Despite their support for the DP over many years, the majority of the English-language-press readers often voted for the NP, especially in the 1983 referendum and 1987 election when the old PFP lost some 10 seats to the ruling NP.

Furthermore, given the sluggish nature of the DP's campaign, the endorsements from the English press lacked vigour or enthusiasm. It was as if many newspaper editors who were morally or conscience bound to put their cross next to Dr Zach de Beer knew at the same time that the party had really not delivered the electoral goods during the campaign. Their support for the DP was half-hearted and muted and was hardly sufficient to make even wavering DP supporters remain with their home party. The voice of South African liberalism, Ken Own, was perhaps most vocal in articulating this message. In his *Sunday Times*[1] column entitled 'Democracy means voting for the least bad choice', Owen chided the DP leadership for being 'shuffle-footed and toffee nosed' as well as 'soulless and isolated in their higher education and higher incomes.' In a devastating indictment on a party that he supported, he added, 'The party has failed to exploit the new opportunities for democracy which Mr De Klerk has exploited and the reason is that the DP is in the hands of a clique; as Dr Zach de Beer has admitted, the top of its list of candidates is dominated by people who have served the party for up to 20 years. Their principal qualification is that they know each other.' Owen did admit that 'the potential of the DP, if it can find the right leaders after the election is exciting' but went on to provide a most lukewarm endorsement by concluding: 'Anyway, I stuck with the liberals when they were almost extinct. I shall not desert them now simply because they are confused.'

The Durban-based *Sunday Tribune* was kinder to the DP,[2] and Johannesburg's mass circulation *Star*[3] newspaper also endorsed the party, albeit with reservations. Significantly, the DP received its more enthusiastic support from the country's two major business publications. *Business Day*[4] newspaper said that 'the DP has the experience and the will to stand up to bad government. Every vote for it will be a vote for the decent South Africa we all want.' The influential *Financial Mail* weekly magazine, in two forceful editorials, promoted the DP as being 'the best opposition to ANC majorities',[5] and further positive support came from long-time allies, the *Argus*[6] and *Cape Times*[7] – both Cape Town dailies.

Although an English-medium newspaper, the Johannesburg daily *Citizen* has always been something of a maverick. Started in the mid-1970s with government funding, the *Citizen*'s initial mission was to wean English-speakers away from the old liberal English press and to new homes in support of the NP. Indeed, it was the funding of the *Citizen* that caused the 'Information Scandal' of 1979, which resulted in the toppling of senior cabinet ministers and even the then President, John Vorster. The *Citizen* for years vilified the liberal opposition and has largely backed the ruling National Party; but, over the last 15 years, the newspaper had progressively become more and more sympathetic to mainstream right-wing causes and was the only English-language daily which did not support the 'yes' vote in the 1992 referendum to endorse the De Klerk reform initiative.

During the months of March and April, the *Citizen* tended to provide an unusual amount of news-space to right-wing movements. In many instances, the front page of the tabloid was dominated by stories relating to the right-wing. On Friday, 22 April 1994, the headline story dealt with 48 former police generals who were now backing the Freedom Front, while the Saturday, 23 April edition gave prominence to a senior police officer, Leon Mellett, who had just joined the FF. However, this time round, the paper took a similar stance to that of its Afrikaans colleague *Rapport* and refused to endorse any political party.

Indeed, it was, to say the least, unusual for *Rapport*, South Africa's most influential and respected Afrikaans newspaper, to fail to officially endorse the NP. In an emotional editorial that called on Afrikaners to be wary of the *godloosheid* (ungodliness) of the communists, *Rapport* warned of the hidden reality within the ANC. It stated: 'The true ANC are yet to stand up, and if they really do in the future, will it perhaps be either the face of a Lenin or a Stalin?'[8]

However, there was little surprise in the editorials of either *Die Burger* (Cape Town)[9] or *Beeld* (Johannesburg).[10] Both have loyally supported the NP, and continued to do so throughout the 1994 campaign. *Die Burger* in particular was staunchly NP throughout the election period and played its dutiful role as an adjunct to the successful NP campaign that resulted in their taking the Western Cape province.

There was some degree of predictability about the press endorsements from the newly emerging black press. Although owned by the same parent companies as their white counterparts, this media sector retained its own editorial independence, albeit tempered to suit its financial bosses. Foremost among the 'black press' was the *Sowetan* newspaper – the only daily newspaper aimed at a predominantly black readership. Although it is an English-medium paper, the *Sowetan's* circulation growth has been impressive; in 1991 it replaced Johannesburg's *Star* as the largest-selling daily newspaper in South Africa, boasting a readership total of some 1.6 million readers.

In contrast with the majority of Argus-owned newspapers that called in some form or other for a pro-DP vote, Aggrey Klaaste of the *Sowetan*[11] favoured the liberation movements in an emotional front-page editorial on the Monday prior to voting. Klaaste wrote:

> We recognise the choice for black voters in this week's elections will be difficult. It is our view, however, there is an undeniable obligation to vote for the liberation organisations. The ANC and the PAC are the only parties for whom our choice should be made.

Regrettably, Azapo is not standing. The liberation organisations were the engine in the struggle that brought about the first all-race democratic elections in SA. Not only did the leaders of these parties spend years in prison, they were subjected to all the terrible onslaughts used by apartheid to destroy entire communities and, in the process, our beautiful land.

New thinking within the pro-NP Nasionale Pers led to this newspaper group buying *City Press*, another predominantly black-readership weekly newspaper in Johannesburg. Even the staunchest NP supporters realised that saturation levels had been reached for the white press and that expansion was needed into the lucrative black market. Ironically, Nasionale Pers had appointed Percy Qoboza, one of the NP's harshest and most articulate critics, as editor of *City Press* until his death in 1988. So while *City Press* had long been a stable companion of NP mouthpieces, its editorial policy had been quite independent. In a front-page endorsement editorial, *City Press* stated that 'While there are many men and women of vision who made this day possible, ANC president Nelson Mandela undoubtedly stands head and shoulders above all who finally took us to this glorious and momentous day. We thank God Almighty. Let us go to the polls on Wednesday and vote for a party we can trust with our lives.'[12]

The 'alternative' press in South Africa represents a market born out of the resistance and struggle years of the 1980s. These newspapers' editorial stances marked a shift to the Left away from the dominant groups like Times Media Limited or the Argus. Of this new breed of papers the *Weekly Mail* is social democratic in persuasion. Started as a desperate effort to maintain journalistic independence following the demise of the much-lauded *Rand Daily Mail,* the *Weekly Mail* offered qualified support to the ANC but was unafraid to speak out against the liberation movement, or any of its personalities, should it deem this necessary. In their endorsement editorial the *Mail* criticised the NP for being 'too burdened by its past and too untrustworthy in its born-again non-racialism'. The DP also received a hammering as being 'plagued by poor leadership' and 'failing to rise above narrow sectional interests.'[13]

In endorsing the ANC, the *Weekly Mail* committed itself to being especially vigilant in watching the new government. 'While we hope the ANC will act more honourably than its predecessors, we will watch it even more closely than we watched the last because we now have higher expectations.' Editor Anton Harber admitted that they were 'deeply troubled by some of the people on the ANC lists, in particular corrupt homeland leaders' but his final message was clearly pro-ANC, arguing that 'South Africa needs a party with the leadership and credibility to unite the nation behind a vision of reconstruction. Only the ANC provides that.'

The more left-wing alternative papers were undeniably trusting of the ANC, which was hardly surprising, given their pro-United Democratic Front position during the State of Emergency years under P. W. Botha. This sector also engaged in vilifying to the greatest degree the challenges of both the NP and DP. The liberal DP was singled out by these papers for some of the harshest attacks of the campaign. Rafiq Rohan, writing in the Cape Town-based *South* on election day, described the DP in the following terms:

> While they [the DP] insist they were opponents of apartheid, they supported the NP government in cross-border raids on our brothers and sisters. They, including the Helen Suzmans, Zach de Beers and Colin Eglins, spent their years as politicians in a tainted parliament that drew up these horrendous apartheid laws and they, although they made a few noises about apartheid, drew fat-cat salaries and did precious little for those suffering under apartheid. They didn't know us then and our votes are all they're after now so they can continue their dubious careers in parliament.[14]

The notion that the DP were simply in cahoots with the apartheid state was also echoed in the *Sunday Nation*.[15] In its editorial, the paper lumped the DP and the IFP together as being 'co-managers of the suppression of democracy with the NP and should not be allowed to postpone the liberation'. It was as if the years of dedicated opposition by the likes of Helen Suzman had brought the DP absolutely no credit. Instead, they were viewed as another oppressor working against the democratic aspirations of the people, and nothing more than partners in apartheid. The association with parliamentary opposition tainted the DP with a 'collaborationist' image and led *Sunday Nation* to advise its readers to 'block the initiatives of these parties [NP, DP, IFP] by strengthening the hand of the ANC, which has behind it more than 80 years of commitment to non-racialism, democracy, accountability and transparency.'

All in all, the election saw a straining of the traditional liberal press's love affair with the DP as a liberal opposition party. These strains do, however, reflect on the nature of the DP as a party rather than on the concept of liberal democracy. Most English newspaper editors would still firmly regard themselves as 'liberals' but would question the effectiveness of the DP in articulating these views. The DP can no longer take for granted any support from these quarters and will have to go back to the drawing board and reassert their role as opposition watchdogs with a social conscience.

The NP also lost ground. Given its past hold over the Afrikaans press as the government of the day, the NP had always been able to rely on patronage for support. While most of its traditional press allies continued in their support, cracks emerged in the case of *Rapport*. This may well reflect the reduced role that the NP now plays in public life. No longer the party of power or privilege, the NP will find that the ties between itself and the print media have steadily loosened and will also undergo considerable review.

Finally, the alternative left-wing media were the most partisan of all sectors of the press. To the virtual exclusion of any positive reporting of either the NP or DP, *South* and the *Sunday Nation* steadfastly promoted the ANC and belittled any moderate opposition. Of interest will be the role of this sector during the next five years. Will they blindly follow the new ANC government or adopt a more social democratic role in opposing controversial decisions?

Electronic Media: Radio and Television

In the old South Africa there was always ample evidence to prove who pulled the strings of the South African Broadcasting Corporation. Over a period of more than three decades, the SABC systematically became the mouthpiece of the ruling National Party, and the introduction of television coupled with the centralisation of power behind the P. W. Botha presidency saw the emergency of even greater government control. Previous elections were characterised by vast discrepancies in the amount of air-time given to non-NP political parties, which negatively impacted upon any potential electoral success they might have had. Both the 1981 and 1987 elections were prime examples of television favouritism, although this was beginning to change by the time F. W. de Klerk took power in 1989.

The most noticeable changes came in the composition of the new board of the SABC, which was announced towards the end of 1993. The previous pro-NP members were shunted aside to make room for new personalities, whose ties seemed equally strong to the once-demonised ANC. Dr Ivy Matsepe-Casaburri was nominated as chairperson of the reconstituted SABC board after the resignation of former PFP leader, Frederik van Zyl Slabbert. Although she had not been a prominent figure in any political party, it was evident from press reports that she was a member of the ANC.[16] However, even more controversial was the appointment of Zwelakhe Sisulu as special assistant to the SABC Chief Executive, Wynand Harmse. The son of ANC Deputy President, Walter

Sisulu, Zwelakhe was also seen as having very strong ANC leanings. He had been detained in the late 1980s and was the former editor of the pro-ANC *Sunday Nation*.

During the election period the entire spectrum of the South African broadcast media was monitored by the Independènt Media Commission.[17] This was chaired by the Hon. Mr Raymond Leon, a retired judge, whose duty it was to oversee the allocation of free air-time for party election broadcasts and to monitor existing paid-for adverts on the various radio services. Political parties received over 150 hours of free air-time in prime-time radio slots often before or after news bulletins – over and above the time paid for by the various political parties. However, the formula on which the allocation of time was based resulted in the ANC and NP receiving almost 19 times more air-time than the smallest provincial party.[18] This election was also unique in terms of South African broadcast history. It was the first time that election radio advertising had been allowed, although political paid-for advertising remained barred from television. It was argued that the financial burden would benefit the larger parties that could afford the advertising, and would so act against the minor players. The same applied to radio, where it was only the ANC, NP and DP that were able to afford multiple spots. These varied from serious policy statements from the ANC to more light-hearted and catchy jingles by the NP. The DP used senior candidates to promote their party. The only television advertising came from non-partisan business interests, who called for South Africans to 'stand up and walk tall' in an emotional series of visually impressive adverts.

There can be little doubt that the television coverage for the election period was remarkably fair. The generally balanced coverage afforded the variety of political parties seemed to substantiate the view that the SABC had shed its shackles of overt or covert government control and was ready to enter a new era of impartiality even if it was just for the short duration of the election. The SABC's premier news programmes, Agenda (TV1) and Newsline (CCV), were extended by up to half an hour each evening, and provided viewers with in-depth analyses and party debates. Both TV1 and CCV covered local provincial debates in the nine new regions, which were lively and entertaining. These afforded all parties air-time although additional time was often given to smaller parties in order to level the broadcast playing-fields.

Regular audience participation programmes were also held: the principle of a fair allocation of questions to each political party was scrupulously adhered to. Unfortunately, little use was made of prominent academics in the run-up to the election, and the SABC rather opted for party spokespeople to articulate policy. One controversial pre-election anchor appointment was the hiring of former *Vrye Weekblad* editor, Max du Preez, as an addition to the news actuality team.

The four years after February 1990 saw the two major TV channels adopt differing characteristics. While TV1 still offered more air-time to President De Klerk, CCV tended to promote the ANC and Nelson Mandela. This continued throughout the campaign, although TV1 slowly moved towards a more inclusive approach and so blurred the distinction between the two SABC channels. The late inclusion of the IFP resulted in some last-minute juggling to provide Dr Buthelezi with a solo interview and additional radio-time. Consequently, a planned appearance of the DP's Zach de Beer had to be postponed to accommodate the IFP leader.

It was as if the SABC had finally matured. Years of supporting one player had been replaced with a remarkably free and balanced approach. However, as in the print media, the visual images presented were confined largely to the ANC and NP. Such domination of the media by the ANC and NP clearly established South Africa's first liberation election as more of a presidential battle. Two major figures were taking to the hustings in a fight for supremacy. Personality and razzmatazz were the order of the day, rather than policy or principle. This culminated in the presidential-style debate between De Klerk and Nelson Mandela on Thursday, 14 April 1994, between 20h30 and 21h45. Both domestic channels, TV1 and CCV, carried the debate live as well as most SABC domestic radio stations, thus offering the nation saturation coverage of the event. The debate was moderated by senior anchor, Freek Robinson, and included an interviewing panel of Tim Modise, Lester Venter and Ferial Haffajee of the SABC and John Simpson of the BBC.

This was a crucial point in the campaign for both the NP and ANC. To date, both were holding their support, neither suffering any major disaster or embarrassment. It was up to the two heavyweights of South African politics to preserve their positions rather than score any telling knock-out blows. However, once it took place, the 'Great Debate', as it had been billed, proved something of a disappointment. Nelson Mandela's approach was fairly confrontational from the outset. He consistently attacked De Klerk on the issues of third-force involvement with the IFP, government corruption and racist electioneering in the Western Cape. Mandela was tough with De Klerk, and this resulted in a series of sharp exchanges between the two leaders. However, De Klerk rarely lost his cool. In a masterly way he deflected some very telling questions and managed to convey integrity and warmth even after some acrimonious personal allegations from Mandela. The debate closed with

WORKING TOGETHER WITH THE PEOPLE, THE ANC HAS WON THE RIGHT FOR ALL SOUTH AFRICANS TO VOTE.

PAN AFRICANIST CONGRESS OF AZANIA		PAC		
VRYHEIDSFRONT – FREEDOM FRONT		VF-FF		
AFRICAN CHRISTIAN DEMOCRATIC PARTY		ACDP		
AFRICAN DEMOCRATIC MOVEMENT		ADM		
AFRICAN NATIONAL CONGRESS		ANC		X
DEMOCRATIC PARTY – DEMOKRATIESE PARTY		DP		
NATIONAL PARTY – NASIONALE PARTY		NP		

* Northern Cape Provincial Ballot Slip.

VOTE ANC ON APRIL 27, AND WIN A BETTER LIFE FOR ALL.

Everything we've worked for over the years comes down to the choice you make on April 27. A vote for the ANC will put a government in place that has a workable plan to create jobs, to ensure 10 years free, quality education for all our children, and to provide the homes and infrastructure our country needs.

Above all, a vote for the ANC means a government that will take responsibility for bringing peace and stability to South Africa. Your vote will win a better life for all. Use it. On April 27, vote ANC.

A better life for all. Working together for jobs, peace and freedom.

Issued by ANC, DIP, P.O. Box 61884, Marshalltown, 2107.

Nelson Mandela taking De Klerk's hand across the studio desk and proclaiming: 'I am proud to hold your hand.'

There was no discernible winner in this debate, which is said to have enjoyed South Africa's highest-ever viewership. Both leaders played to their constituencies first and to undecided voters second. Both remained in control, and neither dented his own personal image or that of his own party. Mandela largely continued to appeal to the black electorate while De Klerk may have pleased his traditional support base and even won a few converts elsewhere. Essentially, both leaders did enough to differentiate their approaches without destroying one another. But what was significant was that the SABC had presented a two-horse race, and thus the choice was finally made for most viewers.

Perhaps the most controversial aspect of the SABC's election coverage was that of its voter education broadcasts. The Democracy Education Broadcasting Initiative (DEBI) often made references to the apartheid past to urge citizens to vote in the election, and used certain personalities who in the past had been associated with the ANC, like visiting American actor, Danny Glover. Although annoying to senior NP candidates and De Klerk himself[19] (resulting in the NP formally laying a charge with the Independent Electoral Commission against the broadcasts),[20] they continued on a nightly basis until DEBI ran up a huge debt of some R3.5 million.[21]

Although there was little discernible bias in news-related broadcasts, many Afrikaners were shocked at the way the broadcast of the final election results was handled. Language parity between English and Afrikaans was always fairly adhered to by SABC-TV, but in a policy shift the corporation announced that while there would be a complete English results service, Afrikaans would share the remainder of broadcast time with the other nine official languages of the country. But after considerable pressure from Afrikaner cultural groups, the SABC moderately increased the Afrikaans share of the air-time. In their final report following the elections, the IMC concluded that the quantitative treatment of the contesting political parties had, from the start of voting, been broadly equitable on both radio and television.[22]

The Party Political Press Advertising Campaigns

It was apparent from early on in the campaign that political advertising would be confined to the larger, more established political parties. While the ANC and NP started running press ads as early as February, both the DP and Freedom Front only began in March. The IFP did insert a full-page ad nationally during March which asked voters to 'Vote IFP when the time comes',[23] but only committed itself to a major press campaign

"I'm a teacher and I'm voting National Party."

"My name is Winnie and I'm going to vote for the National Party. So are hundreds of other black teachers like me. We will not be intimidated.

Now we have the vote, we must put aside the past, and vote on one thing: Who will give us – all of us – the best future?

The answer is the NP.

I am a mother of two young boys; and like all mothers, I wonder what the future will bring for them.

I know for certain that their future will be a lot better under the National Party, than it ever would be under the ANC.

Only the NP has the strength and experience to run the country. The ANC can't. They just don't have the experience.

I have been teaching in a High School in the PWV region for 17 years and, in that time I have seen the ANC and their friends destroy the education of a whole generation of township children.

It makes me so angry, because children are the future of this country.

The ANC are promising that everyone will have free education – but how on earth are they going to afford it? They have no hope of delivering on their promises.

The NP has a proper plan to get the money to build factories and businesses, so that the jobs will come – and _then_ we will be able to build the schools and hospitals we need.

That way ALL our children will get the best affordable education, and we will be able to make the most of their gifts.

Also the ANC don't understand democracy – to them there is _only_ their point of view. No one else is allowed an opinion. They are autocrats.

I try to teach my children to think for themselves. This is vital if we are to have a proper democracy in this country.

A lot of people say that their hearts are telling them to vote for the ANC. I tell them that their hearts are for emotion. This election is not about emotion. It is about the future, our future. Our children's future.

And only one party can deliver that: The NP"

BE _SURE_ OF A BETTER LIFE

Vote for FW de Klerk and the new National Party

We've made the change

once the party had officially entered the election fray in mid-April. However, it was only the ANC, NP and DP that consciously staggered their campaigns into carefully planned and manipulated phases. All three parties also commissioned established advertising agencies, often with considerable international assistance.

The ANC used Applied Marketing and Communications (AM&C), a division of Hunt Lascaris, one of South Africa's most successful agencies. They also drew on the expert guidance of Stanley Greenberg and Frank Greer, who were the media advisers of the Bill Clinton presidential campaign. Saatchi and Saatchi through their divisional representatives, Optimum, assisted the NP. They had experience in successful election advertising in the most recent Conservative Party victories in British general elections. The DP's agency, the Jupiter Drawing Room, was considerably less adept at political advertising although the agency does enjoy a high degree of respectability as a growing player within the South African market.

The ANC began an impressive campaign late in 1993, which publicised the 'people's forums' town-hall-style meetings of the party. The public were advised of the location of these meetings and were encouraged to participate. Cut-out coupons were included for voters to send in specific questions: this gave the ANC the image of a caring, inclusive approach to politics and had the important spin-off of providing the party with vital feedback from its potential constituents. Their official election phase began with detailed policy advertisements. These 'Open Plan' adverts[24] were based upon the tenets of the ANC's Reconstruction and Development Programme, which emphasised jobs, workers' rights, land reforms, housing policies and welfare. While somewhat dry and uninspiring, the adverts nevertheless provided the electorate with a clear alternative to government policy. They portrayed the ANC as ready to govern and well prepared on a broad range of policy issues.

In the latter phases of the campaign, the ANC placed greater emphasis on highlighting past NP failures, although this role was apparently left to COSATU to fill. The ANC adverts had thus far been rather soft on the NP and had shied away from direct conflict or criticism, but the COSATU adverts flighted in the Western Cape were some of the strongest and most revealing of the entire campaign. Images of starving women and dispossessed people urged voters to reject the NP. The adverts were also some of the few to attack the personas of De Klerk and Western Cape premiership candidate, Hernus Kriel. Indeed, the Western Cape stands out for the sheer quantity of ad spend run up in the election. During early April, it was increasingly apparent that the ANC were failing to make inroads into the coloured voters, who formed the

SOUTH AFRICA
We did it for
YOU

YOUR ONLY
ALTERNATIVE

If you want to help us build a better future, you can do
so by supporting us financially. Our account details are:

First National Bank, Greyville
Branch number 22 27 26
Account Number: 6000040444
Account Name: IFP Election Fund

VOTE IFP

A Power for Good

majority in the region. In a desperate attempt to redress the situation, the ANC went for saturation coverage in the Western Cape media. Three to four full-page adverts per day were not uncommon, and in conjunction with sharpened and even more vitriolic COSATU-sponsored efforts, the ANC hit at all aspects of NP rule. Finally, the ANC brought in the respected Cape Town academic, Franklin Sonn, and prominent Muslim community leaders[25] for a series of full-page endorsement ads in a frantic effort to stem the flow to the NP.

Whereas the ANC concentrated most of their efforts on their own policy issues, the NP fought on a more aggressive ticket, attacking both the ANC and the Democratic Party. De Klerk was prominent in many early ads, in line with the certain knowledge that he was the major vote-catcher for the party. Initial ads reflected key target constituencies for the party. As the NP were unable to campaign in many black townships, they relied on press advertising to reach these hitherto uncanvassed areas. Target ads included black women,[26] who were identified as strong potential voters. One emotional advert showed an illustration of a small black child accompanied by a headline of 'Vote ANC and break her heart'. It was in this arena, of emotional comparative advertising, that the NP excelled. Little space was wasted on policy details, and instead readers were treated to a barrage of endorsement ads from 'ordinary citizens'. NP adverts appealed to various economic and social sectors of society. Ads ran the gamut from declaring 'I am a computer operator and I'm voting for the NP' to 'I am a motor mechanic and I'm voting for the NP'. Particularly effective in this series was that headed 'I am a teacher and I'm voting National Party'.[27] The copy of this ad, accompanied by a page-length photograph of a smiling black female teacher, concluded that 'A lot of people say that their hearts are telling them to vote for the ANC. I tell them that their hearts are for emotion. This election is not about emotion. It is about the future, our future. Our children's future. And only one party can deliver that: the NP.'

The NP clearly succeeded in articulating commonly held fears about the ANC in their press campaign. However, during early April they also turned their attention to the DP, following that party's improved showing in the final spate of opinion polls. Both the NP and DP were essentially fighting for the anti-ANC vote, and it was clear that any attempt by the NP to neutralise the DP vote would hurt the latter. In a full-page advert placed nationally in mid-April,[28] the NP declared that they fought the election to be the victor. This ad claimed that the DP was 'content to exist as a minor opposition party, however weak and ineffectual', and was accompanied by further personalised endorsement ads from so-called former supporters of the DP who provided a variety of

HOW YOU CAN PREVENT
HAVING YOUR CULTURE
AND LIFESTYLE SQUASHED

similar reasons why they were now fully committed to supporting the NP.

It should also be noted that one of the few issue-oriented adverts occurred likewise in the Western Cape media. The NP latched onto the decision by both the ANC and DP to give prisoners the vote. They presented an identikit image of the notorious Station Strangler who had terrorised the local coloured community over a period of years and was still at that stage at large. The advert headline read, 'Can you imagine the Cape Strangler having the vote? The ANC and DP can.'[29] This image of a strangler being allowed to vote was effective. The use of an identikit photograph that portrayed the criminal as more black- than brown-skinned also hinted at a racist slant. The NP's Cape campaign had been one of instilling fear about the black majority into the minds of the coloured community. Now the advert confirmed the threat from the majority black population. The ANC did not respond to the advert, but the DP, already suffering a barrage of NP hostility, attempted a response advert that was visually far too similar to the original NP attack and therefore failed to make any impact.

The DP's own press campaign produced a sophisticated yet ambiguous series of adverts. Concentrating on full-page spreads in the daily and Sunday press, the DP were faced with severe budgetary constraints, but still managed to run a sophisticated ad campaign. Images of a soldier waving a white flat in battle were combined with a telling headline, 'When it comes to effective opposition, the Nats have shown their true colours.' Another ad depicted a four-poster bed filmed through romantic soft-focus lens, with a headline reading, 'When the Nats get into bed with the ANC, guess what happens to you?'[30] The DP were also forced to concentrate their campaign on the nature of opposition against the ANC. They claimed to be the only party that could effectively oppose an ANC-dominated government, and they constantly depicted the ANC and NP as being in cahoots to secure power and privilege for themselves.

To this end, the DP were forced repeatedly to keep a hold on their shaky supporters who were deserting them in droves. Only ten days before the election, the DP ran a full-page advert depicting a mother and child above a banner quote, 'I want a party that will stand up to the ANC – Do I have to vote for the Nats?'[31] The copy tried in vain to convince voters that the DP would provide the only really effective opposition, but endless NP attacks to the contrary had drained any credibility from this message.

With their late inclusion on the ballot paper, the IFP were left with only seven days of advertising. This meant that the party had to familiarise the electorate with their corporate image or logo and provide

I WANT A PARTY THAT'LL STAND UP TO THE ANC. DO I HAVE TO VOTE FOR THE NATS?

We know that some of you are still thinking this. You may not like the Nats, or trust them, but you think you have to vote for them or you'll weaken the opposition.

This isn't true. The words "Nats" and "opposition" do not mean the same thing. After the election there will be several opposition parties. All the parties which oppose the ANC will form the opposition.

It's vital to understand that, in Parliament after the election, all the votes of all the parties opposing the ANC will be counted together - irrespective of how those votes are made up.

This means you are free to vote for a party which can

provide really effective opposition. A party which really believes in the things it stands for. A party which, because of this, will fight harder.

This party is the Democratic Party, and if you vote for us, you won't be alone.

People from all over the country are moving to us because they realise only the DP can provide a better calibre of opposition. (Remember, every 1% of the vote puts another 4 Democrats in Parliament). So vote for the Democratic Party. If you think it would weaken the opposition, we'd like to tell you something. The only way to weaken the opposition would be by not voting for us.

DP

DEMOCRATIC PARTY. PROTECTING YOU FROM THE ABUSE OF POWER.

FOR ELECTION INFORMATION, CALL JOHANNESBURG 403 2743, DURBAN 3054820, PORT ELIZABETH 521770, OR CAPE TOWN 461420.

some message that differentiated them from the NP and the ANC. Although often crude and visually uninspiring, the IFP's campaign saturated the weekend press prior to the election. South Africa's largest circulation newspaper, the *Sunday Times,* boated no less than five full-page IFP adverts in its 24 April edition, in stark contrast to the single advert from the ANC.

Following Mangosuthu Buthelezi's decision on 19 April to participate, the IFP ran a full-page advert prominently displaying their logo. The heading read, 'South Africa, we did it for YOU',[32] which emphasised the party's claims that holding out against the major players was the right strategy to follow. Another IFP advert listed the 'achievements' of the party. These included the release of Nelson Mandela, opposition to the old tricameral parliament, resistance to the armed struggle, and the fight against sanctions. In a right-wing approach, the IFP also attacked De Klerk and depicted him amidst two flags – the old South African flag and the hammer and sickle of the former Soviet Union.[33] As awareness often counts as effectively as clever copy, the IFP could be said to have succeeded with their advertising. There was nothing memorable about it – graphically, the ads were a disaster, often reproducing badly in their monochrome tones, but the message that they were now in the election, coupled with an almost victorious sense of accomplishment, may well have helped the party in some way to secure their high figure of 10 per cent of the popular vote.

The IFP were not the only party to adjust their media campaign to reflect party dynamics. The right-wing Freedom Front were themselves hamstrung by the acrimonious split between General Constand Viljoen and the leadership of the Conservative Party. This led to the FF's late inclusion on the ballot paper. The FF's main task was to reach their right-wing constituency and inform them that there *was* an option for them to choose on the ballot paper.

The FF campaign was launched with a large identification advert in mid-March that prominently depicted party leader, General Constand Viljoen. The copy was headed with 'Cometh the hour ... Cometh the man!'[34] Other corporate ads were few and far between until mid-April when the FF launched a series of unusual adverts differentiating themselves from the NP. With the use of striking three-quarter-page monochrome photographs, the FF effectively and innovatively projected themselves well beyond their sectional Afrikaner *volkstaat* appeal. In an advert depicting the undersole of a boot,[35] the FF offered the electorate the ability to 'prevent having your culture and lifestyle squashed'. Another ad showed a close-up photograph of a gavel with the copy reading, 'How do you prevent being hammered by injustice'.

Though original in nature, the FF's ads suffered a similar fate to that of the DP. Clever copy does not necessarily sell political parties, and while both the DP's and FF's ads might be said to have been superior from an ad agency's point of view, their message was perhaps too sophisticated for an electorate that wanted hard fact and fell for emotion.

Some advertising was forthcoming from the smaller players. The Federal Party of Frances Kendall inserted an attractive four-page mini-newspaper into the press shortly before the election. The Soccer Party (Sports Organisation for Collective Contributions and Equal Rights) placed a humorous, tongue-in-cheek advert in the *Sunday Times*[36] which augmented their light-hearted campaign. The PAC, strapped for cash throughout the election, placed a small advert in the community publication, *South*,[37] but otherwise was unable to compete. The two Muslim parties, the African Muslim Party and the Islamic Party, both advertised in the Western Cape press,[38] and a smattering of African Christian Democratic Party ads was evident throughout the campaign. In addition, IEC ads and double-page spreads from the business community complemented those of the political parties in filling the daily and weekly press.

South Africa therefore witnessed a classy round of political advertising such as it had never seen before. The country's ad agencies, assisted by foreign experts, had a field day in attempting to manipulate the electorate. There can be little doubt that the ANC's more reasoned and informative approach did have the edge, although the NP's strident and robust campaign of vilifying their opponents on all sides resulted in this party establishing themselves as the second major player in South African politics. New standards of professionalism emerged but, more important, the relative freedom with which the parties were able to campaign through this medium helped in the promotion of democracy and an open society. South Africa was witness to a 'first-world' advertising campaign to attract a majority of 'third-world' voters. Although a liberation election emphasises the emotional loyalty between the masses and the liberation movement, the past 'oppressors' were able to project a changed image effectively. The ability to retain their current position of influence may in large part be attributed to effective and focused advertising.

The Future Role of the Mass Media

Just as South Africa's political parties were born out of the past apartheid decades, so the media power blocs represent much of the old South Africa. Language and racial divisions still largely dictate which newspaper is bought, although there are now some important changes taking place in this regard. As South Africans become more integrated and English assumes its role as lingua franca, it is possible that both black and white readers will begin to read and enjoy the same print media. This will result in new challenges for the English liberal media, which have always provided the watchdog role in South African society. The question for the future is whether this role will continue. Is it a role that an emerging black readership wants to see, and is it a role that the new government will tolerate?

The electronic media have already taken the step towards greater inclusivity and fair representation. In many ways, the broadcast medium is now ahead of the print. Radio and television have been able to steer a reasonably impartial ship and have perhaps been more in touch with the electorate than many newspapers. But the key issue facing this medium is its ability to retain its independence. After being so long under the thumb of the NP, it has now a new lease of life. In fact, the whole country has tasted political freedom as never before. It will be difficult to return to an era of suppression, given the liberties enjoyed over the last few months. However, there are always forces that will threaten the mass media's ability to expose and inform impartially. The ability of the media to apply unrestrained critical analysis will be the real test of tolerance for the new democratically elected government.

Notes

1. *Sunday Times*, 24 April 1994.
2. *Sunday Tribune*, 24 April 1994.
3. *Star*, 23 April, 1994.
4. *Business Day*, 22 April 1994.
5. *Financial Mail*, 22 April 1994.
6. *Argus*, 26 April 1994.
7. *Cape Times*, 25 April 1994.
8. *Rapport*, 24 April 1994.
9. *Die Burger*, 25 April 1994.
10. *Beeld*, 20 April 1994.
11. *Sowetan*, 25 April 1994.
12. *City Press*, 24 April 1994.
13. *Weekly Mail*, 22 April 1994.
14. *South*, 27 April 1994.
15. *Sunday Nation*, 24 April 1994.
16. *Rapport*, 5 December 1993.
17. Independent Media Commission Executive Summary, Johannesburg, May 1994.
18. *Business Day*, 30 March 1994
19. *Weekly Mail*, 31 March 1994.
20. *Beeld*, 6 April 1994.
21. *Beeld*, 2 April 1994.

22. Independent Media Commission Executive Summary, Johannesburg, May 1994.
23. *Sunday Times*, 13 March 1994.
24. *Sunday Times*, 6 February 1994.
25. *Weekend Argus,* 2 April 1994.
26. *Sunday Times,* 13 March 1994.
27. *Sunday Times*, 17 April 1994.
28. *Weekly Mail*, 22 April 1994.
29. *Argus*, 29 March 1994.
30. *Sunday Times*, 17 April 1994.
31. *Argus*, 16 April 1994.
32. *Sunday Times*, 24 April 1994.
33. *Sunday Times,* 24 April 1994.
34. *Sunday Times*, 20 March 1994.
35. *Sunday Times,* 24 April 1994.
36. *Sunday Times,* 24 April 1994.
37. *South*, 27 April 1994.
38. *Weekend Argus,* 23 April 1994.

9

A US Perspective
of South Africa's
1994 Election

TIMOTHY D. SISK

The end of apartheid unfolded perfectly scripted for a conflict-weary world. As the promises of a new, more peaceful international order after the Cold War's end go unfulfilled – filled instead by the tragedies of a failed settlement in Angola, fruitless intervention in Somalia, helplessness and hand-wringing in Bosnia, and the agony of inaction in Haiti – the historic South African election saga offered the US public a foreign policy event to feel good about: this tragedy ends with burgeoning hope for a new democracy. To make the drama even more compelling, a negotiated settlement of the conflict in South Africa runs counter to the predominant themes of the post-Cold War world. In this instance, unlike elsewhere, a tolerant, inclusive, multi-ethnic world-view prevailed over narrow, chauvinistic, ethnic nationalism. South Africa's election provided proof positive that the propensity towards ethnic strife may not be an invariable feature of the post-Cold War world.

The South African election story was as historically significant in the US as the fall of the Berlin Wall, yet replete with all the elements of a great literary tale: a riveting context; compelling and controversial characters, including real-life heroes and villains; twists of fate and reversals of fortune; deep symbolism and stark imagery; and, above all, a stirring climax. This chapter provides a US perspective of the election, reviewing coverage of the campaign and voting in major US newspapers and the reactions of the public and policy-makers to its outcome – a small but important slice of international opinion. The perspective is put in the context of the evolution of US policy. As the South African election drama unfolded, the American audience could not have been more pleased. Nelson Mandela's journey from prisoner to president, and his steadfast plea for national reconciliation despite the agony of apartheid, seemed to purge the American public's ill-felt emotions.

Indeed, for Americans the South African election produced a cathartic effect, opening the door for a new relationship.

The Setting

Images of South Africa in the American psyche conjure up a mirror image of its own dilemmas, albeit a somewhat inverted reflection. In the US, a white majority subjugated a black majority; in South Africa, it was the opposite. Although civil rights activists in the US fought for inclusion in the political system under the existing constitution and bill of rights, whereas anti-apartheid efforts were aimed at creating a new constitution, many in the US – particularly African–Americans – see the anti-apartheid struggle as part and parcel of their own cause for equal rights and racial justice. Invariably, perceptions of South Africa are oriented within this basic framework, and this was true of the election coverage. This basic orientation gave many Americans an underlying basis for conceptualising the election drama, even if the parallels are not wholly direct or the analogies perfect.

At the outset of the apartheid era, the US was ambivalent towards race relations in South Africa. Beginning in the 1950, however, the civil rights struggle gathered steam in the US just as apartheid was being implemented in South Africa. With the onset of the Reagan administration and its policy of constructive engagement, views of South Africa in the US began to polarise. In 1984, the uprising against the 1984 tricameral constitution provoked a backlash against US policy, and by 1986 the US Congress passed sanctions legislation, the Comprehensive Anti-Apartheid Act, against South Africa over President Ronald Reagan's veto. What was significant about this period was the degree of public involvement in US efforts to impose sanctions against South Africa, in colleges and universities, local governments, unions, and to push for divestment and disinvestment by US corporations. This experience created a large pool of Americans who had direct and personal involvement in the anti-apartheid effort and who therefore had a strong interest in South Africa's 1994 election.

The 1986 veto override on sanctions demonstrates perhaps more than anything else how US perceptions of South Africa are a function of the interplay between domestic politics and international events. It is not by chance that sanctions legislation was passed in the Senate in an election year in which control of the body by the Republican Party was in jeopardy; African–Americans are an important swing vote, and that year their minds were on South Africa. In part as a result of sanctions, and as a result of deteriorating political conditions in South Africa, between 1985 and 1990 some 209 US companies sold their investments or closed their doors in South Africa, leaving only 107 in place. Popular pressure on myriad companies and public institutions around the country persuaded them to disinvest their holdings in South Africa.

As the transition from apartheid unfolded, US attitudes changed with events. The US was strongly supportive when ANC leader, Nelson Mandela, was released from prison in February 1990, pledging support for the transition and shifting the focus of its modest $10 million annual aid package to democracy-building. The focus changed from punitive sanctions to the conditions under which sanctions could be lifted. The Bush administration played a supportive but quiet role in encouraging negotiations. US non-governmental organisations, such as the Aspen Institute for Humanistic Studies, had been holding regular forums for South African political leaders as a way of facilitating dialogue prior to formal negotiation. As negotiations began in earnest, Bush rewarded De Klerk with a Washington summit in September 1990, in which he lent political support for the transition away from apartheid, and − to De Klerk's delight − termed the process 'irreversible'. This angered some in Congress, for example the Congressional Black Caucus, who argued that the white government had not gone far enough to warrant such praise.

By June 1991, following repeal of the Population Registration Act (which classified all persons by race), President Bush lifted some sanctions − notably bans on new investment and loans − declaring that all conditions for their repeal had been met. Following the lifting of sanctions, and indeed preceding it, US policy had begun to place emphasis on economic and development assistance to South African blacks, and training for democracy. South Africa became the largest single recipient of US aid in sub-Saharan Africa.

When President Clinton assumed office in 1993, one of his early acts on South African policy was to telephone Mandela. As constitutional negotiations in South Africa continued into 1993, the US and other Western states were supportive. When right-wing black and white political leaders walked out of talks with the government and the ANC in mid-1993, US diplomats worked actively (but unsuccessfully) to mediate. In mid-1993, Clinton presided over a ceremony in Philadelphia that awarded the Freedom Medal to F. W. de Klerk and Mandela for their efforts to negotiate peace in South Africa, and the President met with both political leaders (albeit separately) during their US stay.

Agreement between the government and the ANC on an interim power-sharing constitution in November 1993, ending apartheid, led the US and other Western powers to welcome South Africa back into the international community. Days after the adoption of the new constitution, Congress passed legislation that repeals remaining sanctions, calls on state and local governments to remove punitive laws, makes South Africa eligible for most-favoured-nation status, and authorises further democracy-building and developmental assistance. The law also encourages and promotes US trade and investment with South Africa, and targets black-owned businesses with aid.

By 1994, the basis of US–South African relations had changed dramatically, and so had perceptions of the country. Indeed, South Africa in 1994 defies traditional definitions of the US interests – South Africa is not a former US colony, no US troops ever invaded there, there are no oil-fields to protect, no military alliances, no Soviets to be countered, and little significant trade – yet there was much at stake in the electoral drama. Success in South Africa would typify the kind of negotiated outcomes that the Clinton administration would like to see take place in myriad other conflicts around the world. Here was one case in which the actual advent of democracy and a culture of human rights seemed to warrant the rhetoric of the promotion of democratic governance as the hallmark of post-Cold War US policy.

Ron Brown, Secretary of Commerce and an African–American, was the most senior official to travel to South Africa since the onset of the sanctions era. Concluding a bilateral finance and insurance agreement with the South African government in November 1993 – and bringing in his entourage US business leaders with a flurry of announcements of new investment – the trip was an important signal that the US would support the South African transition in a tangible way. 'This is part of the Clinton administration's effort to support nonracial, multiparty democracy,' Brown said of his mission. 'We believe that a democratic South Africa will promote peace and prosperity in the entire southern Africa region while simultaneously advancing American interests by expanding the market for US goods and services, even as we create jobs in South Africa through the purchase of increasingly available and sophisticated exports ... We intend to forge a partnership between our two countries that is long-lasting and mutually beneficial.'[1]

The setting for South Africa's election drama in the US was one of substantial national interests, high stakes, higher expectations, and pitched emotions. President Clinton told a group of journalists, which included editor Richard Steyn of the Johannesburg *Star* and Aggrey Klaaste of the *Sowetan:* It's amazing ... think of it – contrast what we see about to happen in South Africa. I believe that if the [South African] election comes off well, it will send a message around the world that there is another way to deal with [the problems of a multi-ethnic society]. If it can be done in South Africa, how can you justify the old-fashioned killing and fighting and dying over a piece of land?'[2] Clinton left no doubt about his happiness to have some foreign policy issue turn his way – his administration had been widely criticised for foreign policy ineptness – and hoped for the best in South Africa. As the election loomed, South Africa was poised to become the America's newest, and possibly closest, ally. The US had a strong interest in a successful outcome.

The US and the Run-up

US non-governmental organisations (NGOs), funded by the government, were deeply involved in voter education programmes as preparations for the election began when the date was announced in June 1993. By far the most intense effort was that of the South African Election Support Project, collectively administered by the National Democratic Institute for International Affairs, the Republican International Institute and the Joint Center for Political and Economic Research (a leading, historically black Washington think-tank). The programme was funded by the US Agency for International Development. Its focus was basic voter education, which included the mechanics of organising and administering the balloting as well as broader civic virtues. An important element of the programme was party leadership training and campaign management. The support project also conducted a comprehensive survey of voter attitudes, released in December 1993. The survey did not assess party affiliation, but rather sought to 'establish a benchmark of attitudes' among potential voters to give the parties a reading on the political environment to help them shape their campaigns.[3]

In mid-1993, a non-profit organisation – the South Africa Free Elections Fund (SAFE) – was created by US business and civic leaders to raise a target of $10 million and thereby channel funds to support 'high-impact, non-partisan voter education initiatives'. Close to $7 million was eventually raised. The organisation awarded grants to South African and US NGOs to educate voters, many of which were distributed in South Africa through the Ecumenical Assistance Trust to programmes run by religious groups, civic associations, women's and youth groups, schools, and community associations.

Coverage of the election campaign for specialists and policy-makers in the US was quite extensive. The Lawyers' Committee for Civil Rights under Law Southern Africa Project produced a noteworthy bi-weekly newsletter – *South Africa: The Countdown to Elections* – beginning in December 1993. The newsletter covered the major transitional, constitutional, election preparation, voter eligibility, voter education, and political violence issues. The director of the project, Gay

McDougall, served as an international member of the Independent Electoral Commission (IEC). Also bombarding specialists' mailboxes was the *Watchdog on the South African Election* newsletter produced by the South African Institute of Race Relations and distributed in the US by the International Republican Institute.

Popular media coverage of the election campaign in major newspapers began in earnest in early 1994. Some of the themes of the election campaign covered by American journalists are listed below. The selection of these topics by the media tended to underscore their understanding of the election in terms of dramatic plot development, irony, and intrigue.

–The campaign of the National Party (NP) for votes among blacks, particularly for the coloured vote in the Western Cape, highlighted the irony of black support for the 'party of the oppressor'. The National Party leader, De Klerk, was often portrayed as a comic–tragic figure as he worked the townships in a seemingly fruitless pursuit of votes. A favourite photo for several papers was the image of De Klerk and his men stumping in traditional African attire.[4] Interviews with blacks that joined the NP were common in many articles, such as this quote from an account of De Klerk's venture into Soweto: 'When people ask me how I can support the party of the oppressors, I tell them they would never have got Mandela if it wasn't for De Klerk.'[5] Just as the American audience appreciated the irony of the situation, it was also amused by images of uncomfortable crowds chanting 'Viva De Klerk! Viva!'

–The role of the communists in the ANC supplied the intrigue. Surprisingly, there appeared little concern in the West that the election of the ANC would also bring to power the South African Communist Party. In a prominently placed op-ed piece, *New York Times* correspondent Bill Keller wrote that 'mainstream western politicians who speak with foreboding of the Communists' resuscitation in Eastern Europe scarcely mention Nelson Mandela's partnership with the Communists in South Africa. Yet if pollsters are even close in their forecasts for South Africa's first free elections ... South Africa will have a higher proportion of Communist Party members in its new Parliament than Russia has.'[6]

–The nuances of key symbolic themes, such as the Sharpeville massacre, evoked strong emotions. 'This is the campaign venue from hell,' the 27 March op-ed by *New York Times* reporter Bill Keller began, describing the squalid and tense conditions in the Sharpeville township. 'But politicians cannot so easily bypass Sharpeville ... [it is a] hellhole with a claim on history.' The piece goes on to describe the appeals of the ANC, PAC and even the NP to lay claim to the legacy of Sharpeville and its potent symbolism.

–Appeals to key swing voters, such as the Zion Christian Church (ZCC), drew fascination from the reader. Keller also wrote an in-depth story on South Africa's 'silent majority', the nearly five million members of the ZCC. Arguing that the church members will be more likely than revolutionaries to mould the future of South Africa, these black South Africans are richly portrayed as politically moderate, God-fearing, hard-working, complacent, and devout. Referring to the 1994 Easter celebrations, when the church invited the leaders of six political parties to come and pray with, but not address, the huge gathering, Keller notes that 'there was no mistaking the affections of the crowd, judging from the joyous murmur that greeted Mandela when he arrived'.[7]

–No drama is complete without the presence of deep conflict, and this element of the dramatisation of the South African transition was found in the ANC–IFP struggle, particularly for Natal. During February and throughout March 1994, when political violence in the townships of the East Rand flared and the battle in Natal grew more intense, many were already predicting that South Africa's pending all-race election would instead deteriorate into inter-racial war. US reporters recounted the bitter politics of brinkmanship: 'Today Chief Buthelezi rallied his followers with war talk, telling them that they were the target of "ethnic cleansing" and calling on them to be prepared to die, but not to vote, to prevent an African National Congress victory.'[8]

Despite the constitutional concessions offered to the IFP and white right-wing in February, the rejectionists continued their expected boycott of the poll. *Washington Post* correspondent Paul Taylor sought to relay the tension and anxiety that built up during those most uncertain of weeks in the final run-up to the election: 'The exhilaration of holding a liberation election coexists with the nerve-wracking reality of intimidation, thuggery and war talk,' he wrote. This perception was echoed by the *Los Angeles Times*'s Johannesburg bureau chief, Bob Drogin, whose lengthy story 'Blood, Bitterness and the Ballot' on the campaign and pending vote appeared in the *Los Angeles Times Magazine:* 'With South Africa's first free elections only days away, the country is a tense, tenuous place, unsure whether it is headed for war or peace. The past is riven with hate, suffering, and the bitter divisions of apartheid. The present is filled with violence, intimidation and fear. And the future is a dream of multiracial democracy.'[9] This contradictory image of South Africa – at once torn by racial hatred, and at the same time coming to terms with itself as a multi-ethnic society – pervaded much of the media coverage and public perception on what the election was all about.

Twists of Fate

The central theme of news coverage in the immediate run-up to the voting was, of course, the expected boycott of the election by the IFP and the white Right – the spoilers. The issue had received widespread attention in the press in the weeks and months preceding the election. It built tension in the plot, ratcheting up anxiety that the birth of the new South Africa would be a bloody one. Political violence had long been an attractive subject for the press, and the expectation that the election would produce an orgy of violence brought many more additional newsmen than might have otherwise covered the story. The prospect raised was not a new one for US observers of international events: yet another promising democratisation process might succumb to the challenge of ethnic rejectionists, portending a civil war or other crisis with which the international system could not cope. If there was to be a flaring of violence during the poll, the US media would be there to cover it.

Reports on the rejectionists – such as the articles that appeared after the rally in Pretoria on 29 January at which the Afrikaner Volksfront declared its shadow government while on the same day, IFP leader, Mangosuthu Buthelezi, urged his supporters to prepare for 'resistance politics' – set up the conflict as leading inexorably toward an armed confrontation. 'Zulu and Afrikaner Leaders Rally the Wrathful,' read the headline in the *New York Times*.[10] As the fruitless negotiations to bring the Freedom Alliance into the election continued through February and into March, a series of articles began to portray the image of stalemate and an impending explosion. One story quoted a South African academic as saying 'there's a whiff of civil war in the air'.[11]

On the one hand, some members of the American public and policy-makers were sympathetic to Buthelezi's claim for a more federal constitution. There seemed to be merit in the call for a devolution of power to the local level, a principle upon which the US constitution was founded. On the other hand, most Americans abhorred the militant ethnic rhetoric, and associated the IFP with violence and opposition to the advent of democracy. There was a general feeling that Buthelezi was taking the right tack substantively, but that his tactics were ill advised. Although the US was not visible in its efforts to influence the inclusion of the IFP in the election poll, surely it brought its weight to bear. Most significantly, however, the US changed its basic attitude towards the Zulu leader. Whereas under the Bush administration, the essential policy was that 'there would be no settlement without Buthelezi', the Clinton administration made it quietly known that it would support the implicit NP–ANC alliance and would back their going ahead with the election if they could not bring the rejectionists along. When Buthelezi and Mandela met for a summit in March 1994, President Clinton (along with British Prime Minister, John Major) sent an appeal urging a successful outcome. The agreement on international mediation that emerged from the summit offered a brief, if faint, ray of hope.

The prospect of international mediation to bring Buthelezi into the process was greeted with guarded expectations in Washington. Reportage on the Independent Electoral Commission's finding in early April that it would be impossible to hold a free and fair election in Kwa-Zulu–Natal – and De Klerk's subsequent announcement of a state of emergency there – heightened the drama surrounding the mediation mission. The shoot-out at Shell House increased tensions and built the suspense. The solemn turn of events on 8 April – the failure of the four-way summit between Mandela, De Klerk, Buthelezi and King Goodwill Zwelithini – reinforced the perception that doom was impending, even inevitable. Finally the failure of the high-profile international mediation left only the conclusion that there would be widespread violence in Natal during and well after the election. US policy-makers began to contemplate what to do if the election were wracked by widespread violence and Buthelezi rejected the outcome and chose civil war.

When the startling news came on 19 April that the IFP would reverse its course and join in the election, the suspense which had so carefully built up was released. President Clinton acclaimed the agreement that allowed the IFP to join, even if it was at the eleventh hour; he called the accord 'one more act of collective statesmanship that bodes well for the prospect of free and fair elections ... and for the success for the future government of national unity.'[12]

A sense of excitement now set in over the prospects for a relatively peaceful poll. The *Washington Post* postulated that the entry of Buthelezi and the IFP 'increased [the] likelihood of polling places being showered with ballots rather than bullets'.[13] With the country flooded with foreign media, and the election itself looking more and likely to be peaceful, reporters were required to look harder for interesting stories. Indeed, the lack of violence during the days of voting in South Africa may account for the large number of human interest stories – personal accounts of what the election meant. These stories revealed to the US public a creative and problem-solving side of South Africa that had not been emphasised while the focus of reportage was on the impending boycott of the IFP and the ongoing political violence.

The Climax

The climax of the drama was election day. As the day neared, papers reported the remarkable drop in political fatalities and the sense of tense optimism that pervaded South Africa. With the rejectionists sidelined, the path was cleared for the plot to work its way towards the act of liberation: casting the ballot. Just prior to the election, each of the major papers ran large stories that gave background on the history of apartheid, anecdotal accounts of ordinary people and places, biographical profiles on key opinion leaders, a summary of major issues, and fact sheets on the country and the 23 million voters. A sense of anticipation permeated the coverage, but also retrospective accounts of how far the country had come in such a short time.

As the voting began, US eyes were turned towards South Africa. All of the major television networks broadcast live from South Africa; the familiar anchors served as narrators of the unfolding drama. Full-page photo-essays ran in most of the major papers; lengthy stories were broadcast on virtually every television and radio news programme. Sample ballots appeared alongside stories about voters who stood patiently for hours in snaking lines for the right to vote, a privilege barely 50 per cent of US citizens regularly exercised. Americans, who have a romantic relationship with democracy, were especially captivated by the scenes. And they were impressed by the resolve of South Africans to go to the polls, a last-minute terrorist bombing campaign notwithstanding. The White House issued a statement that condemned the attack as 'a cowardly effort at intimidation [that] cannot and will not deter the overwhelming majority of South Africans who will vote in the country's first non-racial election'.[14] For each of the four days of balloting US newspapers and media were crowded with articles describing the momentous occasion as black South Africans became liberated through the ballot box.

The US sent an official observer team, led by veteran civil rights campaigner and presidential candidate, Jesse Jackson, supported by a $35 million US government grant. The delegation included key members of Congress and other civic leaders who were instrumental in leading the US to impose sanctions against South Africa in 1986. Sixty-seven Americans participated as officials of the United Nations Observer Mission in South Africa (UNOMSA), which fielded some 1,800 observers from more than a hundred states. A number of US non-governmental organisations also fielded observer teams, as did several historically black churches in the United States and several small university delegations.

Jesse Jackson expressed delight over the inclusiveness of the electoral rules and its enforced power-sharing, noting that there were lessons to be learned for the United States, where new proposals for changing local electoral laws to allow for greater minority representation have blossomed in recent years. While lamenting that the voting process had not been perfect, he said the success of the poll was a cause for world-wide celebration. He praised South Africans for concluding a 'negotiated revolution over a senseless bloodletting ... coexistence over co-annihilation'. Despite the logistical foul-ups, alleged fraud, and charges of ballot stuffing, the US was prepared – even elated – to call the elections substantially free and fair and the South African transition a success.

The Soliloquies

Perhaps no aspect of the election event was covered more than Nelson Mandela's post-election appeal for national reconciliation. During the entire election campaign, the actual voting and in the immediate post-election days, Mandela's beaming face and methodical voice were ubiquitous in the US media. Americans are captivated by Mandela the myth and the man. Earlier, in February, the *Washington Post* magazine had run a cover story on Mandela, written by *Post* bureau chief, Paul Taylor. Leading with an account of the beleaguered 'latest world's hero' at a 'people's forum' campaign stop in KwaNdebele, the article portrays the ANC leader as larger than life, a proverbial man of the people who could indeed measure up to the myth that had been created about him.[15] Focusing on the people's forums, the story covers Mandela on the campaign trail, describing his appearances before myriad audiences from intimate breakfast meetings with white business groups to massive township rallies. Similarly, all of the major media outlets in the United States gained 'exclusive' access to Nelson Mandela in the news-vacuum days between the actual voting and the announcement of the final results. He was interviewed live on Jesse Jackson's CNN television programme.

After the landslide win by the ANC and the complete transition from prisoner to president, Mandela was quickly lauded as one of the great men in history. Columnist Richard Cohen captured the popular feeling when he wrote about the soliloquy Mandela gave as President-elect: 'Mandela refutes an entire historical theory. There are those who believe that no single person is of historical importance. Movements – social, economic, religious – are the engines of change ... The late philosopher Sidney Hook argued otherwise. He said there were great men on their own who changed history. Mandela vindicates Hook.'[16] In sum, in the drama that was the South African election, Mandela was portrayed as the tragic hero. The tragedy of his life under apartheid was overshadowed by his larger-than-life character and the consistency of his moral convictions. Cohen's remarks were reflective of the comments of other analysts who placed the onus of success in South Africa on De Klerk and Mandela. Many columnists and commentators emphasised leadership to the detriment of the broader base of support and yearning for national reconciliation that the political agreements by the party leaders reflected. Visionary leadership is perhaps a necessary condition for a successful transformation like South Africa's, but it is not a sufficient one.

The *Washington Post*'s editorial on 2 May summed up the mood that most Americans felt after watching what was in effect the symbolic passing of power and the end of apartheid: 'The transfer of power from minority rule to the black majority will come about on terms that most South Africans and the international community can accept. The victory represents a brilliant success for South Africans across the political spectrum who set aside their own factional interests and withstood acts of violence and intimidation to make their country's first multiracial election a reality.' Americans were especially impressed by the abdication of the National Party and the eloquence with which De Klerk conceded defeat. So, too, they were enthralled with Mandela's victory soliloquy, in which he reiterated his appeal for national reconciliation and declared South Africans, to Americans' delight, 'free at last.' As the *New York Times* editorialised on 4 May: 'The presence of Dr. King's widow at Mr. Mandela's side during the victory speech underscored the special tie between South African blacks and African–Americans.' Both De Klerk's and Mandela's speeches were replayed for nearly two days on the widely broadcast US public affairs network, C-SPAN, and excerpts were reprinted in major newspapers around the country.

When the final results of the election were announced on 6 May, it was clear that the international community – like the IEC – was primarily concerned with the overall process and not with the precision that the results reflected. Indeed, the US press reported that the final results essentially reflected a 'negotiated outcome'.[17] Senior policy-makers, speaking off the record, acknowledged that they were relieved that the ANC did not achieve a two-thirds share of the votes. They were also pleased that the National Party managed a good showing – vindicating De Klerk's programme of reform – and that the IFP won enough votes for representation in the cabinet. Officials also thought it beneficial that the first and second runner-up parties had won two key regions. In short, the results were seen as having a salutary effect, assuring the US that its new ally would be a stable one. It fits the power-sharing model that US policy-makers have long thought a viable means of conflict resolution in Africa (even if it was not deemed appropriate domestically for the United States). And with Mandela's broadly

inclusive cabinet choices, a number of potentially tough policy choices –
such as what to do with Buthelezi if he stayed an opposition figure –
were taken off the table. Policy-makers breathed a collective sigh of
relief.

Happily Ever After?

With South Africa's successful transition, contrasted with the many
foreign policy crises on the world's plate, South Africa was acclaimed as a
great success for conflict resolution. 'For the past half-century, South
Africa has been the most preached-at country in the world. Now it is
preaching to the world,' *Washington Post* correspondent Paul Taylor
wrote.[18] 'Events in South Africa have made the previously pariah
country the envy of the world ... it is the only place where there is
dancing in the streets,' columnist Mary McGrory echoed. 'In Bosnia,
Serbs have blown up bridges that joined Serb and Muslim areas. In
Rwanda, people are hacking their brothers and sisters to pieces. In Italy,
a new prime minister is giving cabinet jobs to neo-Fascists. And South
Africa is giving lessons in democracy and joy.'[19] What seemed to please
US observers most was the inclusive nature of the outcome, that the
heroic victor (Mandela) had offered his hand in reconciliation to the
vanquished (De Klerk), and that the latter had conceded gracefully.

The notion that Mandela would – in accordance with a constitution
that mandates inclusivity – reach out to his former jailers struck a
responsive chord among an audience used to pathological winner-take-
all conflicts elsewhere in the world. It seemed uncanny. Some, like
columnist Stephen Rosenfeld, wondered aloud if there was a way 'to
capture the essence of what is unfolding in South Africa ... to bottle it
and to inject this elixir into the disruptions and disputes which burden
American foreign policy in other locations.'[20] Most simply attributed the
unexpected success to the Mandela–De Klerk chemistry. Rosenfeld
attributed the success to South Africa's 'broader legitimate consensus goal
... to become a multiracial state'.

Few commentators, however, saw the deeper underlying trends in
South African society – the reality of interdependence and the
willingness to avoid a race war – that produced the onset of negotiation
in South Africa and sustained it during a very turbulent and bloody
transition. Fewer still seemed to appreciate the difficulties of ameliorating
the legacies of apartheid and the obstacle that a 'grand coalition'
government may present for advancing socio-economic reform and the
redistribution of wealth. The American audience expects that South
Africa will live happily ever after, not aware that the ANC will face
tremendous challenges scaling down the apartheid bureaucracy while

creating new provincial and local governments – at the same time, meeting the promises made in the heat of the campaign.

To show US support for the consolidation of democracy, President Clinton announced a new $600 million aid, trade and investment package for South Africa on 5 May, more than doubling the previous annual allocation. Announcement of the assistance, which had been in preparation for some time, was carefully planned – after the peaceful days of voting but before the final election results had been announced – to show US support for the successful election and the negotiated transfer of power. The assistance package was also an inducement to all parties to accept the outcome. Clinton pledged to lobby leaders of other Western states for aid to post-apartheid South Africa and to press for favourable terms at the International Monetary Fund and the World Bank.

The Clinton administration is correct to sense that the new US–South Africa alliance offers tremendous opportunity for US companies. South Africa, unlike the moribund economies of Eastern Europe, has a consumer market of 40 million but with a well-developed physical and financial infrastructure. 'The new South Africa is open for business,' led a story in the *Wall Street Journal* on 2 May. US firms are beginning to respond.[21] Honeywell, IBM and Sara Lee Corporation, for example, have re-acquired some of their equity in South African subsidiaries. Nevertheless, firms seeking to invest in a post-election South Africa will still face the scrutiny of socially responsible activity to which they were previously subject. On 31 March, 1994, the Rev. Leon Sullivan – author of the 1977 'Sullivan Code' of social responsibility guidelines – released a set of 'Post-Apartheid Corporate Responsibility Guidelines'. The Guidelines call for firms to ensure equal opportunity, provide training and education, advance non-discriminatory working and living conditions, support black businesses, and engage in community relations programmes.

Whether it be a simplistic view or not, the peaceful elections represented for many Americans a clear-cut triumph of victory over evil, a relative glimpse of clarity in the world of murky foreign-policy dilemmas. It was a reflection in American society's mirror. Apartheid's end 'is almost a metaphor for the expunging of racist evil, something we can't deal with in our own country', former US Assistant Secretary of State for African Affairs, Chester Crocker, said.[22] The buoyant mood in the US at the outcome of the election reflected the inherent fascination with the history of apartheid and the negotiated path of its demise. There is also a recognition that the US will have a special relationship with South Africa well into the future. In a speech before some 200 US veterans of the anti-apartheid struggle announcing his aid package,

Clinton summed up the US perspective on the election: 'South Africa is free today because of the choices its leaders and people made. Their actions have been an inspiration. We can also be proud of America's role in this great drama.'[23] For Americans, like South Africans, the April 1994 election produced a cathartic effect.

Notes

1. *Southscan,* 3 December 1993.
2. Anthony Lewis, 'Clinton on South Africa', *New York Times,* 22 April 1994.
3. Some of the more important findings showed that during the survey period, potential voters were quite pessimistic. For example, 66% of the respondents thought that 'things were seriously on the wrong track' (a standard US measure of voter satisfaction) and that 75% of respondents thought that white right-wing extremists would start a civil war after the election. See the summary of the survey results in the *Christian Science Monitor,* 28 February 1994.
4. See, for example, the photo of De Klerk being draped in a traditional Sotho blanket that ran with a Bill Keller op-ed in the *New York Times,* 20 February 1994.
5. *Washington Post,* 1 February 1994.
6. *New York Times,* 1 January 1994.
7. *New York Times Magazine,* 17 April 1994.
8. *New York Times,* 14 February 1994. See also the article 'Township in Natal Braces for South African Vote', *Christian Science Monitor,* 29 March 1994.
9. *Los Angeles Times Magazine,* 17 April 1994.
10. *New York Times,* 30 January 1994.
11. *Washington Post,* 1 February 1994.
12. *Financial Times,* 20 April 1994.
13. 'A South African Turnaround', *Washington Post,* 24 April 1994.
14. *Los Angeles Times,* 25 April 1994.
15. 'Mandela's Moment: One Man's Fate and a Nation's Future', *Washington Post Magazine,* 13 February 1994.
16. *Washington Post,* 12 May 1994.
17. *Newsweek,* 16 May 1994.
18. *Washington Post,* 3 May 1994.
19. *Washington Post,* 12 May 1994.
20. *Washington Post,* 13 May 1994.
21. According to a recent survey of US company representatives, business consultants and government officials, US executives are more favourably disposed towards South Africa as an investment prospect than Eastern European countries. *Africa Report,* November/December 1993.
22. *Washington Post,* 26 April 1994.
23. *Wall Street Journal,* 6 May 1994.

10

South Africa
Goes to the Polls

BENJAMIN POGRUND

Day One: Tuesday, 26 April

The first black South African to vote was Noma Paintin, a 50–year-old medical doctor. She signalled the formal end of apartheid at 7 a.m. in Wellington, New Zealand, 11 hours ahead of the start of polling in South Africa. 'I felt marvellous, it felt marvellous,' she said. 'There are no words to describe it. I felt the tremendous responsibility of restoring dignity back to all South Africans. I was determined to be the first black person to vote. Nothing was going to stop me.' A niece of Nelson Mandela and married to a New Zealander, she was surrounded by journalists as she cast her vote. Also on hand was her close friend, New Zealand's Prime Minister, Jim Bolger. He gave her a congratulatory hug. So, said one journalist, would it be impertinent to ask her which way she voted? 'Go ahead, ask me. I am wearing a black, green and gold dress. I voted ANC.'

With the others queuing behind her she was the first among the tens of thousands of South Africans who cast their votes in many parts of the world on the day set aside for 'special voters' – in effect a curtain-raiser to the main event the next day. There were a dozen or so voters in cities such as Montevideo, St Petersburg, Ankara, Libreville and Jutland. Australia had 22 polling stations to serve the thousands of expatriates scattered around the country, and Canada had 12. Those who voted were enthusiastic but there was also much apathy: in Australia and New Zealand, less than 11,000 of the estimated 90,000 South Africans living in these countries cast their votes.

In the United States, the 25 polling stations included two tents on the lawn in front of the United Nations headquarters in New York. The South African embassy in London was one of seven polling stations in the country, and nearly 8,000 voters passed through it. They queued around the block and brought Trafalgar Square alive with cheers and singing. Archbishop Trevor Huddleston, who had last voted in South Africa in 1948 when a priest in Sophiatown and had gone on to become a towering figure in the anti-apartheid movement abroad, had had his citizenship restored only a few days before. Cries of 'Viva Trevor' greeted him, aged 80 and on crutches because of a broken knee, as he was helped into the polling station. It was the first time he had set foot inside the embassy. As with other foreign polling stations, no Inkatha Freedom Party stickers were available: they were supposed to have been put at the bottom of the list of parties on the ballot papers. Instead, and so as not to name any particular party, embassy officials told voters they could write the name of any party they wanted to vote for.

In Israel, Jewish South Africans were described as finding themselves caught between two peace processes, in South Africa and the Middle East. One man, waiting to vote at the Tel Aviv showgrounds, said: 'If the whites and blacks in South Africa can get it together, we should be able to do it here too.' In Hong Kong, the 500 available ballots ran out two hours before voting was due to end, with 150 people still waiting to vote. Officials obtained a swift dispensation from the Independent Electoral Commission (IEC) at home to photocopy ballots and to extend voting hours.

From Athens, Roger Omond reported for the *Guardian* in London: 'In the cradle of democracy, thousands of South Africans struggled to vote ... Socrates and company would have organised it better.' The embassy, he said, had thought 600 to 700 would turn up to vote at the polling station, one of three in Greece. But an hour after polling began at 7 a.m., the officials were overwhelmed and by mid-afternoon some 1,500 South Africans had voted. By then the queue, in places a dozen wide, stretched 50 metres into the street from the embassy. Greek policemen, caught unprepared, tried to control the crowd. 'By 3 p.m. voters who had been queuing all day in the hot April sun in the dusty Athens suburb of Marousi finally made it through the front door. To get that far showed a determination that almost equalled white support for apartheid and privilege. But hundreds gave up ...'

In South Africa it was polling time for hospital patients, pensioners, the aged and infirm, prisoners, pregnant women, handicapped people and security force members. To welcome the event was a statement from Mandela: 'Today marks the dawn of our freedom,' he said as he urged all South Africans to go to the polls. 'Today is a day like no other before it.'

South Africans proved it. In cities, towns and villages, streets were bright with posters put up on lampposts during the campaigning by competing parties, but by decree of the IEC no electioneering was allowed inside a marked-out area around polling stations. Unlike traditional whites-only elections, party supporters were not allowed to solicit voters inside this area; nor were party stalls allowed inside it; not a koeksuster was in sight.

From well before sun-up, people began to queue. They were undeterred by the bombs which had exploded during the previous two days, killing 21 and injuring hundreds. There was a cold-blooded professionalism in the size and placing of the bombs, and this seemed to threaten a level of terrorism never before experienced in South Africa. But not entirely, for the bombers were sloppy in making their getaways: there were eyewitnesses to at least one of the bombers, and this time the police were on the track of those responsible. They issued an identikit of a middle-aged white man, with long blond hair and a dark moustache, whom they suspected of having been involved in setting off a car bomb on Sunday in central Johannesburg in which nine people had died. And in Pretoria, in the early hours of Tuesday, the police shot dead a white man close to where a bomb had exploded a few hours earlier: he and others were seen near the bomb site and had fled when challenged.

The country was awash with rumours and with false reports of AWB attacks. In the Orange Free State, 11 bomb threats were recorded, aimed at polling stations and other buildings. No bombs were found and the police said they suspected possible right-wing attempts at disruption. They appealed to the public to be on the look-out for any suspicious packages. In the Cape Peninsula more than 40 false bomb threats were reported. In Ventersdorp a bomb was reported in the National Party headquarters: it turned out to be a bag of onions. In Johannesburg, the *Sowetan* was inundated with phone-calls asking about rumours that drinking water had been poisoned; the Rand Water Board said it was untrue. In Soshanguve, near Pretoria, the rumour also circulated and set off panic among residents; the Council for Scientific and Industrial Research was called in to test the water and reassure the public.

Despite all of it, and widespread apprehension about the possibility of more violence to come, long lines formed at polling stations. And then across the country, people waited and waited. Some polling stations opened hours late; others did not have ballot papers; or were without the ink used to mark hands and intended to show up under ultraviolet light if anyone tried to vote a second time; or did not have the lightbox which revealed the ink; or, as at Fort Beaufort in the Eastern Cape, 45 ballot boxes lacked lids. People who should not have voted that day arrived at polling stations, crowding out the old and infirm. Fraudulent voter cards were reported. One newspaper report referred to trucks carrying ballot boxes being burnt en route to Katlehong on the East Rand. In

Katlehong and Tokoza, hundreds of people left, because of fatigue and hunger, after queuing for eight hours. In Alexandra, Johannesburg, a blind man of 85 waited in line for five hours and then asked his grandson to take him home. 'I'm too tired now and it's too hot for me here,' he said. 'I'll come back tomorrow or the next day.'

At least in the prisons all went smoothly, overtaking the violence which had erupted in previous weeks while the South African Prisoners Organisation – its existence and dedication to human rights testimony to changed times – had been campaigning for the right of all prisoners, irrespective of the nature of their crimes, to exercise the vote. Some 100,000 of the country's 115,000 prisoners voted. Excluded in a last-minute government decision were murderers, rapists and those accused of fraud, corruption, bribery and armed robbery with aggravating circumstances. One polling station had its own poignancy: Robben Island, where Mandela had spent 18 of his 27 years in jail, and still housing 800 criminal prisoners; all went smoothly there after a late start caused by problems with the ferry-boat from the mainland. However, another small group of would-be voters never had the chance to exercise their democratic rights: they were staff at the remote base of the South African National Antarctic Expedition – scientists and researchers and workers from the Department of Public Works. The base did not feature on the list of the IEC's foreign polling stations.

Some parts of the country were barely touched by the first day of polling. In Matjiesfontein, 280 km from Cape Town and well known for its renovated colonial-era hotel, there were not enough potential voters to justify special polling. Only five election posters adorned poles along the one tarred street, all for the National Party. The two policemen guarding the polling station did not know that bombs had been exploding elsewhere in the country.

In the Transkei, within hours of the start of voting, a furious complaint was lodged with the IEC by Major-General Bantu Holomisa of the ANC: he said 602 out of the more than 1,500 polling stations in the area had no voting equipment, and he demanded an extension of polling. The day's voting had been 'completely lost and is of no value to our electorate', he said. The ANC in the Border region also called for an extension: a spokesman voiced suspicion about the 'seemingly deliberate' efforts of some IEC officials to 'slow down or completely sabotage' voting. In the Northern Transvaal, the same sort of complaint was expressed by the Pan Africanist Congress.

The late entry of the Inkatha Freedom Party (IFP) into the election caused obvious strains, as the IEC struggled to put an extra 500 polling stations into place in KwaZulu-Natal. The IEC issued statements explaining how the hastily printed sticker bearing the IFP name and Mangosuthu Buthelezi's photograph should be stuck to ballot papers, at the bottom, after the National Party's listing. But Tony Leon of the Democratic Party reported at least 15 polling stations in the Johannesburg area which lacked IFP stickers, in addition to a shortage of ballot papers and materials such as ink. He, too, proposed an extension of special voting following what he said were wide-ranging disruptions. In KwaZulu-Natal an IFP spokesman referred to a 'deep election crisis'. Buthelezi complained that violence and lack of transport had impeded the vote. 'It savours of sabotage,' he said. He asked for a three-day extension of polling. The Inkatha call would be carefully considered, said the IEC's vice-chairman, Dikgang Moseneke. 'Natal is a special case ... we may well have to consider an extension,' he said, acknowledging that the commission had 'hopelessly underestimated' the problems of running free and fair elections. That day, and throughout the rest of the election, the Department of Home Affairs went on issuing temporary voter cards after identifying people as South African citizens. For many blacks, however, voting offered the chance for one final – and positive – use of the old *dompas* for identification purposes, thus giving a two-fingered salute to apartheid.

President F.W. de Klerk, too, expressed concern about the lack of performance of the voting system, especially in the Natal and Pretoria–Witwatersrand–Vereeniging (PWV) area. Some polling stations had not opened by late in the afternoon, said a National Party official. In the Western Cape, a Pan Africanist Congress representative claimed that the polling had been 'rigged' and demanded that two IEC officials, who allegedly had told people whom they should vote for, should be immediately dismissed. 'ANC party agents were instructing people inside polling stations which party to vote for. And the ANC has up to five agents while other parties are allowed only one,' said Patricia de Lille, the PAC's candidate for the region's premiership. 'We suspect this was done in conspiracy with IEC officials.' But the IEC said no problems had been experienced at 89 per cent of the Western Cape's 680 polling stations, and voting took place in 'a peaceful and routine' manner despite a number of cases of congestion. The IEC chief analyst in the region, Wilmot James, said that mainly logistical problems had been encountered at 11 per cent of polling stations, and 3 per cent of stations had been forced to close down completely. 'We are satisfied overall, but there is certainly room for improvement,' he said at the end of the day.

But even as angry complaints were aired and the snags reported, it began to dawn on South Africans that something strange and beautiful was happening – that the threats, the fears and the murderous bombs which had gone off were only a small part of the whole, and that in fact peace reigned through most of the country. Even the criminal robbers and killers had drawn back. People of different colours were meeting in the patiently waiting queues at polling stations and were finding each other in an unaccustomed way.

Stories about the spirit of the people began to circulate. In Katlehong, despite the hours-long wait, Magdalene Kutoane emerged after casting her first-ever vote at the age of 85 and said: 'I think my dignity has been restored.' Friday Mavuso, 45, crippled by a police bullet when he was 22, declared: 'I have said all my life we shall overcome, and we have.' An old man, waiting in a queue for an hour, said: 'I waited for years, what is an hour?' At Natalspruit Hospital, Stella Malinga, 80, of Katlehong, said after a wait of many hours: 'I'm very excited. I am also tired and hungry but I'm not leaving. This is my first and maybe last chance to vote.' At Hillbrow Hospital, Lillian Lepheane, 77, struggled for about an hour to walk from the out-patients' department to the special polling station in the hospital. Using a walking-stick, she had a brief rest before slowly making her way up the stairs to get to the hall being used for the poll. She eventually arrived, smiled, nodded her head and said: 'I've made it at last. I've waited long for this day to come. I've never voted before and to me this vote symbolises the need for peace.' As 75-year-old Mary Molobi of Alexandra voted, she said: 'It's like I'm born again.' For the babies actually born that day, Nkululeko (Freedom) was a favourite name.

To Judge Johann Kriegler, the IEC chairman, none of the damage experienced during the special voting was irreparable. There were still two days of voting, and there was enough time and materials for everyone to vote. 'A truly momentous day,' he summed up. 'In terms of quality, spotty. Generally good; some areas of concern.'

To the business world it was all good news. That day, investors rushed to buy on the Johannesburg Stock Exchange as 'pre-election jitters were swept aside on positive voting sentiment,' wrote Ari Jacobson in the *Cape Times*. 'Buying was indiscriminate as the long wait for South Africa's first democratic elections ended.' The JSE indices rocketed with the Industrial Index surging 226 points, or 3.8 per cent, to 6257.

Reinforcing that confidence and responding to the pictures and reports pouring out of South Africa, President Bill Clinton in Washington congratulated South Africans on the start of the elections. He said that the 'images of South Africans, black and white, going to the polls in the face of intimidation by vicious opponents of democracy inspire the imagination and are a stern rebuke to the cynics of the world.'

'It was a glorious day for freedom,' Michael Hamlyn reported for *The Times* in London after visiting Soweto. 'The sun shone from a cloudless sky. Young men kicked footballs in the dusty streets. Even white policemen smiled as they guarded the polling stations. Millions of South Africans were exhilarated to be allowed to vote for the first time in their lives ...' The *Financial Times* reported in sober terms: 'South Africa made a disorganised but largely peaceful start to democracy ...'

At the end of the day, Archbishop Desmond Tutu, with a few words, captured the feelings of happiness, surprise and excitement which were sweeping across the country. He was 'walking on clouds', he said. 'It is an incredible feeling, like falling in love.'

Day Two: Wednesday, 27 April

The day began at midnight: the flag of the old South Africa was ceremonially lowered and the new multi-coloured flag was raised in the nine provincial capitals. In Cape Town, outside the Cape Provincial Administration building in Wale Street, now to be the seat of the new provincial government, a crowd of several thousand started chanting before midnight: 'Now, now' and 'Down, down'. The provincial co-ordinator for the Western Cape, Rod Solomons, had prepared a 50-second speech for the occasion. He got as far as 'This symbolises the commencement of a new era ...' before the impatient crowd drowned him out with shouts of 'Mandela for President'. A choir singing 'Die Stem' was outshouted by chants of 'ANC, ANC, ANC'. And then the moment came: the new flag was hoisted as the crowd sang 'Nkosi Sikelel' iAfrika.' Alan Boesak, the ANC candidate for premier of the Western Cape, said: 'I feel great. One has to see tangible signs of the death of apartheid, and tonight was such a sign.' And on the other side of the political fence, Hernus Kriel, the National Party candidate for the premiership, said he 'obviously had some nostalgia' about the old flag, but one should look to the future. 'It is the end of an era and the start of a new era. It is only fitting that we should start the new with a new flag.' In Pietermaritzburg, the flag-raising ceremony led to fierce criticism of the ANC's 'offensive behaviour' by the National Party. The party's Natal division said in a statement: 'Its flagrant abuse of what could have been a dignified ceremony, which could have contributed to the process of nation-building and reconciliation, is disgraceful.'

In Johannesburg, 300 people were outside the Civic Centre to watch. They fell silent as a band played 'Die Stem' but cheered as the old flag was slowly brought down at 11.59 p.m. As the new flag was hoisted, 'Nkosi Sikelel' iAfrika' was played. Corporal Anton Jooste, the soldier who lowered the old flag, said of it afterwards: 'It meant a lot to me, but I'm quite prepared to serve under the new.'

Not everyone who wanted to could raise the new flag: many flagpoles were bare because of the acute shortage. Manufacturers had been working overtime to produce more than 100,000 flags needed outside government offices, police stations, courts, military bases, prisons and municipal buildings – as well as for people holding 'New South Africa' celebrations. Because of the late agreement on the flag's design, production was well behind what was needed. The South African Bureau of Standards had made its contribution by rushing out its specifications, within five days, on colours, size and material. The Bureau worked to the stipulation by the Transitional Executive Council that shades of the colours be distinctly different from similar colours on the old flag. Only hours before the hoisting ceremonies, the new flag featured in a court case: a Pretoria businessman said he had a government contract for 22,000 flags and he had subcontracted two women to make flags, paying R14 for a small one and R21 for a big one. Later they had increased their fees to R40 and R80, and stopped work after he said he could not pay the money. The court ordered the women to hand over all their finished and unfinished flags. As the flag went up at midnight, it also signalled the inauguration of the new constitution, establishing democracy and expunging racism. Also born at that moment, to replace the South African Defence Force, was the South African National Defence Force.

With the dawn, the morning newspapers set the scene. 'Freedom in our lifetime,' yelled the headline in the *Sowetan*. 'Today marks the end of a long nightmare for South Africans and the beginning of a new future filled with hope and promise,' wrote Tyrone August of the newspaper's political staff. In Cape Town, the *Cape Times* proclaimed in the biggest headline type possible: 'V-Day'. Its front-page report reflected the anxiety carried over from the previous day about arrangements for the full voting: 'Millions of South Africans will stream to the polls for the first time today amid fears by political parties that the long-awaited celebration of democracy could degenerate into chaos in some areas,' wrote Anthony Johnson and Barry Streek. 'But', they added, 'the Independent Electoral Commission last night played down concerns that the problems which marred special voting in a number of areas yesterday would be repeated today and tomorrow.'

Far greater numbers than the day before streamed to polling stations. There was an 'avalanche of voters', said the *Argus* in Cape Town. The scene was a common one in the country: when polling began at 7 a.m. queues already stretched for hundreds of metres, and in some cases for kilometres. Priority was given to the old and infirm who had not voted

the previous day as well as to pregnant women and women with babies. At one polling station in the Transvaal, newspapers reported, an eagle-eyed official spotted that the same baby had come through for the fourth time, always with a different 'mother', as a means of beating the queue. Officials of some parties feared that the queues would have a negative impact and that people would get tired of the long wait and go off. But again, as on the day before, there was a new and unexpected spirit among South Africans, and waiting for long hours in queues became, for many, if not exactly a pleasurable experience, then part of sharing in the historic day.

Desmond Tutu, who went to Guguletu, near Cape Town, to vote – and had to wait until 7.30 a.m. for the polling station to open because of the late arrival of ballot papers – again vividly expressed popular feeling: he felt 'more than two inches taller,' he said. It would no longer be possible to refer to the government as the illegal regime because all people, black and white, had elected it. 'We are the rainbow people. We want the whole world to know that we have done it.' Asked which party he had voted for, Tutu said: 'I've known ever since the day I was born which party I would vote for but I'm not going to tell you.' In his exuberant way he said he had woken at 2 a.m. feeling 'very fantastic' – 'I could have touched the sky because of my happiness. The day I have been waiting for has eventually arrived.'

But not long after the polls opened, the country was stunned by news of the explosion of yet another powerful bomb. This time it was a car bomb set off at 7.20 a.m. outside the international departures area at Johannesburg's airport. An eyewitness said a white man had run from the car and then the interior of the vehicle began smoking. As traffic officers moved to clear the area, the car exploded. There were no fatalities, but about a dozen people were injured and a hole was ripped through a wall into the departure area. The airport building was extensively damaged. Incoming aircraft were kept in the air, circling the airport for an hour before being given the all-clear to land.

Again it was an ominous portent that worse might come. It seemed that whoever was responsible – and suspicion centred on the extreme right-wing – was more organised and prepared than had been realised. No doubt there was support for the bombers among those on the extreme Right who were boycotting the election. But among the mass of people it was clearly an unpopular, meaningless cause. In Laingsburg in the sheep-rearing Karoo, a National Party official did not bother to give the bombers any political credibility; he simply dismissed them as 'mad'.

The police swiftly issued an identikit of an alleged bomber – and as swiftly went on to arrest 31 people and to seize a large amount of arms and explosives. Most of those arrested were members of the AWB's Ystergarde (Iron Guard Unit), said the police, and some were held in connection with the Johannesburg airport bombing. The Commissioner of Police, General Johan van der Merwe, told a press conference in Johannesburg: 'Investigation teams have been working around the clock over the past few days to hunt down those responsible for recent terror blasts and in an attempt to prevent further blasts.' The arrests, he said, had been carried out in Rustenburg, Ventersdorp and Pretoria. Newspapers speculated that the R1 million reward which the police had offered early in the week – the largest in the country's history – as well as the work of undercover policemen inside right-wing organisations, had led to the arrests.

As a significant footnote to the day, the Commissioner of Police noted that the men had been arrested, not detained under Section 29 of the Internal Security Act which provided for detention without trial. There was no Section 29 any longer – it conflicted with the charter of fundamental rights in the new constitution.

There were other lesser episodes of violence, including two houses damaged by an explosion near Postmasburg in the Northern Cape; a bomb found outside Potchefstroom's main polling station and rendered harmless before it could explode; the cutting of telephone lines between Three Sisters and Victoria West in the Karoo; and nails thrown on the road at Ermelo in the Transvaal, puncturing the tyres of cars heading for polling stations. In Alexandra there was sudden fear when a young couple drove up and hastily abandoned their small car; it turned out that they were from Pretoria and in a hurry to get into the queue before polling closed. None of the incidents, real or imagined, affected the election, and there was no further large-scale terror after the day's arrests.

Extensive action had been taken to prevent attacks on polling stations and to maintain peace: 100,000 policemen were on duty; administrative staff were switched to the operational beat and 12-hour shifts were worked. Police 'sniffer' dogs and their handlers were worked to the limit checking out bomb hoaxes – there were still dozens – or suspicions. The South African Defence Force had issued a call-up for Citizen Force members. Although only 43 per cent responded – another sign of the times – the SADF said it was not unduly worried, as it had enough men for its needs.

There were other types of armies spread around the 9,000 polling stations: monitors appointed by the Independent Electoral Commission to watch over the electoral process; another 15,000 monitors trained by the National Peace Secretariat to keep the peace; some 5,000 observers from the United Nations, the Organisation of African Unity, the United States government, the Lawyers Committee for Human Rights, the European Community and other groups. 'The whole world is watching ... through the eyes of 5,000 observers,' said Gay McDougall, one of the five foreign commissioners with the Independent Electoral Commission. The observers – their origin identified by blue, orange or turquoise bibs – roamed from one polling station to another, incidentally furthering friendships across colour and national lines with black and white South Africans teamed together, or a black Canadian with a Russian, or a Norwegian with a Ghanaian.

There were also journalists – reporters, commentators, columnists, photographers, TV anchormen and women, camera and sound crews – plus hosts of freelances also meeting the appetite of the world's media to record the passing of white rule. Apartheid had been a sustained issue of interest for so many decades that its ending rated among the media mega-events of the century. Several thousand journalists – some said as many as 3,000 – reported on every twist and turn.

A good number of them were on hand for one of the dramatic moments of the election – when Mandela cast his vote. He did so at Ohlange High School in Inanda, north of Durban – burial place of John Dube, founding president of the ANC in 1912. Mandela used the opportunity again to stress his insistent theme: 'We are starting a new era of hope, reconciliation and nation-building.' De Klerk, his tenure as president running to a close, voted at the Arcadia Primary School in Pretoria, hailing the golden era that lay ahead for South Africa. He declared his shock at the airport bomb blast and reiterated his previous assurance that extensive measures had been taken to make polling stations secure.

The heavy turn-out of the morning did not halt. Literally millions surged to the polling stations, ignoring the news of the morning bombing, the heavy rain in some places, and fear of violent intimidation in some areas. People were stoical and patient. After the lesson of the previous day many came prepared with folding chairs, picnic baskets, flasks of coffee and books. At the Golden Grove Primary School polling station in Claremont, Cape Town, neighbourhood children played cricket in the street to cheers and shouts of 'Howzat!' St John Ambulance staff, on duty at Cape Peninsula polling stations, reported that the only casualties they attended to were people who fainted from hunger in the queues. At Elsie's River, a woman was rushed to hospital when she started giving birth while walking to the polling station.

Swanieville, the squatter camp near Krugersdorp, defied its notoriety as a flashpoint for violence between political factions, and voted almost without incident. Thousands of people were standing in queues as the polls opened. A large number tried to push their way into the polling station, but IEC monitors and policemen quickly calmed the crowd. The atmosphere then became jovial, and not even the dust or long hours of waiting in the sun dampened spirits. A woman hawker profited from selling fruit and sweets to queuers. Unlike so many areas where the number of voters had been underestimated, in Swanieville there seemed to be an overestimation, or else many stayed away: less than half the anticipated 15,000 voted. People who went to the polling station at the Tarlton International Raceway had a more comfortable time than most because the drag strip, designed to handle crowds of thousands, had toilets, water and a café. By mid-morning the queue was hundreds of metres long. 'It's the biggest crowd we've ever had at Tarlton,' said Mick van Rensburg, the man known as South Africa's Big Daddy of drag racing.

But chaos was reported in the town of Alberton. 'Bad planning was the order of the day,' said a local newspaper, the *Alberton Record*. There was a lack of ballot papers, it said, even though IEC officials gave public assurances that ballots had been delivered. There was no communication with voters and people queued for hours on end at polling stations, not knowing why the queues were not moving. The *Boksburg Advertiser* reported 'an air of friendliness and co-operation' in its town. 'For many voters it was a time of excitement, anticipation and happiness,' it said. 'They stood in long queues for many hours under the hot baking sun. In many cases there were no toilet facilities, and water, when available, was often far away.' There was a shortage of ballot boxes, and officials improvised, using a cardboard box which had contained toilet rolls. When the box was full the ballot papers were transferred to a metal trunk and sealed under the watchful gaze of party officials and IEC monitors. At the town's Dawn Park polling station, the queue stretched for about six kilometres and in places people stood eight abreast. 'But no one seemed to mind too much. There were complaints, but on the whole they were good-natured and the atmosphere was happy and relaxed.' It remained so among white voters when busloads of blacks, seeking escape from even longer queues, came from the township of Vosloorus.

On the West Rand, voting stations generally experienced few or no logistical problems, noted the *Roodepoort Record*. 'The sun was hot, the queuing was hard and long ... yet smiles, humour and good spirits prevailed as Roodepoort residents queued at the city's 20 voting stations.' And crime, violence and unrest 'ground to a virtual standstill'. However, in Pilanesberg, in what had been Bophuthatswana, voting was held up by intimidation: IEC monitors moved in and fears were resolved.

At the Wilderness, on the Garden Route, former president P.W. Botha and his wife, Elize, arrived to vote. There 'was a certain irritation in the air', said a newspaper report, when they jumped the queue. Botha refused to speak to reporters afterwards. For some, the outgoing foreign minister, Pik Botha, was also an unpopular queue-jumper when he went to Soweto. 'They may have given us the vote but they still think they run this place,' a woman grumbled as she rubbed her feet, sore from standing for four hours.

Near Pietersburg in the Northern Transvaal, a number of farm labourers claimed they had been refused leave by their right-wing employers to vote. The *Sowetan* said that a reporter had tried to speak to the labourers but they said they were too frightened. 'What happens if I lose my job because of you people?' one asked. A group of white farmers confirmed having taken their workers' identification documents so that they could not vote. 'I can release them but they should not come back to my farm after voting for Mandela. Mandela should give them jobs,' said a farmer. In Viljoenskroon, where the AWB had recently defiantly erected watchtowers and barriers, and the notice, 'Dit is ons volkstaat' (This is our people's state) appeared below the town's name, long lines of black people voted unhindered at the magistrate's court. Elsewhere, white right-wingers voted in large numbers, according to Corné Mulder of the Freedom Front. There was intimidation, especially in rural areas where supporters of the Freedom Front were known, but there was more anonymity in the urban areas, he said. The spirit of the day was much in evidence at the Bloemfontein City Hall: polling began smoothly and some whites said how happy they were to have blacks join them in the polling queues. 'It feels lekker,' said a 68-year-old veteran of ten whites-only elections.

Johannesburg's Hillbrow flatland suburb, its streets usually vibrant with people and hawkers, was silent and empty. Many shops were closed and people had gone to the polls. Prostitutes were not at their usual places. In Bree Street in the city, the scene of the murderous blast on Sunday, a few tourists filmed the scarred buildings. In the suburbs, employers took their maids with them as they drove around seeking the shortest queues. 'Masters' and 'madams' queuing with their domestic servants was a feature of the day. In a commentary on relationships, one employer said he had learnt more about his maid during the day than during the ten years they had lived in the same house.

At Committee's Drift, near Grahamstown, a fierce south-westerly wind blew away half a polling station: it consisted of two tents and one blew down. 'Our planning did not include the wind,' said an IEC official. Voting was moved to a tennis clubhouse nearby. In KwaZulu-

Natal, the IFP claimed that voters were able to remove the invisible ink on their hands with hairspray – not just any hairspray, but the Alberto VO5 brand. Nonsense, said the IEC, tests showed that Alberto VO5 made the mark even more luminescent.

At Nqutu in northern Natal, the patient line stretched in two directions, crossing a road and dwindling over a rise, reported Drew Forrest in the *Weekly Mail and Guardian*. 'Most people had been there since the small hours, and were using the blankets they had brought to keep out the cold as protection from the midday sun. Some were special voters who had waited in vain from dawn to dusk the previous day.' At the nearby Nqutu stadium, voting began at 12.30 p.m. With Nqutu known as IFP territory there had been fears of violent intimidation and a voter stayaway. 'Neither happened. As in other parts of the Newcastle electoral district, there was no violence or harassment of voters or election officials by the right, left or centre. Polling was free, fair – and chaotic.' But another *Weekly Mail* report, by Farouk Chothia, quoted David Ntombela, the IFP Natal Midlands chairman and noted as a firebrand, as railing against the 'corrupt and biased' IEC for having failed to provide IFP stickers for ballot forms, in addition to delays in opening polling stations and a shortage of voting materials, near Elandsdorp, in the Pietermaritzburg district. At one point, an IEC official arrived back after rushing to the IEC's regional headquarters in Pietermaritzburg to collect materials: he brought a rubber stamp-pad instead of a rubber stamp, and this too delayed the start of voting.

In the Orange Free State, Patrick 'Terror' Lekota, the ANC candidate for premier, rushed around ten different towns and concluded angrily: 'Something is going on in this province. There must be something going on in this province.' He suspected that National Party members were trying to cook the results, and alleged they had taken over IEC structures at grassroots level. In Jagersfontein, ANC officials complained to him that the IEC and other electoral officers were all white. In Excelsior, a farming town, he found that not a single ID document had been issued. 'No man, you can't do that,' he burst out. 'How can you do that to my people? I am going to report this matter. It is criminal.' The official explanation included the statement that there was a shortage of photographic paper in the Orange Free State. ANC members also claimed that a priest working with the IEC was cheating the blind and the illiterate. The ANC had sent 12 members who pretended they were blind and asked the priest to cast their votes for the ANC. 'They all opened their eyes after the priest had cast the vote and saw that he had voted for the National Party,' said an ANC member. Confronted by Lekota, the priest told him not to make wild allegations which could not be substantiated.

Soweto still had problems. In the morning, two polling stations in Tshiawelo lacked ballot papers and voting materials. 'Some people started queuing from 4 a.m.' said a resident. 'As a result thousands of people went home.' A presiding officer explained that ballot papers had only been received at about 12.30 p.m. 'We hope the people who left will come back as they live nearby,' he said. From Tokoza, Sharon Chetty reported for the *Sowetan*: 'It was an "open day" no one had expected. At the end of Tokoza's Khumalo Street – dubbed the death drag – is the Madala Hostel, usually a no-go area ringed by security forces. But this bullet-ravaged compound took on an air of festivity that stunned even the people who live there. Inside the complex that has often served as an IFP fortress, it felt like an open day at school ... Everywhere there were people milling about, chatting, smiling and enjoying the sunshine ...'

Reporting in the *Star* after a helicopter tour, Helen Grange wrote: 'Around voting stations all over the Reef, people could be seen snaking single-file for up to 5 km. The queues stretched along dusty township roads, circled and recircled city blocks and formed huge clover-shapes on tracts of peri-urban land. Beneath the autumn sun the people were patiently waiting, moving a step at a time. Two hours later, and only ten steps further, they were still waiting – still dignified and patient – to languidly traverse the 1,000 steps to go.'

But as the day wore on, anxiety mounted over the organisational problems, with warnings of the danger of violent reactions in several areas. Mistakes and blunders, including shortages of ballot papers, many of which were still without IFP stickers, were widespread, causing lengthy delays and frustration among voters. The turn-out and the problems created severe bottlenecks, especially in city areas. In areas like the Mitchell's Plain voting district, which included Khayelitsha, conditions were often chaotic.

The IEC extended voting hours and asked the army for overnight help in printing and distributing ballot papers. Millions more ballot papers were printed in Port Elizabeth and sent to polling stations in the Eastern Cape. To meet public worries that many people would not be able to vote that day, presiding officers were given the right to extend polling hours. The IEC sent an urgent memorandum to officials telling them to use postbags if they ran out of ballot boxes; if invisible ink ran out they were to sign voters' identity documents to indicate clearly that they had voted and also apply some sort of indelible ink to voters' cuticles.

Late in the afternoon De Klerk, still exercising presidential powers in the transition period, declared the next day a public holiday. Businessmen reacted glumly, expressing worry about the cost to the country of 'hundreds or millions of rands' in lost productivity. There was also uncertainty how employers would deal with the issue of pay: Would it be a paid holiday? And what about people who would not know it was a holiday and arrived for work? Anglo American Corporation's gold and uranium division said that work would continue on its mines: about 80 per cent of workers had already gone to polling stations on its properties, and voting would continue.

Buthelezi added to nervousness with a threat of walking out if the problems bedevilling the poll were not urgently met. 'I cannot rule out the possibility of our withdrawing from the election,' he said in Ulundi. He noted that it was grossly unfair to expect millions of illiterate voters to write the name of his party on ballot papers because not enough IFP stickers were available. He said that delays and organisational confusion demanded a further day of polling – a view separately endorsed by the Democratic Party's leader, Zach de Beer, and the ANC's election chief, Jay Naidoo. But, said De Klerk, that was irresponsible talk by Buthelezi. 'When we discussed his joining the process only a week ago he was informed that it would be a matter of crisis management and that his late entry would cause chaos. Everything is being done to accommodate voters and ensure that all logistical problems are resolved.' That night the Home Affairs Minister, Danie Schutte, flew to Ulundi to defuse the crisis, promising additional officials and resources to support the election machinery.

The Freedom Front added its share of complaint, with its general secretary, Joseph Chiolé, accusing the IEC of being 'totally incompetent' to manage a general election. Calling for polling to be extended by at least one day, he said that at various polling stations in 'white' areas thousands of voters had been sent home after waiting in vain for hours for ballot papers to be delivered. There were allegations that many of the ballot papers meant for 'white' areas were taken to 'non-white' areas instead.

One indication of the problems emerged in Cape Town, with a businessman revealing that ballot papers had been 'dumped' at his storeroom near the airport on Monday night. He said the boxes of papers arrived in trucks from two well-known transport companies. He was told they consisted of IEC 'material' and he was asked to store them. He said he was later astonished to discover that the boxes contained about 900,000 ballot papers, and he phoned the police and the IEC to tell them to remove the ballots. The police took them away. An IEC official said 'serious misplacement [of ballot papers] had taken place and we have asked the police to investigate'. To cap the mystery, the businessman said he had received an anonymous death threat – for what reason it was not clear.

By the evening, Kriegler was conceding that organisation had been 'poor' and that if this was repeated in the PWV area the next day, and only 70 per cent efficiency was attained, he would consider declaring the elections in the region unfree and unfair, to be re-run within 12 weeks. Reviewing the day, the IEC said it had received 10,087 reports from polling stations indicating no hitches at all; it had also received more than 2,000 reports about a wide variety of problems, including failure of some polling stations to open at all. Northern Cape was the only one of the nine regions which had achieved 100 per cent normal polling, followed by North West with 95 per cent and Western Cape with 94 per cent. Orange Free State achieved 87 per cent, Eastern Cape and Eastern Transvaal 80 per cent, Northern Transvaal and KwaZulu–Natal 75 per cent.

'We never promised you [the voter] a rose garden,' Kriegler told a press conference. 'We promised an adequate and respectable election, not a 12-cylinder supercharged election.' De Klerk echoed that sentiment: 'If we cannot have a 100 per cent perfect election, we must go for a 95 per cent perfect election.'

Day Three: Thursday, 28 April

Early voting on the second full day of polling was a pleasure in the Western Cape, the *Argus* reported. There were none of the long queues which had marked the previous day's frenzied voting. Most polling stations opened on time and had plentiful voting material. Only at Strandfontein did would-be voters find the gate shut and a notice: 'Closed until further notice'. An official of the Independent Electoral Commission said that no ballot papers were available, and people were being sent to other polling stations. But a local man, Sammy Maritz, would have none of it and refused to go elsewhere: 'I'm going to stay here. If I don't get a chance to vote here, I don't vote,' he said.

The dramatic change came about as a result of an all-night rescue drive by the IEC. It included the printing of some 9 million extra ballot papers carrying the Inkatha Freedom Party candidacy, and a South African Air Force airlift to hundreds of polling stations, the declaration of Thursday as a public holiday, and deciding to keep polling stations open until everyone wanting to vote had done so. Some Christians still would not vote, however, because they said the invisible ink which would be put on their hands was 'a mark of the beast': the IEC refused to give way on this.

In the Johannesburg area, IEC officials breathed sighs of relief when they arrived to find only modest queues. But shortages of ballot papers were experienced at some polling stations in the North West province because of delays in flying in fresh supplies. Voting in KwaZulu-Natal also again began with long queues and a shortage of ballot papers. Many polling stations were still closed because of lack of voting materials. But Buthelezi said he was satisfied with the IEC's actions and the balloting crisis had been resolved. Here again there was a general sigh of relief as the threat of a walk-out was dropped.

But that the country was not entirely at peace was evidenced by reports of several incidents in the Western Transvaal, the heartland of white conservatism and marked by the AWB for an Afrikaner *volkstaat*. A white man who opened fire on voters at a polling station at Taung was severely burnt when angry voters set his car alight. He was under police guard in hospital. In Rustenburg, white and black government soldiers lined the streets as an AWB convoy of about 100 cars moved through the town for a rally; there were reports of the security forces and AWB members levelling their weapons at each other. These episodes were said to be behind the declaration during the day of 15 magisterial districts in the Western Transvaal as 'unrest areas'. A police spokesman said the decree had been issued 'mostly because of the right-wingers, but also because of possible violence that may occur.'

Most attention, though, was focused on six former 'homelands' – Transkei, Ciskei, Venda, Lebowa, Gazankulu and KwaZulu. Persistent chaos was reported, with many polling stations still not functioning properly. The IEC was deluged by complaints or irregularities lodged by the political parties. Nelson Mandela spoke of 'massive sabotage' of the voting in some areas, and the ANC said the KwaZulu police had set up 'pirate' polling stations. Inkatha made its own accusations of partisanship and fraud. The Pan Africanist Congress complained again of vote-rigging in the Western Cape. The National Party accused IEC officials of partisanship.

Kriegler held a five-hour meeting with party representatives, and the Transitional Executive Council then decided to allow an extra day's voting in the six affected 'homelands'. Kriegler also held out the possibility of the election being extended by another day or two, if necessary. The ANC's election chief, Jay Naidoo, estimated that between one and two million voters would have been effectively disfranchised if the polls had closed as scheduled. De Klerk said that the National Party had insisted, and it had been agreed, that all the votes cast on the additional day would be kept separate so that in the event of disputes they could be separately assessed. 'In the final analysis we must be able to say that all South Africans who wished to take the trouble to vote were given the opportunity,' said De Klerk. 'If we don't do that, the election result will right from the beginning be in total jeopardy.'

But in most of the country it was clear that those who had wanted to vote could vote. As a mood of relief and relaxation spread, at Bellville, in the Western Cape, IEC officials sang 'Happy birthday' to a voter when his birthdate was spotted in his identity book.

Day Four: Friday, 29 April

All was peaceful during the extended voting in six 'homelands', while in Johannesburg that day, after further arrests, 34 AWB members appeared in court charged with 19 counts of murder and 191 allegations of attempted murder. The charges arose out of the bombings earlier in the week.

After meeting Nelson Mandela and F.W. de Klerk, Judge Kriegler announced: 'I reported to them that the extension had served its purpose and that substantial electioneering had been conducted in areas which had not been adequately covered in the previous days.'

It was not a totally perfect picture: because of poor weather, not enough ballot papers reached parts of northern Zululand. Voting was extended to midnight in some areas of KwaZulu, and ANC complaints were rising, alleging Inkatha malfeasance. In Transkei, there were still delays in delivering voting material in a western district, and voters went to other polling stations. But it was over, and in a magical way that, a mere few days before, no one could have anticipated. The headline in the next day's *Star* in Johannesburg caught the mood of most South Africans as it exulted: 'It's a people's victory.'

Notes

Information in this chapter is derived from:

South Africa: *Cape Times*, the *Argus*, the *Star*, *Sowetan*, *Die Burger*, *Beeld*, the *Citizen*, *Sunday Times*, *Weekly Mail and Guardian*, *New Nation*, *Roodepoort Record*, *Southern Courier*, *Sandton Chronicle*, *Northcliff–Melville Times*, *Krugersdorp News/Nuus*, *Alberton Record*, *Boksburg Advertiser*, *Kempton Express*.

Britain: the *Independent*, the *Guardian*, *The Times*, *Financial Times*, *Sunday Telegraph*, *Observer*, *Mail on Sunday*, *Independent on Sunday*.

11

The Results

ANDREW REYNOLDS

The Long Wait

When Judge Johann Kriegler finally read out the national election results at 2.30 p.m. on the afternoon of 6 May, one could almost hear an audible collective sigh of relief emanating from the people of South Africa. It was not just that the announcement was the trigger for a much-needed release of tension which had built up over the previous week through seemingly endless delays in releasing ongoing tallies of provisional results, increasing criticism of IEC ineptness and widespread mudslinging between parties accusing each other of 'election irregularities.' More important, when Kriegler announced the ANC's national percentage of 62.6%, the country realised that no one party would be able to fundamentally change the negotiated constitution without reference to others in the new parliament.[1] F. W. de Klerk and the National Party, Chief Buthelezi and Inkatha, and a handful of significant other parties certainly feared such an outcome. But interestingly enough, the greatest sigh of relief that the ANC had not won two-thirds of the national vote came from the ANC themselves. The President-elect, Nelson Mandela, argued that such a result would have only created fears that the ANC wanted to write the permanent constitution unfettered and would therefore railroad all others in the new National Assembly. He argued that the government of national unity should in no way be an 'empty shell' for opposition parties.[2]

* This chapter is the product of a larger collaborative research project (with Bernard Grofman of the University of California, Irvine, and Arend Lijphart of the University of California, San Diego) on Electoral Laws, Electoral Lists, and Campaigning in the First Non-racial South African Elections, supported by the National Science Foundation of the United States, Award No. SBR-9321864.

TABLE 1. RESULTS OF THE SOUTH AFRICAN NATIONAL
ASSEMBLY ELECTIONS, APRIL 1994

Party	Votes	National %	Nat. Assembly Seats
ANC	12,237,655	62.65	252
NP	3,983,690	20.39	82
IFP	2,058,294	10.54	43
FF	424,555	2.17	9
DP	338,426	1.73	7
PAC	243,478	1.25	5
ACDP	88,104	0.45	2
AMP	34,466	0.18	0
AMCP	27,690	0.14	0
DPSA	19,451	0.10	0
FP	17,663	0.09	0
MF	13,433	0.07	0
SOCCER	10,575	0.05	0
ADM	9,886	0.05	0
WRPP	6,434	0.03	0
XPP	6,320	0.03	0
KISS	5,916	0.03	0
WLP	4,169	0.02	0
LUSO-SA	3,293	0.02	0
Total	19,533,498	100 %	400

The counting process for this momentous election had been characterised by nearly as much chaos as the voting procedure which had gone before. The first problem faced by IEC counting agents was that the reconciliation process (i.e. reconciling all the materials which went out to polling stations with the materials which were returned to the counting centres) took much longer than expected and eventually was abandoned by the IEC in some areas, with the promise that the checking procedure would be completed after the party votes had been counted. The underestimation of the time it would take to begin counting, combined with the slowness of the IEC results processing department, meant that the press and public became increasingly frustrated as days dragged on and the provisional result tallies were still only being released in dribs and drabs. Then, after three days of releasing results, the IEC discovered that a computer hacker had gained entrance to the IEC's database and installed a virus which would incrementally increase the totals of three of the minor parties in the election. Judge Kriegler did not admit who the lucky parties were, but the ANC was clearly not one of the beneficiaries of this high-tech piracy. However, the problem was quickly dealt with, and the results began to flow a little quicker as the week dragged on into Thursday and Friday.

Adding to the IEC's counting difficulties were a number of disputes between parties about the illegality and irregularity of some ballot boxes which held up the process. In the Port Elizabeth, Northern Transvaal and KwaZulu–Natal areas it was claimed that certain ballot boxes arrived with neatly stacked ballot papers – a clear sign of tampering – and in other regions there were complaints of ballot boxes arriving at counting stations in private cars, from pirate stations and without official seals. It is clear that the local IEC monitors let many of these irregularities pass, especially in the northern and midland areas of KwaZulu.[3] Finally, the counting of ballots and releasing of results were slowed by organisational inexperience, general weariness and stress on the part of IEC officials. This is not unsurprising considering that the previous whites-only electoral system, handling 2–3 million votes, was never geared up, nor had the infrastructure, to deal with the extra 16–17 million South African voters whom the authorities were faced with in April 1994.

The Overall National Picture

The people spoke on 26, 27 and 28 April, and in overwhelming numbers they said 'Mandela'. By any objective standard the African National Congress won a resounding electoral victory in the first non-racial democratic parliamentary elections in South Africa's history. The 62.6% of the national vote the ANC obtained was a full 42% ahead of their nearest rivals, the National Party, and left them with a majority of 104 seats over all others combined in the new National Assembly. Such a high vote could only be achieved as a result of the ANC winning a huge proportion of the votes of the black South African community, which in itself was overwhelmingly dominant among the groups that constitute the people of South Africa. The fact that SWAPO only won 57% of the national vote in the first Namibian elections of 1989 (against much weaker opposition than the ANC had to face) puts the ANC's achievement into some perspective. In Western democracies govern- ments rarely, if ever, win competitive elections by such a large margin. No ruling party in the United Kingdom in the twentieth century has ever come close to winning 60% of the popular vote,[4] and even under electoral systems of national proportional representation, such as in Israel, governments almost never come into office with the support of more than 50% of the electorate.

But in the face of the ANC's victory, F. W. de Klerk could also feel some satisfaction and bask in the knowledge that his party had successfully pulled off an illusion of Houdini-like quality to transform themselves into a majority non-white party (in respect of their electoral base) and retain a high degree of influence in the new democratic dispensation. The simple mathematical fact that only 15% of South Africa's electorate is white and that De Klerk's National Party managed to win over 20% of the popular vote immediately tells us that many people who had never voted Nationalist before, because they had never been allowed to vote before, did so in spite of years of repressive and blatantly racist apartheid legislation directed at them. It is highly probable that De Klerk won the Indian and coloured communities in South Africa by as large a margin as he won the white community, and it was only the lack of inroads into the votes of black South Africans which failed to push his party's vote up even higher than its already considerable base. If it was not indicated by the events of the past five years, the election results certainly confirmed De Klerk's position as the consummate politician.

Chief Mangosuthu Buthelezi's Inkatha Freedom Party could also feel well pleased with their efforts. Having rejoined the electoral process at such a late stage, they only had five days to campaign officially (despite the fact that they had been unofficially campaigning since 1975 – so any serious talk of Inkatha's campaign disadvantage in the election is at best a misnomer). The IFP's half share of the KwaZulu–Natal region gave Buthelezi not only a provincial base to rule but also (along with a scattering of votes from outside of KwaZulu) over 10% of the national parliamentary seats, enough to catapult this mercurial political personality back onto the national stage.

Even General Constand Viljoen's Freedom Front could take some comfort in their fourth place, despite that fact that Viljoen's 400,000 plus (white) votes only translated into 2% (and 9 seats) of the national total. For, in the most important respect, Viljoen achieved all he set out to do. He split the white Right down the middle, thus mitigating the danger of Afrikaner anti-system violence, bred from exclusion, which certainly was a more pressing possibility before he brought his moderates into the democratic process. He put the issue of an Afrikaner *volkstaat* firmly on the agenda, and many would argue this is all he wanted to do. Being a rational man, Viljoen realised the concept of a *volkstaat* was always a non-starter, but he appreciated that by debating the issue over the next five years the threat of immediate and possibly violent secession by small pockets of white right-wingers in the *volkstaat* heartlands of the Transvaal and North West would be reduced.

The only clear losers in this watershed election were the minor parties. The Democratic Party failed to break out of their suburban white base and so, because of the new realities of the franchise, were resoundingly crushed in the electoral fray. The Pan Africanist Congress had far more potential but far less competence. Their election campaign was a textbook case of how to squander an increasingly favourable position through leadership ineptness, detachment from the community and organisational disarray. In the supposed PAC heartland of the Western Cape, they failed to outpoll even the tiny African Christian Democratic Party, and in the Xhosa-dominated Eastern Cape they came in behind the Democratic Party. In fact, the ACDP was the one minor party which could be pleasantly surprised by its success – winning 88,000 votes on the national level, entitling the party to a surprising 2 National Assembly seats.

In the end the election results resembled a gloriously inclusive pass the parcel game with everyone getting a small prize along the way as they unwrapped another piece of the fabric of the old society. De Klerk won a Deputy President spot along with a pack of ministers in the new cabinet of national unity. Buthelezi won KwaZulu–Natal (some would maintain he was given KwaZulu–Natal) and three cabinet ministers; and a handful of smaller parties got a few parliamentary seats and encouraging words on how they would not be ignored in the new dispensation; but of course, no one ever really doubted who would be unwrapping the big prize at the end.

Estimated Electorate and Turnout

Probably the only benefit of the old South Africa's Population Registration Act and Group Areas Act, those universally despised pillars of apartheid legislation, was that they did give the psephologist and political observer some idea of the ethnic diversity of the country and therefore a pretty good idea of the ethnic breakdown of the electorate in the first non-racial elections, although the vote made quite rightly no reference to race, colour or creed. While there is a strong argument that we should no longer concentrate upon such ethnic breakdowns or racial divides, it is true to say that the realities of South African life and party politics continue to require us to assess the scene with reference to such differences. This is not a negative thing, nor a divisive approach. It merely recognises the positive diversity within this country and the fact that parties in this new non-racial South Africa are overwhelmingly divided along racial lines. In assessing each political party's vote in regard to support won among each ethnic community, we garner important clues about the character of a party's constituency (or support base) and therefore how we might expect them to act in the future. If, say, one party's votes came almost entirely from the Indian community, then we might well expect that particular party to predominantly advocate the Indian community's interests within parliament and tailor their political priorities to that group's objectives. While a party's electoral support base does not tell us all (its electoral base may be very different from its leadership composition), it does give us a useful starting point in assessing party political motivations.

However, in saying that, there have historically been serious problems with census-taking and population group estimation in South Africa. These stemmed from distrust of the Department of Home Affairs, a fragmented homeland and self-governing territory system, and the randomness and variability of racial classification under the apartheid regime. For these reasons, and others, the estimates of the total South African population, the total electorate size, and the proportionate size of the ethnic groups that would constitute such an electorate have always been disputed. The 1992 government census (adjusted from the 1985 census)[5] estimated there were just under 21 million eligible South African voters, of whom 68.5% were black, 18.8% white, 9.8% coloured and 2.9% Indian. By 1994 the Independent Electoral Commission had upped that figure to 22.7 million, with 73% of the total constituted by black South Africans, 15% white, 9% coloured and 3% Indian. It appears from the vote (with 19.7 million South Africans casting their ballots – or 86% of the estimated electorate) that the IEC's figures were about right.

TABLE 2. TURNOUT AND ESTIMATED ELECTORATE[6]

Province	Poll	Proportion of poll	Estimated electorate	Estimated turnout	Proportion of total
Western Cape	2,137,742	10.9%	2,405,919	87%	10.6%
Northern Cape	403,772	2.1%	439,149	92%	1.9%
Eastern Cape	2,908,906	14.9%	3,176,970	92%	14.0%
North West	1,572,142	8.0%	1,763,445	89%	7.8%
Orange Free State	1,354,266	6.9%	1,636,581	83%	7.2%
PWV	4,198,250	21.5%	4,862,117	86%	21.4%
North. Transvaal	1,920,260	9.8%	2,287,105	84%	10.1%
East. Transvaal	1,326,068	6.8%	1,552,775	85%	6.8%
KwaZulu–Natal	3,664,324	18.8%	4,585,091	80%	20.2%
Total	19,533,498	100%	22,709,152	86%	100%

However, even if we have faith in the IEC's total figures, this does not necessarily mean that 73% of those who voted in April 1994 could be identified as black South Africans. In the months leading up to the poll, many observers expected there to be a high degree of differential turnout in these first all-inclusive elections: white voters would be able to vote in far higher numbers (as a proportion of their total) than non-whites. All the factors which could possibly suppress the turnout on the day seemed to be directed against the black community. Firstly, there was the expectation that violence and intimidation would keep many blacks from going to the polls, especially in the violence-torn areas of KwaZulu and the East Rand. Secondly, the levels of identity paper ownership among black citizens were still unknown, and there remained the possibility that up to a million potential voters could be disenfranchised because of a lack of official documentation. Finally, among those actually making it to the polls, a high spoilt ballot paper rate was expected among illiterate and more rural South Africans who had been denied access to schooling in the past and voter education in the present. The Matla Trust, one of the leading voter education organisations, said they expected anything up to a 10% spoilt ballot paper rate among blacks and a negligible rate among non-blacks.

However, on the day the vast majority of these fears failed to materialise. It appears as if the momentous nature of the election did enable black voters to overcome obstacles they might have faced and turn out in equal proportions to their white, coloured and Indian countrypeople. On the first day of official polling, 27 April, it was much more difficult to vote in black areas than in white. Where there were ballot papers and staff, the queues were huge, but throughout large areas of the Transkei, Ciskei, KwaZulu, Northern Transvaal and the North West there were considerable logistical problems, which meant delay and frustration for many first-time voters. But the patience and goodwill of the people overcame these problems. As a result of the extension of voting into Friday, 29 April in the worst-affected areas, the vast majority of South Africans who wished to cast their votes did so. The level of political and indeed non-political violence was also gratifyingly low over the polling period itself. Some police commented that it was the quietest week they had had for years. Even in the heartlands of low-intensity conflict, i.e. KwaZulu and the townships of the East Rand, there appeared to be little threat of immediate violence for voters making the trip to the polling station. It is quite possible that potential ANC voters did not vote in IFP strongholds, NP supporters didn't risk it in liberation movement breeding grounds, and PAC voters stayed at home in ANC heartlands. But on the day, these perceived threats of retribution for voting against the hegemonic power of an area were certainly not supported by overt actions of violence. For that reason we can assume that most South Africans who might have been disenfranchised through their own fears of violence were, on the day, happily able to exercise their democratic right.

The results showed that the province of KwaZulu–Natal (76% black) did have the lowest turnout of 80%, but the very highest turnouts came from those provinces with the highest proportions of black voters (Northern and Eastern Cape). Such a nationally high turnout illustrated that even if there was a drop-off among black voters it could not have been large. Interestingly, the Conservative Party's boycott appears to have had minimal effect on the white share of the vote, and equally AZAPO's boycott had negligible effect on the black vote. Finally, the spoilt ballot paper rate was remarkably low in a country where illiteracy is a major problem and voting by the mass of the people was a new and often bewildering experience. The less than 1% spoilt ballot rate was a testament either to the quality of voter education in the pre-election period or to the political intelligence of the people: one has to lean towards the latter explanation.

TABLE 3. SPOILT BALLOT PAPER RATES

Province	No. of spoilt ballots	% of total
Western Cape	10,704	0.5%
Northern Cape	3,534	0.8%
Eastern Cape	13,248	0.5%
North West	18,974	1.2%
Orange Free State	10,286	0.8%
PWV	25,383	0.6%
Northern Transvaal	13,702	0.7%
Eastern Transvaal	12,631	0.9%
KwaZulu–Natal	39,369	1.0%
National	193,081	1.0%

All in all, these factors seemed to have balanced out across the ethnic groups. Combining them with the probability that the black share of the electorate was marginally underestimated in the first place, we can predict with some confidence that the IEC's original estimates of the vote were to a fair degree correct, and that of those 19.7 million South Africans whose votes were counted, 73% were black, 15% were white, 9% were coloured and 3% Indian. This then allows us to move on to assessing the regional and national party vote percentages. Using our knowledge of community support for different political parties gained through opinion polling and other means, we have an excellent starting point to estimate how each party's vote broke down along ethnic and regional lines.

TABLE 4. ESTIMATED ETHNIC BREAKDOWN OF NATIONAL VOTE

	Black	White	Coloured	Indian	Total
% share of vote	73%	15%	9%	3%	100%
Vote	14.2 million	2.9 million	1.8 million	0.6 million	19.5 million

A further interesting aspect of South African election demography was not only the large black proportion of voters, but the consistent growth of the white vote since 1983. The estimated number of whites entitled to vote in this election was higher than the 3.2 million in 1992 because of the expatriates enfranchised and the influx of exiles and permanent residents who had been unable to vote in South African general elections before 1994.

TABLE 5. WHITE ELECTORATE 1981–94

Year and election	Number Voting	
1981 General election	1,361,172	
1983 Referendum on tricameral constitution	2,051,800	
1987 General election	2,038,659	
1989 General election	2,140,336	
1992 Referendum on negotiations	2,799,805	(3,293,691) [a]
1994 Estimated white vote in non-racial election	2,930,000	(3,406,373) [a]

[a]Estimated total electorate.

The African National Congress

Despite the ethnic and racial balance in the leadership of the ANC, their vote in these first non-racial elections was almost entirely racially based. Of the 12.2 million votes cast for Nelson Mandela and the ANC, around 11.5 million (or 94% of the total) were cast by black South Africans and predominantly by speakers of Xhosa, Sotho, Venda, Ndebele, Tswana and Tsonga combined with one-third of the Zulu-speaking vote. This partly reflects the dominance of black South Africans within the electorate as a whole, but is also indicative of the ANC's failure to make inroads into the votes of the white, coloured and Indian communities. The best estimates put the ANC's share of the coloured vote at around 30%, and a little less for the Indian community's votes. However, the ANC, even as the majority party in the new government, failed to win more than 2–3% of the white vote: it is here that the reins of economic and administrative power still lie and will do so for some time to come.

TABLE 6. HOW THE ANC'S VOTE WAS CONSTITUTED[7]

Community	% of ANC's total vote	Approximate vote
Black	94% [a]	11.5 million
Coloured	4%	0.5 million
Indian	1.5%	150,000
White	0.5%	50,000
Total	100%	12.2 million

[a]Predominantly Xhosa, Venda, Sotho, Tswana, Tsonga and Ndebele, but between 6–7% Zulu mostly polled in KwaZulu–Natal.

That the ANC was able to win such a massive proportion of black votes was testament to a shrewd and straightforward campaign message, which highlighted the ANC's position as the liberation movement that would deliver the majority of the people from apartheid and into the promised land. They were able to corner the market as the only viable liberation party, partly because of the historical truth of the statement, partly because of the AZAPO and Black Consciousness Movement boycott of the elections, and partly because of the failure of the PAC, who were the only party contesting the elections that could legitimately lay claim as well to the ANC's liberation mantle.

The ANC's national, and Eastern Cape and North West provincial, vote was also dramatically improved by the collapse of the homeland dictatorships of Lucas Mangope in Bophuthatswana and Brigadier Oupa Gqozo in the Ciskei in early 1994. These two areas were effectively no-go areas to ANC campaigners before 1994. As such, over one million potential ANC votes could have been placed in jeopardy if those puppet governments had not crumbled in the face of civil service strikes and pressure from ANC supporters.

The lack of violence and intimidation on the polling days also enabled the ANC to maximise their vote. The only rider to this came from KwaZulu–Natal, where it seems that polling stations in the IFP-controlled north were set up in such a way as to protect Inkatha hegemony and discourage ANC supporters. Furthermore, in the ANC-aligned townships around Durban the turnout was far lower than in comparable areas, but it is not clear whether this was due to intimidation, apathy, logistical problems in the polling or merely ANC inefficiency. But once ANC voters got to the polls, their ballots were over-whelmingly valid, which was not the expectation of international and domestic voter education experts. As I noted earlier, anything up to 10% of the ballots cast by black South Africans were expected to be spoilt, with the vast majority of these translating into lost votes for the ANC. Such a scenario would have sliced off well over one million votes (or 5%) from the ANC's national share of the vote. The less than 1% spoilt ballot paper rate in the election helped the ANC enormously.

Finally, there was clearly an *uhuru* or liberation aspect to this first election, which may never be repeated again. The vast majority of South Africans had waited all their lives for such a moment in the polling booth, and they weren't going to waste the moment now it had arrived on a minor party unable to deliver the liberation and political transformation they had long dreamt of. This factor clearly advantaged the ANC over all others. And while many ANC supporters voted with their heads and hearts in equal measure, on balance the ANC's historic victory was a collective vote of the heart born out of black South Africa's hope for a better future.

The National Party

South African politics has a habit of turning up curious anomalies. No more so than in the first democratic elections of 1994, for the party most approaching real multi-racialism in its electoral base was the party which created, designed and operated apartheid. While the NP's leadership remains fundamentally white, Afrikaner and male (with a few token non-whites in positions of party responsibility), the NP represents a constituency which still can be characterised as conservative, religiously motivated and fearful of communism, but now, with a slight majority, is non-white.

TABLE 7. HOW THE NP'S VOTE WAS CONSTITUTED[8]

Community	% of NP's total vote	Approximate vote
White	49%	1.9 million
Coloured	30%	1.2 million
Black	14%	0.5 million
Indian	7%	0.3 million
Total	100%	3.9 million

The surprising NP dominance among the coloured community of the Cape (by far the largest group in that area) was picked up early by a series of opinion polls. In December 1993 the 'Launching Democracy' report of the Institute for Multi-Party Democracy estimated that 45% of coloured voters in the Western Cape would support the National Party, and that figure increased to 68% in a subsequent report of February

1994.[9] The final national results and Western Cape provincial result did indeed indicate that the NP had won 60–70% of the coloured vote (or 1.2 million coloured votes out of a national total of 1.7 million). Thus just under one-third of the NP's national votes came from those people on whom apartheid had previously conferred second-class citizenship. That the National Party was so successful in garnering coloured votes was testament to a well-planned campaign to highlight coloured fears about their position in the new order in relation to the overwhelming black majority of the country. The NP in the apartheid and post-apartheid period had utilised a divide and rule strategy that set disenfranchised coloureds apart from disenfranchised blacks, and encouraged racist stereotypes within each community. Many working-class coloured voters clearly saw the ANC as a black party, dominated by communists and ready to usurp what limited influence was still left them within society. There is also the often-overlooked linguistic factor, white and coloured Afrikaners being brought together by their common mother-tongue. All these factors combined to give the NP's Hernus Kriel the premiership of the important Western Cape region, delivered on the back of two-thirds of the coloured vote (by far the largest ethnic voting bloc in the Cape).

Perhaps equally interesting is the estimation that approximately 14% of the vote for F. W. de Klerk came from black South Africans. Even though this translates into only 3–4% of the total black vote, it nevertheless represents a bridgehead into the black community which the National Party might hope to capitalise on in the 1999 election. Opinion polls before the election indicated that what small number of black votes there were for the NP came from older, more conservative and often rural black South Africans who had been severely affected by the upheavals in their communities and the most extreme actions of the ANC-aligned comrades.

The National Party were also successful in presenting themselves to the white community as the only viable alternative to black majority rule and parliamentary subservience. While the Freedom Front and Democratic Party fought hard for white votes, the NP appear to have won their largest-ever share of the white electorate since their unrivalled two-thirds dominance in the whites-only general election of 1977. Their 1.9 million white votes equalled the number of white South Africans who voted 'yes' to further constitutional negotiations in the referendum of March 1992. However, in that poll the DP urged their supporters to vote yes, and some CP supporters disobeyed their party's call for a no to further negotiations. The evidence indicates that many white voters who had previously supported the DP or CP in 1994 turned out for De Klerk and the NP in the belief that their former parties were now spent forces. The difference between the results of the national and regional ballots also backs up this point: the figures show that the extra 215,000 FF votes gained in the provincial ballot (over and above their national 424,000 votes) combined with the DP's extra 200,000 votes (over their 338,000 national votes) make up a large proportion of the NP's 490,000 drop in votes from the national to provincial level. What this implies is that many white voters supported De Klerk on the national ballot, but stayed true to their traditional electoral home on the regional level.

TABLE 8. THE EVOLUTION OF THE NP'S WHITE VOTE

	Total vote	% of white vote
1981 General election	777,558	58
1987 General election	1,075,454	53
1989 General election	1,031,557	48
1994 Non-racial election	1,900,000 [a]	65 [a]

[a]Estimated

The Inkatha Freedom Party

Inkatha's 10% plus of the national vote surprised all observers except those who had made a close study of the politics of clientelism in the former self-governing territory of KwaZulu and Mangosuthu Buthelezi's cross-over appeal to conservative whites in South Africa. There is a pervasive argument that Inkatha's vote could well have been in the 15–20% range if he had not played the role of spoiler in the constitutional negotiations and had begun building his electoral base long before 19 April 1994. Since 1990, and particularly through 1993–4, Buthelezi let slip the considerable sympathy that international governments and the white business community had displayed for his leadership during the previous decade. This support had been shown openly despite the ever-increasing evidence of the KwaZulu government's collusion with the National Party regime and its involvement in violent ethnic attacks and resulting regional instability.

As a result, the 1994 election showed Buthelezi's Inkatha Freedom Party to be the most ethnically and geographically exclusive and isolated party in the country. Up to 85% of Buthelezi's votes came from black South Africans, of which almost all were Zulus. Furthermore, the IFP won a full 86% of its national total from KwaZulu–Natal, with only 14% coming from the national ballots of all the other eight provinces combined. They did hold on to 5–6% of the white vote (a higher share than the ANC and the highest white vote among any of the historically black political organisations contesting the elections) but this only translated into 10% of Inkatha's national total. The rest of the IFP's vote was constituted by those Indians in Durban and Natal as a whole who decided not to cast their ballots for De Klerk or Mandela.

Inkatha's best showing outside of KwaZulu was in the predominantly Zulu migrant-hostel areas of the PWV region, where they managed to garner over 170,000 votes, giving them 4% of the country's most populous province. However, elsewhere they were unable to reach more than 2%, and it is likely that these were all white votes in areas with a scarcity of Zulus.

The Freedom Front

I am not alone in holding the opinion that General Constand Viljoen, regardless of his motivations and regardless of the eventual status of an Afrikaner *volkstaat* in South Africa, did the greatest service to the cause of peace and stability in South Africa when he entered into the electoral fray with his embryonic Freedom Front party in early 1994. His splitting of the white Right into two adamantly opposed groupings, one inclusive and effectively pro-system (or at least accepting of the system) and another smaller and violently anti-system, left Afrikaner unity in disarray and any hopes of sustained para-military opposition to the new state just for the dreamers. As Conservative Party spokesman Cyrus Smith admitted, the prospect for winning a *volkstaat* through intimidation and threats of armed resistance was now gone. 'We said that when General Viljoen was still with us, but without him it was no longer possible,' Smith argued.[10]

However, despite General Viljoen's optimistic projections of gaining one million votes for a *volkstaat*, when the results were announced his Freedom Front only managed to poll 424,000 on the national level and 639,000 ballots within the provincial legislative elections. Viljoen himself did make the appeal for whites to vote provincially for the FF so as to make it possible to assess the demarcation and boundaries of where support for a *volkstaat* might lie. His national total represented 14% of the estimated white vote, but regionally the FF polled a far more satisfying 22%. Numerically, this compared well with the heady days of the CP (the former repository for white Right – predominantly Afrikaner – votes) in 1989 when that party had won 670,000 votes (admittedly on a much lower poll). Interestingly, Viljoen was unable to hold on to the 875,000 white voters who had said no to negotiations in the referendum of March 1992. This clearly implies that some of even the die-hard white supremacists had capitulated to the inevitable march of history and progress (and voted for De Klerk) in the election of April 1994.

TABLE 9. THE EVOLUTION OF THE WHITE RIGHT'S VOTE [11]

	Total vote	% of white vote
1987 General election	547,559 [a]	27
1989 General election	673,079 [a]	31
1994 Non-racial election	420,000 [b]	14 [c]

[a]The Conservative Party (CP).
[b]The Freedom Front (FF).
[c]Estimated.

The Freedom Front's best showings came in the PWV, Northern Cape and Orange Free State regions, which provide homes to most of the small, rural Afrikaner communities that form the core of General Viljoen's vote. In all three of these provinces the FF won around 6% of the vote, giving them 2–5 seats in each provincial legislature. When one assesses the issue of electoral support for a *volkstaat*, there was clearly no substantial area of the country which could boast majority support for the Freedom Front or a combination of white parties. However, this was to be expected, as whites form absolute majorities in only five of the old magisterial districts in South Africa and the FF did not even win a majority within these districts. Any future proposal for a viable *volkstaat*, in any geographical area, must clearly now accept that its creation is based upon the moving of local people off their land to make way for such an ethnically homogeneous state. That is why, in my view, the new South African government will never seriously consider such a proposal and why morally it must never seriously consider such a proposal. In the Northern Cape, one of the leading sites for a *volkstaat*, the *volkstaat* concept won the support of 6 out of every 100 voters.

The Democratic Party

In May 1974 Colin Eglin sat in the whites–only House of Assembly as the leader of seven white members who, as Progressive Federal Party representatives, were to prove unfailing critics of apartheid. In one way the election of April 1994 was also the ultimate victory for those courageous white liberal critics of apartheid – such as Suzman, Eglin, Boraine, De Beer, Andrew and Van Zyl Slabbert – who, first as Progs and then as Democrats, had argued for the political liberalisation which would ultimately lead to the first non-racial elections in South Africa. But the spectacular failure of the DP to become more than just a white liberal think-tank, or more than just sand in the oyster of government, was graphically illustrated by the sight, twenty years on, of Colin Eglin leading seven white faces yet again as they were sworn in as DP members of the new non-racial National Assembly.

Few observers of the new political scene expected the DP to win much more than the 5% national threshold of votes to be entitled to a cabinet position. But the DP's eventual 338,000 votes (1.7% of the total) surprised many, no more so than the campaign strategists of the DP themselves who were expecting to surmount the 5% barrier and had heady hopes of reaching 7–9% if things went their way. On the day, things did not go their way, and the DP failed to break out of their core liberal white suburban constituency. Between 80 and 90% of the DP's vote came from the white community, and predominantly the white community in the metropolitan suburbs of Cape Town, Johannesburg and Durban, which had consistently returned liberal MPs in the old constitutional dispensation. The approximately 300,000 white votes the DP polled in 1994 represented roughly 10% of the white share of the total vote, or half of their figure in the 1989 and 1981 general elections. However, even hanging on to this proportion of the white vote was a considerable achievement in the light of the two-party race which the campaign inevitably became in 1994. Clearly, many former DP voters placed their cross against the face of F.W. de Klerk in the belief that the National Party was the only viable bulwark against the hegemony of the ANC and the only party that would be able to defend white economic and cultural interests in the new South Africa. There was also a sense of appreciation for De Klerk for initiating (or at least following through) the political reforms which had removed the pariah status of South Africa.

At first glance the difference between the national and provincial voting figures seems to illustrate the point that many DP supporters remained true to their political roots at the regional level but split their ballots to cast a vote for the Nationalists in the national poll. In the Western Cape provincial parliamentary election the DP gained 6.6% of the vote, but in the national ballot they only gained 4.2%. In the PWV area they polled 5.3% in the provincial poll as opposed to 3.0% on the national level, and in KwaZulu–Natal the DP's vote increased from a paltry 1.6% in the national ballot to a slightly more respectable 2.2% on the provincial level. In the Western Cape the NP's vote decreased by a similar amount when the provincial and national tallies were compared and in the PWV region the NP's vote dipped by a commensurate amount, representing the DP's and Freedom Front's gain, from provincial to national ballot. If the DP's provincial results are tallied from across the country, they total 538,000 (or 200,000 more votes than their national total). This represents 18% of the white vote and a reasonably successful performance among the white share of the electorate.

TABLE 10. THE EVOLUTION OF THE DP'S WHITE VOTE

	Total vote	% of white vote
1981 General election	265,297 [a]	20
1987 General election	288,547 [a]	14
1989 General election	430,199	20
1994 Non-racial election	300,000 [b]	10 [b]

[a]As the Progressive Federal Party (PFP).
[b]Estimated.

The great failure of the DP in the first non-racial election was its inability to reach out to the non-white communities in South Africa. Despite the prominence of a number of coloured politicians in the leadership of the DP, such as Joe Marks, Richard van der Ross and Chris April, they were unable to capitalise in any way on the votes of the large coloured community based in and around Cape Town. This community's vote was clearly divided between the NP and ANC, with a small proportion going to the two Islamic parties. The DP picked up no more than 5% of coloured votes nationally. Similarly, the DP seemed to have won only a small fraction of the Indian community's votes (overwhelmingly based in Durban). Here the competition was even higher: Inkatha and Amichand Rajbansi's Minority Front joined the ANC and NP in the battle for the hearts and minds of this small but politically influential community. Among the black community the DP were totally lost: there were no real black DP leaders with experience to speak of, and in the townships the DP were perceived as a white elitist party which had little to offer the dispossessed in terms of substantive material change in the new South Africa. As the NP also found, political intolerance meant that a large proportion of black South Africa was off-limits when it came to spreading the DP's liberal gospel.

The Pan Africanist Congress
The PAC's final total in the great South African liberation election of 1994 was an unmitigated disaster and immediately set the wheels in motion for fundamental change in the leadership and style of this once-proud organisation. Their pathetically low vote, 243,478 (or 1.25% nationally), left them with only 5 members of the new National Assembly and only 3 provincial assembly members shared between the

KwaZulu–Natal, PWV and Eastern Cape regional parliaments. The poor showing surprised many observers who felt that, even though opinion polls were not picking it up, the PAC had substantial core support within the black community as a hangover from their role in the liberation struggle of the 1950s and 1960s. As it was, the PAC's election campaign was built on the twin pillars of racism and extravagant promises, and conducted with the most spectacular organisational ineffectiveness and ineptness. The PAC leader, Clarence Makwetu, made rare public appearances, and the most visible leader, Western Cape premier candidate Patricia de Lille, was seen often but always ended up alienating potential supporters by yet another racist jibe or attack on the townships' beloved ANC. All in all, the PAC's campaign was a great travesty and betrayal of the legacy of Robert Sobukwe.

The PAC's highest vote came from their Xhosa heartland of the Eastern Cape. But even here they were beaten into fourth place behind the white liberal Democratic Party. After, and indeed during, the elections Pan Africanist spokespeople made it plain that they viewed the 1994 elections as a dress rehearsal for the real battle in 1999 when they would be able to pick up alienated ANC supporters who had not seen fundamental change in their lives after the dismantling of apartheid. The argument went that these black voters would naturally turn to the more radical PAC to answer their immediate concerns about shelter, jobs and land. However, such a strategy for the future relies upon some degree of organisational efficiency from the PAC – a talent which to date they have shown no signs of cultivating.

The Others

There were remarkably few surprises from the also-rans in this election, and all 11 non-seat-winning parties combined polled only 0.82% of the popular vote. The one successful new party was the African Christian Democratic Party of the Rev. Kenneth Meshoe which appealed to the deep Christian roots of a large proportion of the South African population. Their 88,000 votes gave them 2 seats in parliament and 3 seats in the provincial legislatures. The only other minor party able to win a provincial seat was the Minority Front in KwaZulu–Natal, where Amichand Rajbansi managed to poll enough Indian votes in Durban to get a spot in the regional legislature.

Frances Kendall, leader, founder and almost everything else of the Federal Party, was thought to stand a chance of winning a single seat for herself in parliament. In the end her 17,000 votes (almost entirely polled from the PWV region) left her less than halfway to achieving the required total. Perhaps South African voters are not immediately attracted to political leaders who claim to have been nominated for the Nobel Peace Prize when they have so many other leaders to choose from who have really won it![12] Of the former homeland parties (outside of Inkatha), the Dikwankwetla Party of QwaQwa performed best by winning 19,000 votes but no seats.

Ironically the two Muslim parties in the Western Cape provincial election would have succeeded in winning a legislative seat if they had combined together. The African Muslim Party won 21,000 votes in this region and the Islamic Party won 17,000 votes. Such an alliance would have ousted the one ACDP member of the provincial legislature – a small electoral victory for one religion over another.

An Overview of the Regional Results

The provincial legislative results showed a slight improvement for the minor parties in comparison with the national ballot. This was translated into an extra percentage of seats for both the FF and DP. However, the hegemony of the three main parties was as striking on the regional level as in the national picture: the ANC, NP and IFP managed to take a full 92% of all the regional parliamentary seats and 98% of the provincial cabinet portfolios. This large-party dominance left the ANC in control of six of the nine provincial parliaments, the NP and IFP in control of one each, and the Northern Cape equally balanced between the ANC and the combined opposition of the NP, FF and DP.

TABLE 11. PROVINCIAL SEATS WON AND LEGISLATURES CONTROLLED

Party	Seats won	% of total	Legislatures controlled
ANC	266	63%	6
NP	82	19%	1
IFP	44	10%	1
FF	14	3%	0
DP	12	3%	0
PAC	3	1%	0
ACDP	3	1%	0
MF	1	0%	0
No overall control	–	–	1
Total	425	100%	9

The ANC's largest legislative majorities came, not surprisingly, in those regions with the largest number of black (but non-Zulu) voters. In the five provinces of the Orange Free State, Northern and Eastern Transvaal,

Eastern Cape, and North West, all regions where blacks constitute over 80% of the electorate, the ANC won over 80% of the popular vote.[13] The province with the largest combined white and coloured vote, the Western Cape, was taken by the Nationalists, and likewise in the Zulu heartland of KwaZulu–Natal the Zulu-based Inkatha Freedom Party was victorious. That this was predominantly a racial democratic election was highlighted by the fact that the most closely fought provinces were those in which no one ethnic group made up more than 70% of the electorate.

TABLE 12. ETHNIC DISTRIBUTION OF VOTERS WITHIN PROVINCES[14]

Province	Black	White	Coloured	Indian
Western Cape	19%	25%	55%	1%
Northern Cape	31%	18%	51%	0.2%
Eastern Cape	84%	8.2%	7.5%	0.3%
North West	85%	12%	3%	0.3%
Orange Free State	82%	15%	3%	0%
PWV	69%	26%	4%	1%
North. Transvaal	96%	4%	0.2%	0.1%
Eastern Transvaal	83%	16%	1%	0.5%
KwaZulu–Natal	76%	10%	1.6%	13%
Total	73%	15%	9%	3%

The Regions in Detail

(a) Western Cape

The Western Cape, historically considered the most liberal part of the old South Africa, was the only province in April 1994 to elect a white provincial premier. Perhaps incongruously, the man chosen, Hernus Kriel of the National Party, had held one of the key apartheid cabinet portfolios, the Ministry of Law and Order. As noted earlier, the NP were highly successful in fanning the racial divides between coloured and black in the Cape. Helped by a poor regional campaign performance from the ANC, they managed to sweep nearly two-thirds of both the white and coloured vote in the Western Cape, which gave them 53% of the total votes and 23 of the 42 seats in the provincial legislature. The ANC, under the leadership of Allan Boesak, were able to add approximately 27% of coloured voters to their 90% of black voters, but because the Western Cape has by far the smallest number of black South Africans (only 19%) these votes only translated into a third of the

ELECTION RESULTS:
NATIONAL AND PROVINCIAL
LEGISLATURES

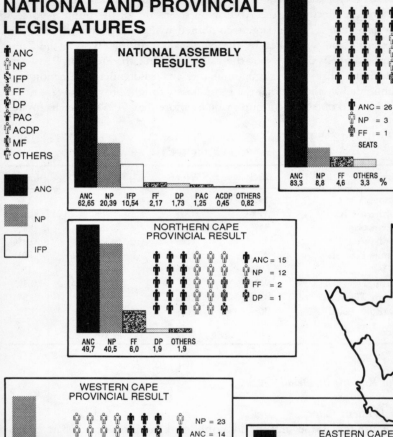

ANC
NP
IFP
FF
DP
PAC
ACDP
MF
OTHERS

■ ANC

▨ NP

□ IFP

NATIONAL ASSEMBLY RESULTS

ANC	NP	IFP	FF	DP	PAC	ACDP	OTHERS
62,65	20,39	10,54	2,17	1,73	1,25	0,45	0,82

NORTH WEST PROVINCIAL RESULT

ANC = 26
NP = 3
FF = 1
SEATS

ANC	NP	FF	OTHERS	%
83,3	8,8	4,6	3,3	

NORTHERN CAPE PROVINCIAL RESULT

ANC = 15
NP = 12
FF = 2
DP = 1

ANC	NP	FF	DP	OTHERS
49,7	40,5	6,0	1,9	1,9

WESTERN CAPE PROVINCIAL RESULT

NP = 23
ANC = 14
DP = 3
FF = 1
ACDP = 1

NP	ANC	DP	FF	ACDP	OTHERS
53,3	33,0	6,6	2,1	1,2	3,8

EASTERN CAPE PROVINCIAL RESULT

ANC = 48
NP = 6
DP = 1
PAC = 1

ANC	NP	DP	PAC	OTHERS
84,4	9,8	2,1	2,0	1,7

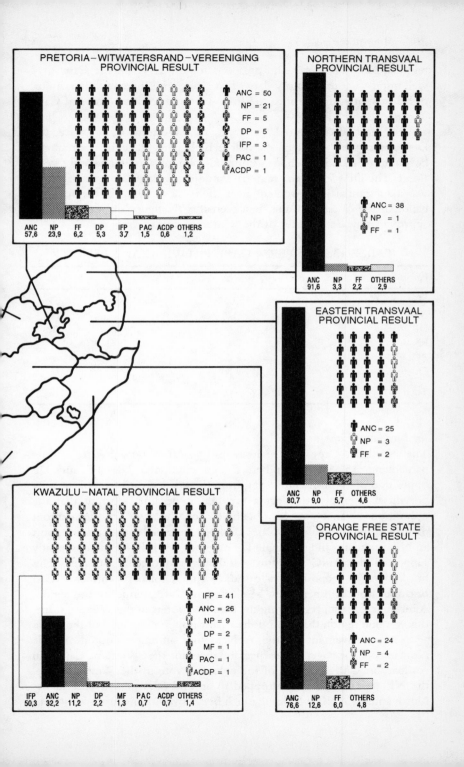

regional total. However, the prospects for the ANC in the Cape may well improve as the century draws to a close, with the continuing influx of black South Africans into the townships and squatter camps of Cape Town.

The most disappointed party in the Western Cape were the Democrats, who expected to poll a high percentage in their liberal boroughs of Rondebosch, Sea Point, Claremont, Constantia and Green Point. The DP's 7% of the regional vote (giving them 3 provincial seats) was a substantial improvement over their 4% showing in the national ballot in the Western Cape, but even the 7% figure only represented approximately one-quarter of the white votes in the region.

TABLE 13. WESTERN CAPE PROVINCIAL RESULT

Party	% vote	Seats
NP	53.3	23
ANC	33.0	14
DP	6.6	3
FF	2.1	1
ACDP	1.2	1
Others	3.8	0
Total	100	42

(b) Northern Cape

The Northern Cape is the closest South Africa now has to a hung parliament: 15 ANC members face a combined NP, FF and DP opposition of 15 more. However, from the first legislative act of the new provincial assembly, to elect a premier, it became apparent that the opposition alliance would not hold, for the two Freedom Front members, led by Professor Carel Boshoff, abstained rather than support an NP candidate, and the single DP member, Ms Ethne Papenfus, tacitly supported the ANC in return for being proposed as Speaker. This breakdown in opposition allowed Manne Dipico, a former NUM organiser from Kimberley, to be elected as ANC premier of the region. After their great success among the coloured voters of the Western Cape, this was one region that the NP had great hopes of taking, but there was a clear improvement in the ANC's vote among coloureds in the Northern Cape over their performance in the Western Cape. In comparison with 65% plus of the coloured vote in the Western Cape, the NP appeared to have dropped to around 58% of that vote in the North and the ANC was doing much better by winning just over 40% of the coloured vote. The Freedom Front won approximately one-third of the white vote in the Northern Cape: this was, comparatively speaking, their best provincial performance in the country. In the subsequent provincial cabinet announced by Dipico on 16 May, the ANC were allotted five portfolios, the NP four and the FF one. In effect, the ANC were magnanimously giving up one of their cabinet positions to the Freedom Front in exchange for some sort of multi-party co-operation in the provincial parliament.

TABLE 14. NORTHERN CAPE PROVINCIAL RESULT

Party	% vote	Seats
ANC	49.7	15
NP	40.5	12
FF	6.0	2
DP	1.9	1
Others	1.9	0
Total	100	30

(c) Eastern Cape

In the ANC's Xhosa heartland, which includes the former homelands of the Transkei and Ciskei, the deputy chairperson of the SACP and Rivonia trialist, Raymond Mhlaba, was easily elected as provincial premier, for the ANC swept the board with 84% of the vote and 48 of the 56 regional assembly seats. This huge ANC landslide was not unexpected, considering that the black community constituted 84% of the electorate in the Eastern Cape and over 90% of those were Xhosa-speakers. Xhosas have historically been the backbone of the ANC, and Nelson Mandela, Walter Sisulu and Thabo Mbeki all consider the region their ancestral home. The two electoral surprises in the region were that the combined NP, DP and FF vote of 13% far exceeded the white electorate of 8%, and that the PAC, in what was considered to be one of their strongest regions, only gained 2% of the vote and one seat in the provincial parliament. The success achieved by the predominantly white parties of the region was either due to a high degree of differential turnout – whites being able to turn out in far higher numbers than their black neighbours – or to a significant number of black or coloured South Africans voting for the National Party. There were, indeed, some major polling problems in the more rural areas of the Transkei and Ciskei which could have suppressed voting numbers, but the high turnout of 92% seems to suggest that the extra voting days did enable the vast majority of Eastern Cape residents to vote. Therefore we must come to the conclusion that the NP picked up a significant number of non-white votes (around 4%) in the region – although it is true to say that other provincial ballots would indicate that the majority of these votes were cast by coloureds rather than black South Africans. Although the NP dipped below the 10% required for a position in the regional cabinet, Raymond Mhlaba did appoint the NP Eastern Cape leader and former Deputy Minister for Constitutional Affairs, Dr Tertius Delport, to the portfolio of Agriculture in his new cabinet.

TABLE 15. EASTERN CAPE PROVINCIAL RESULT

Party	% vote	Seats
ANC	84.4	48
NP	9.8	6
DP	2.1	1
PAC	2.0	1
Others	1.7	0
Total	100	56

(d) Orange Free State

In what had long been considered one of the bastions of white Afrikaner conservatism, the new political realities of South Africa saw whites declining from being 100% of the electorate to only 15%. The ANC dominated the Free State regional vote with 77% of the ballot and 24 of the 30 provincial seats. Here the NP and FF vote (of 18%) equalled almost exactly the number of whites and coloureds eligible to vote, but

TABLE 16. ORANGE FREE STATE PROVINCIAL RESULT

Party	% vote	Seats
ANC	76.6	24
NP	12.6	4
FF	6.0	2
Others	4.8	0
Total	100	30

this was nowhere near enough to stop the ANC gaining the premiership and 8 of the 9 cabinet positions. ANC regional leader, Patrick 'Terror' Lekota, was sworn in as premier and immediately began to speculate about possible name changes in the region, including that of

Bloemfontein. This was another result of the electoral disappointment for the Freedom Front, for their 81,662 represented only 88% of the white Right voters who had opposed negotiations in the March 1992 referendum.

(e) North West

The North West province of the new South Africa takes in much of the former homeland of Bophuthatswana. The collapse of Mangope's puppet government there allowed the ANC to organise in an area of over one million voters which had previously been off-limits to all but the authoritarian government and its business friends. Within less than a month, the ANC managed to turn this region, once considered an electoral disaster area, into one of their strongest reservoirs of popular support. Before Mangope's fall, they would never have been able to garner anything like the 1.3 million votes from the North West, which gave them an extra 7% of the national poll. As it was, the ANC swept the black community, which constitutes 86% of the region's voters, and won 26 of the 30 provincial seats.

The ANC's provincial premier was Popo Molefe of their elections department: he has had an interesting political evolution, first as a founding member of AZAPO, then a leader of the United Democratic Front, and finally one of the accused in the famous Delmas trial. The North West also takes in many of the most conservative white areas of the former Western Transvaal. The Freedom Front were thus disappointed to win only 5% of the popular vote, which gave them just one regional seat and no representation in the cabinet. It seems plausible that in this area at least there was a significant stayaway by some of the most reactionary white supporters of the Conservative Party and AWB.

TABLE 17. NORTH WEST PROVINCIAL RESULT

Party	% vote	Seats
ANC	83.3	26
NP	8.8	3
FF	4.6	1
Others	3.3	0
Total	100	30

(f) PWV

The Pretoria–Witwatersrand–Vereeniging region was as hotly contested as any other of the big three, but here the ANC triumphed with a comfortable parliamentary majority and well over 55% of the popular vote. With 50 elected members out of 86, Tokyo Sexwale easily became the first black premier of Pretoria and Johannesburg – a fitting personal victory for a man imprisoned for terrorism in 1977. He spent 13 years on Robben Island before being released, only to see his close friend Chris Hani assassinated at the very dawn of the new South Africa.

The PWV provincial assembly became host to the largest number of political parties. No less than seven took their seats in the second week of May. The NP's 24% of the vote and 21 seats entitled them to two members of the regional cabinet positions, which were filled by Olaus van Zyl (Public Transport and Roads) and John Mavuso (Agriculture and Conservation). All other posts were filled by ANC members. Interestingly, in a province that was only estimated to be 26% white, the NP, DP and FF combined achieved 36% of the vote: this clearly indicates a level of black support for De Klerk and the National Party. If the ANC's share of the 69% black vote had not been reduced by the NP, Inkatha and PAC, they could have well reached a two-thirds majority in this, the most populated and economically important region of the country.

TABLE 18. PWV PROVINCIAL RESULT

Party	% vote	Seats
ANC	57.6	50
NP	23.9	21
FF	6.2	5
DP	5.3	5
IFP	3.7	3
PAC	1.5	1
ACDP	0.6	1
Others	1.2	0
Total	100	86

(g) Northern Transvaal

The Northern Transvaal provided the ANC with their largest provincial vote of 91.6%. This translated into a hegemonic 95% or 38 of the 40 assembly seats. The late Oliver Tambo's speechwriter, Ngoako Ramathlodi, was elected premier. One of his first acts was to invite Johan Kriek (the one Freedom Front member of the Northern Transvaal assembly) into his cabinet with responsibility for public transport. This was despite the fact that the National Party had marginally won more votes than the Freedom Front, and (with 3.3% and 2.1% of the votes respectively) neither party had been constitutionally entitled to a cabinet position. The vote seems to have split along racial lines in this province: the ANC and PAC combined won 93% of the vote in an area which is 96% black, and the NP, FF and DP won 5% in an area estimated to be 4% white.

TABLE 19. NORTHERN TRANSVAAL PROVINCIAL RESULT

Party	% vote	Seats
ANC	91.6	38
NP	3.3	1
FF	2.2	1
Others	2.9	0
Total	100	40

(h) Eastern Transvaal

The ANC were clearly dominant in this province, which is noted for its Afrikaner conservatism, game parks and remoteness from the urban (and possibly more liberal) centres of South Africa. Bordering Mozambique and ringing much of Swaziland, the Eastern Transvaal region had long been an entrance post for returning ANC exiles and MK cadres. It was an ANC lawyer formerly based in Mozambique, Mathews Phosa, who was sworn in as provincial premier at the head of the newly elected regional parliament.

TABLE 20. EASTERN TRANSVAAL PROVINCIAL RESULT

Party	% vote	Seats
ANC	80.7	25
NP	9.0	3
FF	5.7	2
Others	4.6	0
Total	100	30

Again the vote split very much along racial lines: the ANC, PAC and IFP took just over 83% of the vote in a province which is 83% black, and the NP, FF and DP took just over 15% of the vote (the electorate being 16% white). However, the majority African languages in the Eastern Transvaal are Swazi (38%) and Zulu (27%). This implies that the ANC won a substantial number of Zulu votes in the more rural areas of the

Transvaal where Inkatha's influence is less pervasive.

With 25 seats out of 30, the ANC will be able to dominate both the provincial assembly and executive council without real opposition from the tiny NP and FF caucuses. The National Party's 9% of the popular vote did not entitle them to a position in the ruling provincial executive. But there were rumours that, in the name of reconciliation, Mathews Phosa would offer a position to the leading NP candidate – perhaps in the area of farming and agriculture to appease the prominent white landed interests in the area.

(i) KwaZulu–Natal

The worst election irregularities, and possibly the best case for the invalidation of an election, came from the conflict-torn province of KwaZulu–Natal. The *Weekly Mail* of 6 May reported that in some areas of northern KwaZulu ballot boxes, when opened, contained neatly stacked piles of ballot papers with exactly 2,000 votes for Inkatha and only a handful for the ANC. There were also reports of pirate voting stations in IFP-controlled areas, accounting for anything up to 500,000 votes; the forced removal of IEC and ANC polling monitors from stations; and the issuing of voter cards on a widespread basis to children under the age of 18. However, the ANC's hands were not completely clean in the region either, as thousands of ANC supporters in the Transkei were bused over the KwaZulu border to vote in the neighbouring provincial election. It is unclear whether this was an overt attempt to sway the result of the KwaZulu–Natal regional election or merely a response to the vast logistical difficulties the IEC was facing

TABLE 21. KWAZULU–NATAL PROVINCIAL RESULT

Party	% vote	Seats
IFP	50.3	41
ANC	32.2	26
NP	11.2	9
DP	2.2	2
MF	1.3	1
PAC	0.7	1
ACDP	0.7	1
Others	2.1	0
Total	100	81

in the eastern Transkei. In the end, after a fair degree of secret negotiation between the ANC, IFP, NP and IEC, the ballots were counted largely as they were, and few, if any, of the massive election irregularities caused ballots to be discarded. To some extent this ensured the wafer-thin majority that Inkatha would subsequently gain in the provincial assembly. With 50.3% of the vote and 41 (of the 81) legislative seats, Dr Frank Mdlalose, chairman of the IFP and well-regarded moderate, was elected as KwaZulu–Natal premier, and he quickly set about the task of rebuilding bridges with his defeated foe and now opposition leader, Jacob Zuma, the leading Zulu in the hierarchy of the ANC. Inkatha's one-seat majority is actually far more secure than at first glance because of the close ties that the Natal National Party has historically had with Chief Buthelezi and the KwaZulu government. The 9 NP regional MPs are likely to support Inkatha on most issues. This gives their informal alliance a much more comfortable 19-seat majority in the legislature. The ANC's 32% of the provincial vote translated into around 40% of the Zulu vote, with the IFP winning just over 55%.

The New Parliament

Eighty-seven former MPs from the whites-only constitutional dispensation made it through to the new 400-member non-racial National Assembly. Even though some had been reincarnated as white IFP, FF and even ANC members, they must have all been slightly bewildered or unnerved by the sea of new faces which the historic parliamentary building in Cape Town now accommodates. Where De Klerk and Botha once sat now appear Mandela and Mbeki, and in the Speaker's chair, so long the domain of establishment white males, sat Dr Frene Ginwala who bucked all precedent by failing to be male, white or wig-wearing. The swearing in of the new parliamentary members in the second week of May was a stunning visual demonstration of Tom Lodge's book title, *All, Here and Now:* black sat with white, communist with conservative, Zulu with Xhosa, and Muslim with Christian. Cyril Ramaphosa and Albertina Sisulu stared across the floor from the government benches at Mangosuthu Buthelezi and General Constand Viljoen who occupied their front row seats in the opposition's front bench. Much as in the election, Clarence Makwetu kept well out of sight in the back, and the minor parties were lost in obscurity, vainly trying to peer over the heads of Nats and Inkatha members, who had swiftly monopolised all the prime seating.

However, while this was undoubtably the most representative and democratic parliament South Africa had ever seen, it was not a mirror of the nation in the exact sense. Black South Africans were still dispro-portionately under-represented, and whites and Indians flush with an embarrassment of members over and above what one would expect them to have in line with the ethnic population distribution of the country. Just over half the new National Assembly members were black (as opposed to 73% of the electorate) compared with well over 100 white members, which represented 27% of the new parliament (whites constitute 15% of the electorate). Admittedly there are whites, blacks, Indians and coloureds sitting in all areas of the House and from all parties, but the ethnic imbalance of the Assembly as a whole illustrates the continuing influence of non-blacks over and beyond their population size in South Africa. The Indian community were by far the most well represented in having 40 MPs (as opposed to the 12 their population size might have indicated). Indians were also elected to the prestigious agenda-setting positions of the Speaker (ANC) and the Deputy Speaker (NP).

There was a great improvement in the number of women members of parliament if one compares the old and the new South Africa. This was largely due to an influx of ANC women MPs, who now constitute over a quarter of their parliamentary party. But the other parties failed to fulfil the same promise of gender equality. Women in the new National Assembly still only represent 22% of the total.[15]

The New Cabinet

President Mandela's first Cabinet of National Unity announced on Wednesday, 11 May proved to deliver all that the constitutional engineers had hoped for when drawing up their power-sharing arrangements. Along with the Presidency and first Deputy Presidency (Thabo Mbeki), the ANC took 18 of the 27 ministerial portfolios and 8 (out of 12) of the deputy positions. This represented a share proportionate to their national vote total. But the crucial aspect of the new cabinet was the way in which senior portfolios were allocated to opponents of the ANC, in marked contrast with the parliamentary systems of, say, Britain and Canada where ministers are solely drawn from the ruling party. The ANC ministerial appointments provided few surprises: UWC's Dullah Omar got the Justice Ministry, which was perhaps his choice over a position on the Constitutional Court; the affable head of uMkhonto weSizwe, Joe Modise, became Defence Minister; and Pallo Jordan (the ANC's head of information) was rewarded with the Ministry of Posts, Telecommunications and Broadcasting. Steve Tshwete, the doyen of integrated sport in South Africa, became Minister for Sport and Recreation, and Trevor Manuel, one of the few appointments from the Western Cape, received the all-important Trade and Industry portfolio. The biggest surprise was the appointment of ANC stalwart Alfred Nzo as Foreign Minister, a position which had been expected to remain in the hands of the National Party and, specifically, the (former) longest-serving Foreign Minister in the world, Pik Botha. However, even as the cabinet was being announced there were clear signs that Nzo's appointment was little more than a short-term reward for years of service in exile to the ANC, and Botha may well reclaim his position as South Africa's man on the world stage before the next elections are due in 1999.

The National Party were given six ministerial positions (excluding F. W. de Klerk's Deputy President spot), and through considerable horse-trading they managed to retain some influential posts. The widely respected Derek Keys retained the finance portfolio, a move to reassure foreign investors rather than the NP, and it was expected he would work in tandem with the far less experienced Trevor Manuel. The NP's lead constitutional negotiator and blue-eyed boy, Roelf Meyer, returned to a position he had previously held in the old government as Minister of Constitutional Development. However, this time the portfolio was combined with Provincial Affairs, a post which had originally been promised to the ANC's highly talented Professor of Constitutional Law, Kader Asmal, who was unceremoniously shunted into the Ministry of Water and Forestry after Meyer's appointment. Pik Botha was asked to bide his time at Mineral and Energy Affairs, and Kraai van Niekerk was briefed to reassure and co-opt white farmers as Minister of Agriculture. Perhaps to maintain their multi-racial pretensions, the sixth NP ministerial position went to Abe Williams, a coloured politician from the Cape who had been one of the first non-whites to defect to the National Party when membership was opened up to all races. Williams became Minister for Welfare and Population Development, a post likely to grow in importance in the new South Africa.

As a reward for his fine showing in the elections, Chief Mangosuthu Buthelezi was given the influential Minister of Home Affairs position, which was the next-best thing to an executive Deputy President position. Inkatha's 10% of the national vote also entitled Buthelezi to nominate two other IFP members to the cabinet: Dr Ben Ngubane became Minister of Arts, Culture, Science and Technology, and Sipho Mzimela gained the Correctional Services portfolio.

The Deputy Minister positions were designed to balance specific departments. In a number of cases an ANC minister was asked to work closely with a Deputy from the NP. The ANC's land expert, Derek Hanekom, was positioned to work in tandem with the NP's Dr Kraai van Niekerk; and ANC negotiator Mohammed Valli Moosa was given the Deputy spot under Roelf Meyer at Constitutional Development. Joe Matthews of the IFP, the son of a former ANC president, was asked to deputise to Sydney Mufamadi at Safety and Security. In return the ANC's Penuell Maduna would work with Mangosuthu Buthelezi at Home Affairs. Sealing a quite remarkable political comeback, Winnie Mandela, the estranged wife of the State President, was sworn in as Deputy Minister for the Arts, Culture, Science and Technology.

The ethnic composition of the new cabinet of national unity was as diverse as the country, but sadly the gender balance remained heavily skewed in favour of men. Only 5 of the 42 possible senior governmental appointments went to women, and 3 of these were at the lower level as Deputy Ministers. Those persons of Indian extraction fared particularly well in gaining cabinet posts: the 4 ministerial positions filled by ANC members who happened to be Indian (or 15% of the total) compared highly favourably with the 3% of South Africa that the Indian community constitutes. This influential role of Indian South Africans in the leadership of the ANC, and now the government of national unity, has much to do with the historical role played by Mahatma Gandhi, Yusuf Dadoo and the Indian Congresses in South African political opposition to apartheid and colonialism. Whites are also disproportionately represented in the cabinet: 7 out of the 27 portfolios (or 26%) being taken on by five Nationalist white ministers and two ANC white ministers. It must have been a heady day for Joe Slovo, for so long the communist bête noire of the South African regime, as he was sworn in as Minister of Housing on 11 May 1994. Four of the white ministers are Afrikaans-speaking, but one should be aware that politicians of the likes of Carl Niehaus and Jan van Eck have put paid to the old stereotype that Afrikaners are genetically NP supporters.[16]

Both the coloured and black communities are proportionately under-represented in the first cabinet. This is one of the trade-offs for not having simple majority rule in the new constitutional dispensation. Only 2 of the 27 Ministers (or 7%) are coloured, while 14 (or 52%) are black South Africans. Of those 14 black ministers, Mrs Nkosazana Dlamini Zuma (the wife of the ANC opposition leader in KwaZulu–Natal) joins the 3 IFP members as the fourth Zulu in the new cabinet.

How Alternative Electoral Systems Might Have Worked

The effect electoral systems have upon translating votes cast into seats won is an often overlooked factor in the dynamics of constitutional design. Political parties can be quite diffident about the issues involved until they realise that their electoral futures can turn upon the vagaries of a particular election system. There was little debate in South Africa that a proportional representation-type system (i.e. one that roughly awards parties a number of seats in parliament commensurate to their proportion of the national vote) was best, because the alternative, a plurality or first-past-the-post single-member constituency-type system would have hugely over-represented large parties to the detriment of minority groupings. Until we have exact figures for each of the 700 plus counting streams which provided the results for the first non-racial South African elections, we cannot be exact, but it is safe to say that given their 62% of the popular vote, and the homogeneous nature of South African living areas, we could expect the ANC to have won between 80 and 90% of the parliamentary seats under a Westminster-type constituency system. Professor Kader Asmal, the ANC author of the electoral system which was used in April 1994, recognised what such a result would spell for conflict resolution and inter-racial reconciliation in the new South Africa, and so magnanimously gave up any claims the ANC might have made for a Westminster system.

TABLE 22. SEATS WON UNDER DIFFERENTIAL PR THRESHOLDS

	No Threshold	1% Threshold	3% Threshold	5% Threshold
ANC	252 (63%)	254 (64%)	268 (67%)	268 (67%)
NP	82 (20%)	82 (20%)	87 (22%)	87 (22%)
IFP	43 (11%)	43 (11%)	45 (11%)	45 (11%)
FF	9 (2%)	9 (2%)	– –	– –
DP	7 (2%)	7 (2%)	– –	– –
PAC	5 (1%)	5 (1%)	– –	– –
ACDP	2 (1%)	– –	– –	– –
Other	400 (100%)	400 (100%)	400 (100%)	400 (100%)

However, there are numerous types of electoral systems which fall into the PR family. As such, it is interesting to see how alterations to the system which was eventually used could have affected the final results. The most important variable is that of the size of the threshold for representation; this imposes a base level that small parties must surmount to be entitled to representation in any given parliament. Countries such as Germany have a 5% threshold for representation, while in Israel the figure is 1%. Professor Asmal himself argued for a threshold of between 3% and 5% so that parties in the National Assembly would have a 'national and realistic profile'.[17] In the end the constitutional negotiators agreed not to impose a threshold higher than the effective one which would arise out of the 200 national seats and 200 provincially allotted seats to the National Assembly. That meant that a National Assembly seat was won with approximately 48,500 votes or 0.25% of the total vote.

(The ACDP benefited from the largest-remainder method of calculation, which gave them two seats for just over 44,000 votes apiece, or 0.22% of the national poll.)

As can be seen from the accompanying table, a 1% threshold (similar to that used in Israel and Namibia) would have excluded only the ACDP from parliamentary representation and would have reallocated their seats to the ANC – thus marginally increasing the ANC's already large majority. However, the use of a 3% (the Democratic Party's proposal) or 5% threshold would have dramatically altered the final composition of the National Assembly. Only the ANC, NP and IFP would then have been entitled to parliamentary seats. Conversely the Freedom Front, DP and PAC would have all been excluded from representation. But perhaps even more crucially, the ANC with 62.6% of the votes cast would have won a clear two-thirds, or 268 of the National Assembly seats, giving them the legal opportunity to draft aspects of the new constitution without reference to other political parties. As few people, particularly the ANC leadership themselves, wished to see the ANC have such domineering power over the new Assembly, we can applaud the decision not to impose a threshold for representation for these elections. Furthermore, the low effective threshold did allow a diversity of opinion to be represented in the National Assembly. There are 23 MPs from minor parties who may act as an important balance during the political evolution of the new South African state. This aspect of the electoral system will, however, come up for re-negotiation in the Constitutional Assembly, and it is to be hoped that the large parties do not allow power to go to their heads and try to impose a higher electoral threshold for the elections of 1999.

There are fundamental changes to the 1994 electoral system which could be made to increase democratic accountability and the representativeness of the members of parliament. It was widely accepted that this first non-racial election was more of a referendum about which parties should draw up the new constitution. But in 1999 and subsequent years, the elections will be about constituting a representative parliament, and the electoral system needs to be altered to take this into account. Without greatly increasing the difficulty of the ballot, voters can be allowed to choose between candidates as well as parties, without the PR character of parliament being affected in any way. MPs can be elected by smaller multi-member constituencies in order to maintain some sort of geographical tie between electors and their representatives. At the moment the regional lists represent areas so large that any form of local advocacy is entirely lost; but if a constituency was, say, the size of Cape Town or Pretoria, then a number of MPs would be returned with some knowledge of, and empathy with, their local constituency and constituents.[18]

Electoral Prospects for Parties in the Future

The results of the first non-racial democratic South African elections have set the stage for a fascinating period of party system evolution which is likely to proceed well into the next century. In the 1994 elections only three parties really succeeded and only one dominated, but their respective electoral bases illustrate the potential for a high degree of flux in voter loyalty given to parties in the future. As I maintained before the election, the second election, to be held in 1999, will be the most interesting mirror of electoral support for competing political ideologies.[19]

There are two down-sides to the ANC's huge victory. Firstly, they may well have peaked in electoral terms and may never be able again to reach over 60% of the popular vote. Their 90% plus of the black share of the popular vote will be almost impossible to improve upon. Any gains among the much smaller white, coloured and Indian communities will be almost certainly off-set by losses among their black core vote. The simple reality is that visible change, for a host of reasons, will be incredibly difficult for the ANC government to demonstrate to the majority of previously disenfranchised South Africans. The second down-side is that the very success of the ANC, and their resulting huge parliamentary majority, fan the expectation of change even more. When alienation sets in, some of these voters may turn to the radicalism of the black Left or the conservatism of De Klerk and the new National Party. That means President Mandela's government has a window of opportunity, stretching over the next five years, to introduce real change into the South African polity and civil society. If they are unable to do so, because of the restraints of the new constitution, the involvement of international finance and the realities of wealth ownership in South Africa, and squander this chance, they may never again be as well placed to reverse the inequalities of apartheid and colonial rule. The ANC's dilemma is that their constituency is black South Africa, but the constitution (and the world) say they must take into account the wishes of white South Africa. These two community needs are not always in direct conflict, but often they are, and the expectations of black South Africans are so high that any pandering to the old regime's interests will undoubtedly alienate a large chunk of the ANC's vote. The ANC could seek to alter the constitution to allow any party with 50% plus of the parliamentary seats to rule unfettered and similarly take out the power-sharing clauses for the executive. Yet it seems likely that the political costs, both domestically and internationally, would be too high for them ever to attempt such a change.

In one sense De Klerk and the National Party should be very happy with their 1994 election showing, because they have positioned themselves nicely to be influential in this parliament and ever more powerful in the next. If the NP can hold on to their white, coloured and Indian majority votes (around 65% of each community), then they can begin to build on their small bridgehead into the black voting community. Their 3–4% black vote in this election may seem minuscule but they only need to add another 10–20% to become far more of a threat to the hegemonic power of the ANC. However, such a foray into the world of black politics is not a luxury for the NP: it is essential, as the demographics of South Africa indicate that the white share of the electorate is dropping at a dramatic rate. Presently, whites make up 15% of the electorate; early on next century this will fall to below 10%, and then there is no other constituency to go to realistically than the black community. The slogan 'adapt or die' could not be more relevant to the National Party's campaigning plans for the next five to ten years.

There are some political observers, Lawrence Schlemmer of the HSRC included, who believe that the best growth potential in terms of electoral support lies with the Inkatha Freedom Party of Mangosuthu Buthelezi. The argument goes that Inkatha will not be tainted in the same way as the ANC and NP as being inside government, and therefore be blamed for any failures the new government has the misfortune to encounter. The ANC will be blamed for not delivering, while the NP will be blamed for the government taxing the rich. Among it all Buthelezi will be able to run elections and whisper 'I told you so' in the ears of disgruntled white voters. However, the problem inherent with this scenario is that Buthelezi's growth potential is really to a large extent limited to the white community, and the historical divisions between Zulu and non-Zulu mean that Inkatha will find it exceptionally difficult to attract the votes of Xhosas, Vendas, Sothos, Ndebeles and Tswanas for a long time to come. As I have already noted, the white community's share of the electorate is on the decline and so, even if Buthelezi remains the dominant vote-drawer in the Zulu community, he is unlikely to poll more than 15% nationally without the support of black South Africans who are not Zulus.

The only future for the Democratic Party lies in their ability to break out of the white suburbs. If the new government is very corrupt and blatantly abusive of human rights, they might have a chance. But realistically some sort of realignment needs to take place outside of parliament to create a liberal centrist party which has cross-over appeal to all communities in the land. Such an option has been touted and names mentioned like Oscar Dhlomo (of the Institute for Multi-Party Democracy), Mamphela Ramphele (of UCT), Frederik van Zyl Slabbert, Franklin Sonn (of the ANC in the Western Cape) and Vincent Maphai (of UWC). But none of these academics, however, have shown the slightest inclination to engage in such a realignment, and so for the time being it will remain the stuff of day-dreams on the campuses of UCT, Wits and Natal. In the immediate future the DP are faced with a bruising leadership battle, since the post-election retirement of Zach de Beer, between the brash firebrand of Houghton, Tony Leon, and the considerably less brash DP establishment figure, Ken Andrew, from Cape Town. It seems unlikely that either of these white males has the potential for cross-over appeal into the non-white community. So until a new leader, new image and new focus are found the DP appear set to remain as a thorn in the side of big brother government rather than an effective opposition to it.

The electoral prospects for the Freedom Front are similarly bleak: both possible white Right scenarios over the next five years would entail Viljoen losing votes. Firstly, General Viljoen could deliver the impossible and win a *volkstaat,* in which case much of the Freedom Front vote would emigrate to the *volkstaat* until they realised how miserable and culturally stifling it was. Or, secondly, Viljoen could fail to pull off the impossible and not get a *volkstaat,* in which case he would alienate his core vote, and the white Right, as in many other parts of Africa, would fade into the African sunset. If the first government of national unity was a particular disaster, De Klerk and the Nationalists might lose some of their Afrikaner support to the Freedom Front. But the former State President has shown himself to be particularly adept in distancing himself from the misdeeds and failures of governments which he not only was involved in but in many cases led. Finally, the Pan Africanist Congress do have the potential to be the receptacle for alienated ANC voters, but as I noted earlier this will depend upon a marked development of their organisational efficiency.

On the provincial government level, the prospects for the future are equally interesting. While it is unlikely the ANC will lose their dominance in the provincial legislatures of the Eastern Transvaal, Northern Transvaal, Eastern Cape, Orange Free State and North West, they could well lose control in the Northern Cape and the PWV region in the next elections. However, in contrast, the ANC may be able to make gains in the Western Cape and KwaZulu–Natal regions. This would force those legislatures into the type of no overall control position which faces many local governments in Great Britain today. It is quite likely that as a result of the second round of elections for these bodies, four of the nine provinces will have alliances of different parties in government rather than one-party overall control.

Notes

1. While it was true that any party in the parliament (National Assembly and Senate combined) could in theory amend the constitution unhindered with a two-thirds majority, such fears fail to take into account the role of the Constitutional Court, which would have to vet any fundamental changes, and also ignore the informal constraints of the government of national unity which would make it highly unlikely for a dominant party to follow such an alienating course of action.

2. *Cape Times*, 7 May 1994, p. 1.

3. See the *Weekly Mail* of 6–12 May, p. 2.

4. The highest being the Conservative Party's 54% of the vote in 1935.

5. As quoted by the *President's Council Report on a proportionate polling system for the new South Africa* (1992), pp. 96–97.

6. Estimated electorate figures supplied by the Independent Electoral Commission.

7. Author's estimates calculated from turnout, regional support and opinion poll indications.

8. Author's estimates calculated from turnout, regional support and opinion poll indications.

9. *Launching Democracy (First Report) on Opinion Survey in the Western Cape during Nov/ Dec 1993* and *Launching Democracy (Sixth Report) on Issues Relevant to a Free and Fair Election Feb 1994* (both sponsored by the Institute for Multi-Party Democracy).

10. As quoted by Jan Taljaard in the *Weekly Mail* of 13–19 May 1994, p. 5.

11. From Johann van Rooyen, *Hard Right: The New White Power in South Africa* (London: I. B. Taurus, 1994), updated by Reynolds.

12. Chief Albert Luthuli, Desmond Tutu, and De Klerk and Mandela.

13. The only exception being the Orange Free State, where the ANC won 77% out of an electorate which was 82% black.

14. Estimated electorate figures supplied by the Independent Electoral Commission and the Delimitation of States/ Provinces/Regions Commission.

15. I am indebted to Donald Simpson's article 'An Embarrassment of Pale Faces' in the *Argus* of 16 May 1994 and Edyth Bulbring's piece, 'Side by Side, the Old and the New' in the *Sunday Times* of 15 May 1994.

16. Both Carl Niehaus and Jan van Eck are white, Afrikaans-speaking ANC members of the National Assembly. Niehaus became a spokesperson for the ANC after his release from prison, and Van Eck was a leading DP MP in the white parliament who defected to the ANC after its unbanning.

17. Kader Asmal, *Electoral Systems: A Critical Survey* (Bellville, Centre for Development Studies, UWC, 1990), p. 17.

18. See Andrew Reynolds, *Voting for a New South Africa* (Cape Town, Maskew Miller Longman, 1993), ch. 9–10.

19. See *Voting and Democracy Review*, vol. II, no. 2 (Washington DC: Center for Voting and Democracy, April–May 1994).

12
Prospects for Power-sharing in the New South Africa

AREND LIJPHART

During the 1970s and 1980s, I was always guardedly optimistic about the chances for peace and democracy in South Africa. This cautious optimism was based on my conviction that a consociational or power-sharing system – I shall use these two terms interchangeably – offered an excellent and quite feasible democratic solution to divided societies in general and to South Africa in particular.[1] I had discovered power-sharing in the comparative research that I did on my native country of the Netherlands and other European countries, in the late 1960s. I was, of course, not the only or even the first scholar to analyse power-sharing and to recommend its use in divided societies. The credit for the first scholarly analysis belongs to the Nobel Prize-winning economist Sir Arthur Lewis, a native of St Lucia and of African descent, who advocated power-sharing for the ethnically divided countries of West Africa in his famous Whidden Lectures in 1965.[2] But I was the first to apply the concept specifically to South Africa and to introduce it to South African audiences in the numerous lectures and seminars I gave and the many conversations I had during my first visit to South Africa in 1971 (a six-week visit under the auspices of the Netherlands–South Africa cultural exchange treaty).

Perhaps it would be more accurate to say that I was an 'optimistic pessimist'. I often told my friends and colleagues that anyone familiar with South Africa's huge differences, divisions, inequalities, and

* This chapter is the product of a larger collaborative research project (with Bernard Grofman of the University of California, Irvine, and Andrew Reynolds of the University of California, San Diego) on Electoral Laws, Electoral Lists, and Campaigning in the First Non-racial South African Elections, supported by the National Science Foundation of the United States, Award No. SBR-9321864.

animosities could only be a pessimist. But among these pessimistic observers of South African politics, I always belonged to the least pessimistic or most optimistic – not because I thought that a democratic solution along consociational lines was probable, but because I regarded it as not at all impossible and, in fact, as having great potential. After the release of Nelson Mandela and other leaders from prison and the unbanning of the African National Congress and other organisations in 1990, I shifted from optimistic pessimism to full-scale optimism. This optimism, I believe, has been validated by the adoption of the interim constitution and by the first universal-suffrage election held in April 1994.

The next question, of course, is: Will South Africa's first democratic system work? I remain an optimist. While there is no guarantee for its success, there are four reasons why I think that the outlook is highly promising. The first reason is that the newly founded democracy is clearly a consociational democracy. Second, it is not only a power-sharing system but close to the optimal power-sharing system that could have been devised. Third, the background conditions for its satisfactory operation have become considerably more favourable than they were in the 1980s. Fourth, the outcome of the April 1994 elections augurs very well for South Africa's democratic future. Let me elaborate on each of these points in the remainder of this chapter.

South Africa's Power-sharing Democracy

In my previous writing, I have repeatedly emphasised that consociational democracy is the type of democracy that is much better suited to divided societies than majority-rule democracy – and the *only* workable type of democracy in very deeply divided countries – and that it can be defined in terms of four basic principles: (1) government by 'grand coalition', that is, by a broadly representative coalition of all significant groups; (2) group autonomy by means of territorial and/or non-territorial federalism and decentralisation; (3) proportionality, especially with regard to political representation; and (4) minority veto power concerning issues of vital and fundamental importance.[3] The new constitution embodies all of these basic principles.

First of all, Article 88 provides for a 'government of national unity' in which all parties with a minimum of 5 per cent of the seats in the National Assembly may participate – a clear instance of government by grand coalition. Second, group autonomy in the vital realm of education is guaranteed by Article 32, which states that 'every person shall have the right ... to establish, where practicable, educational institutions based on a common culture, language or religion, provided that there shall be no discrimination on the ground of race.'

Third, proportionality is the leading principle for election and representation. Election by proportional representation (PR) is prescribed for both the National Assembly (Article 40) and the provincial legislatures (Article 127), and proportionality also guides the indirect selection of Senators by the parties represented in the provincial legislatures (Article 48) and the composition of the 'government of national unity' (Article 88). Fourth, the minority veto appears in the form of the two-thirds majority requirement for amending the constitution and for adopting a new constitutional text by the Constitutional Assembly, composed of the members of the National Assembly and the Senate (Article 73). Moreover, a number of fundamental principles, like proportional representation and 'collective rights of self-determination in forming, joining and maintaining organs of civil society, including linguistic, cultural and religious associations', cannot be infringed even by two-thirds majorities (Article 71 and Schedule 4).

Of course, the constitution with which South Africa embarks on its first experience with democracy in 1994 is only an interim constitution, and the 'government of national unity' is prescribed for only the first five years. However, the power-sharing provisions in the interim constitution are reinforced by strong informal agreements and understandings. For instance, in his meetings with the press at the end of April 1994, Mandela stated: 'Even if we may emerge with a landslide victory, we have to be very careful and not create the fear that the majority is going to be used for the purpose of coercing minorities to accept the policy of a particular party which has emerged victorious.' And he indicated that ethnic minority schools would not only be permitted, as guaranteed by the constitution, but – even more important – would also continue to be subsidised by the government.[4] The general expectation is that the final constitution will bear a strong resemblance to the interim constitution. And, if the 'government of national unity' turns out well during the first five years, it may well be continued on an informal basis even if it is not constitutionally required.

The one weakness of the interim constitution is that it is not a federal constitution. To be sure, there are some federal features, such as the equal representation in the Senate of all nine provinces (ten Senators each) in spite of the unequal populations of the provinces – a feature normally found only in clearly and strongly federal constitutions like those of the United States, Australia and Switzerland. Furthermore, the interim constitution contains several provisions that are much more typical of federal than of non-federal constitutions: a bicameral legislature with a reasonably strong second chamber, judicial review by a special constitutional court, and the requirement of extraordinary majorities for constitutional amendment. But, in addition to the fact that the formal label of 'federalism' is lacking – a matter of considerable symbolic importance – the constitution does not provide for a great deal of decentralisation. Mangosuthu Buthelezi has complained that the powers of the new provincial governments will not even match the limited power of his old KwaZulu homeland government. There is still a good chance, however, that the constitution will be amended in the direction of at least a semi-federal system.

That South Africa's democratic constitution is fundamentally a consociational document also becomes clear when we compare it with the major alternatives: the Westminster model of majoritarian democracy and Donald L. Horowitz's advice to the South African constitutional engineers in his 1991 book *A Democratic South Africa?* For instance the South African constitution specifies rules and institutions that contrast sharply and fundamentally with those of British democracy: one-party majority cabinets, winner-take-all elections (according to the first-past-the-post or plurality method), a two-party system, and a flexible (unwritten) constitution amendable by simple majority rule and unprotected by judicial review.

Similarly, the constitution does not contain either of Horowitz's principal recommendations: holding elections according to a special majoritarian method (the so-called alternative vote) and instituting a popularly elected and very powerful president.[5] Soon after Horowitz's book was published, I wrote an extensive critique of it in the South African political science journal *Politikon*.[6] My objective was partly the traditional academic one of engaging in a scholarly debate, but it was also to some extent political: I hoped, directly or indirectly, to reach some of the South African constitutional engineers, and to convince them that Horowitz's proposals were deeply flawed and dangerous and not a serious alternative to power-sharing. Although I do not regret making this effort, it turned out not to have been necessary.

An Optimal Power-sharing System
Power-sharing is compatible with a wide variety of institutional alternatives. It is defined in terms of a set of general principles, rather than specific rules and institutions. This does not mean, however, that all institutional alternatives are equally effective and desirable power-sharing devices. In particular, although a consociational system can be made to work in a presidential system, as in Colombia from 1958 to 1974, a parliamentary system is vastly preferable: cabinets in parliamentary

systems are collegial decision-making bodies in which grand coalitions can flourish, in contrast with cabinets in presidential systems which typically consist of mere advisers to a pre-eminent president. Similarly, although power-sharing can coexist with a winner-take-all electoral system, as in Malaysia since 1955 where the partners in the grand coalition have manipulated the nominations in the single-member districts in such a way as to achieve nearly proportional results, the more straightforward and more accurate – and hence vastly preferable – method to obtain proportionality is to use the electoral system of proportional representation (PR).

Thirdly, a consociational constitution or pact may explicitly name the population groups that will act as the principal partners in power-sharing, such as the Dutch-speakers and French-speakers according to the Belgian constitution, and the Maronite, Sunni, Shiite and other sects in the Lebanese National Pact. But, instead of this kind of predetermination, the better method is to allow the groups to define themselves by such means as PR elections that allow ample scope for any self-selected minority group to gain political representation, and the right of cultural, linguistic and religious groups to establish and run autonomous but publicly subsidised schools. Self-determination works much better than predetermination because it is a neutral and flexible method; moreover, it avoids the frequently controversial question of how the divisions and groups in a divided society should be defined and identified.

On the basis of the above arguments, my 1985 *Power-sharing in South Africa* recommended a number of 'optimal consociational guidelines for South Africa', the first three of which I should like to quote: '1. The segments should be allowed to emerge spontaneously by means of PR elections ... instead of being predetermined ... 2. Proportional representation should be used for legislative elections at all levels – federal, state, and local. 3. The executives at all levels should be proportionally constituted ... collegial bodies.'[7] stipulates that the President Clearly, the framers of the South African constitution have made the optimal choices in all three respects: a power-sharing cabinet in a parliamentary system, proportional representation, and self-determined groups.

As far as parliamentarism and PR are concerned, I need to add some further comments. Because the constitution stipulates that the president is both head of state (Article 76) and head of the government (Article 88), the system appears, at first blush, to be a presidential instead of a parliamentary one. However, the president is neither popularly elected nor elected for a fixed term, as presidents in presidential systems are. Instead, Article 77 prescribes election by the legislature, and Article 93 gives the legislature the power to force the president to resign by adopting a vote of no confidence. This means that the president is an office-holder similar to a British prime minister or a German chancellor in a parliamentary system. But it was an extremely clever and creative invention by the framers of the constitution to call the chief executive a 'president', since this title carries much greater prestige than that of a mere prime minister or chancellor – and still design a clearly parliamentary system.

The interim constitution also proves a point about the differences between presidential and parliamentary systems that I have argued for quite some time. It is often stated that a major difference between the two types of systems is that presidential systems have a single chief executive who is both head of state and head of government, whereas parliamentary systems have a dual executive; that is, a separate head of state and head of government. My argument has been that this may be an empirical difference that we find between the two types in contemporary democracies, but that the dual executive is by no means 'an essential ingredient of parliamentarism', and that 'it should be possible for a prime minister to be the head of both the government and the state in parliamentary systems.'[8] I am pleased that South Africa's constitutional engineers have proved me right on this small theoretical point!

PR is the best electoral method for power-sharing democracies, but since there are many forms of PR, we must also ask: Which of the PR methods is the optimal form for South Africa? I addressed this question in a paper originally presented at a 1985 conference in Pretoria and later published in Robert Schrire's *Critical Choices for South Africa* (1990). My bottom line was to recommend 'list PR in large districts' on the grounds that list PR is less complex than the main alternative (the single transferable vote or STV, in which voters have to rank-order individual candidates); that STV can only be applied in small districts; and that large districts are necessary in order to maximise proportionality.[9] The two-tier PR system that was used for the April 1994 election is completely in accord with this advice: a list PR system in which all 400 seats in the National Assembly are proportionally allocated to the party lists on a nation-wide basis – that is, in the largest possible district.

Credit for making these optimal consociational decisions belongs first and foremost to the wisdom and good sense of the constitutional negotiators. At the same time, it must also have helped that South Africans have paid a great deal of attention to other divided countries and the efforts that these countries have made to manage their divisions and conflicts. In fact, the establishment of South Africa's consociational democracy is unique in this respect. When other prominent cases of agreements to institute power-sharing are examined (such as those in the Netherlands in 1917, Lebanon and Switzerland in 1943, Austria in 1945, Malaysia in 1955, Colombia in 1958, Cyprus in 1960, Belgium in 1970, and Czechoslovakia in 1989), the striking conclusion is that all of them were arrived at completely independently of each other. None of these power-sharing agreements were inspired by the example of an earlier agreement of this kind; each time, power-sharing had to be re-invented. For instance, in 1958 the Colombian peacemakers were totally ignorant of, and hence did not learn any lessons from, the so-called Peaceful Settlement in the Netherlands in 1917 or the 1943 Lebanese National Pact.

In South Africa, on the other hand, the idea of consociational democracy already began to be discussed as a promising model for democratic reform as early as 1971.[10] Ten years later, in 1981, political scientist Denis Worrall stressed the pervasive influence of consociational thinking on South African democratic reformers: 'Consociational democratic theory rules the theoretical roost in political science in this country, [and] its domination of constitutional theory is almost as complete.'[11] In its First Report, issued in 1982, the National Party-dominated Constitutional Committee of the President's Council under Worrall's chairmanship stated that it 'followed Lijphart's reasoning closely'.[12] Unfortunately, the Committee and the National Party then proceeded to distort the idea of power-sharing into an excuse for perpetuating white minority rule: the new 1983 constitution established nothing but, in the words of the German consociational sociologist Theodor Hanf, a 'sham consociation'.[13]

In roughly the same period, however, two genuine power-sharing plans were launched by major political groupings: the 1978 constitutional proposals of the Progressive Federal Party (the predecessor of the Democratic Party), and the final report, issued in 1982, of the Buthelezi Commission of which I was one of the two non-South African members. These proposals were not just thoroughly but also optimally consociational: both contained the key elements of power-sharing cabinets, proportional representation, and self-determination of groups. Therefore, without taking away any of the credit due to Nelson Mandela and F.W. de Klerk, they were only 'Johnny-come-lately' consociationalists, and it would not have been inappropriate if their Nobel Peace Prize had been shared with 'Johnny-come-earlies' like Buthelezi and Progressive Federal Party leader F. van Zyl Slabbert.

The New Spirit of Reconciliation and Accommodation
In my comparative research on consociational democracy, I have tried to

assess the probability of the establishment of power-sharing in divided societies and, once established, the likelihood of its success. My conclusion was that nine conditions conducive to the institution and satisfactory operation of consociational democracies can be identified. The two most important of these are the absence of a solid majority group – since majorities tend to prefer majority rule to power-sharing – and the absence of large socio-economic differences among the groups. Other favourable conditions include overarching loyalties that counter-balance the divisions of a divided society, a relatively small overall population size, and pre-existing traditions of compromise and ac-commodation.

In my 1985 book *Power-sharing in South Africa,* I showed that, contrary to the conventional, deeply pessimistic wisdom concerning South Africa's future, these background conditions were, on balance, not at all unfavourable in South Africa's case. As far as the two most important conditions are concerned, for instance, I argued that the huge socio-economic inequalities constituted a clearly unfavourable factor, but that it was wrong to interpret South Africa's diverse society exclusively in racial terms and that, when cultural, linguistic and regional differences were taken into consideration, the spectre of a solid majority bent on unrestrained majority rule disappeared. When the pluses and minuses of all nine condition were added up, I showed that South Africa was approximately in the middle of the continuum between highly favourable and highly unfavourable background conditions – roughly in the same situation as Belgium, Lebanon and Malaysia, less favourable than Switzerland, but more favourable than Cyprus.[14]

Furthermore, my cautious optimism was based on my conviction that the nine background conditions should be regarded as favourable conditions instead of necessary conditions. This means that power-sharing is possible even in countries with highly unfavourable conditions, and that highly favourable conditions do not guarantee either its institution or the success. The establishment of power-sharing is generally the result of what I have called a 'self-negating prediction'; a prediction of an undesirable event that motivates the predictor to make an effort to prevent this event from occurring. In divided societies, political leaders may have the wisdom not only to forsee, but also to forestall, the 'undesirable events' of violent conflict and democratic failure by turning to power-sharing.

The explanation of power-sharing in terms of the self-negating prediction has given rise to a great deal of scholarly controversy. In particular, my former University of Leiden colleague Hans Daalder has claimed that the 1917 Peaceful Settlement in the Netherlands was the result of long-standing traditions of political accommodation instead of a deliberate, rational decision based on a self-negating prediction.[15] My own theoretical bottom line is that both factors are important. As stated above, a pre-existing tradition of accommodation has become one of my nine favourable conditions. But I continue to think that crucial decisions on power-sharing are inspired to a large extent by the judgement that the alternatives to power-sharing are simply too horrible to contemplate.

It seems to me that both factors are important in interpreting recent events in South Africa. In my numerous conversations with National Party politicians between 1971 and 1990, I always emphasised that the party was making a big mistake if it thought that the choice was between a broad sharing of power and maintaining exclusive power for the white, especially Afrikaner and National Party, minority; their only real choice, I argued, was between sharing power and losing power. The acceptance, long overdue, of this argument can explain much of De Klerk's 1989 'conversion' from apartheid and white minority rule to multi-racial universal suffrage and power-sharing.

Since 1990, the weak traditions of accommodation in South Africa have been strengthened immeasurably and very rapidly. In my *Power-sharing in South Africa,* I showed that such traditions were already present to some extent before 1990, mainly in the form of traditional patterns of consensual decision-making in the African community and the growing sentiment in favour of power-sharing in various quarters, but that these encouraging elements were counterbalanced by a long history of white domination and black exclusion and by the continuing influence of the British majoritarian model. However, in the remarkably short period of four years since 1990, a new spirit and tradition of accommodation have become firmly established.

The African National Congress has responded to De Klerk's 'self-negating prediction' in an admirably moderate and accommodating fashion. In particular, it readily consented to elections by proportional representation even though, as the putative majority party, it stood to gain a lot of additional seats in first-past-the-post elections. And it agreed to PR without even using this agreement as a bargaining chip to obtain concessions on other matters. The ANC's high-minded stance on PR runs completely counter to the conventional wisdom that political parties act on the basis of their narrow partisan self-interests – putting political scientists who operate on this assumption to shame! Nelson Mandela's basic approach to governing, as laid out at press conferences in late April 1994, is characterised by *New York Times* reporter Bill Keller as 'a vision of his Government as a grand negotiating forum in which every party will have a voice, past crimes will be forgiven and the power of the majority will rarely be used.' And Mandela sounded like a true consociationalist when he said that 'we believe that by recognising diversity we will actually be uniting the people of South Africa.'[16]

Happy Election Results

Finally, I see the outcome of the April 1994 elections as a favourable factor for the next five years and beyond. The ANC won the solid victory that, as the main agent of South Africa's liberation, it clearly deserved. It would have been highly ironic and unsettling if the ANC had fallen short of a parliamentary majority and, even more, if an anti-ANC alliance had been able to defeat the ANC. It is fortunate that such a 'shock in the making', suggested as a possible election outcome by Andrew Reynolds and Bernard Grofman about a year ago, did not take place. At the same time, the fact that the ANC won a solid majority but not a two-thirds majority was a positive development. Even though there is no reason to believe that the ANC would have used this majority, required for writing the permanent constitution, in order to impose its will on the minority parties, facing one party with unlimited constituent authority would have been at least somewhat unnerving to these other parties.

It is also fortunate that the highly proportional PR system without any formal threshold – which meant that a party with as little as one-fourth of one per cent of the total national vote could win a seat in the National Assembly – did not lead to a high degree of party fragmentation. Two other parties, the National Party and the Inkatha Freedom Party, emerged as strong counterweights to, and power-sharing partners of, the ANC. That, in addition, the NP and IFP emerged as victors in two of the nine provinces – the Western Cape and KwaZulu–Natal – further enhances the prospects of a stable power-sharing equilibrium. And this result was achieved in an optimally democratic and legitimate way: the electoral system gave the amplest possible chances for small parties to gain representation and did not artificially exclude anyone. My only feeling of sadness is that the voters did not see fit to reward the Democratic Party for its and its predecessor's strong and long-standing efforts, since 1978, to introduce power-sharing.

As I stated in the beginning of this chapter, it was difficult to be an optimist about South Africa before 1990 because of the country's huge differences, divisions, inequalities, and animosities. Now, in 1994, most of the animosities have been replaced by the new spirit of reconciliation, but most of the differences, divisions and inequalities remain. While there can be no guarantee that the new power-sharing government will succeed, the new consociational institutions are just about the best that could have been designed. If they do not succeed, it is unlikely that any other structures could have worked either.

Notes

1. In recent South African usage, power-sharing is sometimes narrowly equated with an absolute minority veto power on all issues. However, I shall continue to use the term 'power-sharing' as I have always used it: as a synonym of 'consociational democracy', defined, as indicated below, in terms of four basic features, only one of which is a strictly limited minority veto.

2. W. Arthur Lewis, *Politics in West Africa* (London: George Allen and Unwin, 1965).

3. See, for instance, Arend Lijphart, *Democracy in Plural Societies: A Comparative Exploration* (New Haven: Yale University Press, 1977), pp. 25–44.

4. Bill Keller, 'Mandela Speaks of Reconciliation', *New York Times,* 20 April 1994, p.5.

5. Donald L. Horowitz, *A Democratic South Africa? Constitutional Engineering in a Divided Society* (Berkeley: University of California Press, 1991).

6. Arend Lijphart, 'The Alternative Vote: A Realistic Alternative for South Africa?' *Politikon,* vol. 18, no. 2 (June 1991), pp. 91–101.

7. Arend Lijphart, *Power-sharing in South Africa,* Policy Papers in International Affairs, no. 24 (Berkeley: Institute of International Studies, University of California, 1985), pp. 80–81.

8. Arend Lijphart, *Democracies: Patterns of Majoritarian and Consensus Government in Twenty-one Countries* (New Haven: Yale University Press, 1984), p. 73

9. Arend Lijphart, 'Electoral Systems, Party Systems and Conflict Management in Segmented Societies', in Robert A. Schrire, ed., *Critical Choices for South Africa: An Agenda for the 1990s* (Cape Town: Oxford University Press, 1990), pp. 11–13.

10. See W.B. Vosloo, 'Pluralisme as teoretiese perspektief vir veelvolkige naasbestaan in Suid-Afrika', *Politikon,* vol. 1, no. 1 (June 1974), pp. 4–14.

11. Denis Worrall, 'The Constitutional Committee of the President's Council', *Politikon,* vol. 8, no. 2 (December 1981), p.33.

12. Constitutional Committee of the President's Council, *First Report* (Cape Town: Government Printer, 1982), p. 32

13. Theodor Hanf et al., *South Africa: The Prospects of Peaceful Change* (London: Rex Collings, 1981), p. 419 (emphasis added).

14. Lijphart, *Power-sharing in South Africa,* p. 120.

15. See, for instance, Hans Daalder, 'The Consociational Democracy Theme', *World Politics,* vol. 26, no. 4, (July 1974), pp. 604–21.

16. Keller, 'Mandela Speaks of Reconciliation'.

Appendix
The New Cabinet

Executive State President	Dr Nelson Mandela
Deputy Executive State Presidents	Mr Thabo Mbeki
	Mr F.W. de Klerk

Ministers

Justice	Mr Dullah Omar (ANC)
Foreign Affairs	Mr Alfred Nzo (ANC)
Home Affairs	Chief Mangosuthu Buthelezi (IFP)
Defence	Mr Joe Modise (ANC)
Finance	Mr Derek Keys (NP)
Provincial Affairs and Constitutional Development	Mr Roelf Meyer (NP)
Safety and Security	Mr Sydney Mufamadi (ANC)
Trade, Industry and Tourism	Mr Trevor Manuel (ANC)
Education	Mr Sibusiso Bhengu (ANC)
Labour	Mr Tito Mboweni (ANC)
Housing	Mr Joe Slovo (ANC)
Health	Mrs Nkosazana Dlamini Zuma (ANC)
Posts, Telecommunications and Broadcasting	Dr Pallo Jordan (ANC)
Transport	Mr Mac Maharaj (ANC)
Land Affairs	Mr Derek Hanekom (ANC)
Public Enterprises	Ms Stella Sigcau (ANC)
Public Service and Admin	Dr Zola Skweyiya (ANC)
Public Works	Mr Jeff Radebe (ANC)

Correctional Services	Mr Sipho Mzimela (IFP)
Agriculture	Dr Kraai van Niekerk (NP)
Sport and Recreation	Mr Steve Tshwete (ANC)
Water Affairs and Forestry	Professor Kader Asmal (ANC)
Environmental Affairs	Dr Dawie de Villiers (NP)
Mineral and Energy Affairs	Mr Pik Botha (NP)
Welfare and Population Development	Mr Abe Williams (NP)
Arts, Culture, Science and Technology	Dr Ben Ngubane (IFP)
Minister without Portfolio	Mr Jay Naidoo (ANC)

Deputy Ministers

Foreign Affairs	Mr Aziz Pahad (ANC)
Provincial Affairs	Mr Valli Moosa (ANC)
Justice	Mr Chris Fismer (NP)
Home Affairs	Mr Penuell Maduna (ANC)
Arts, Culture, Science and Technology	Mrs Winnie Mandela (ANC)
Finance	Mr Alex Erwin (ANC)
Welfare	Ms Sankie Nkondo (ANC)
Environmental Affairs	Mr Bantu Holomisa (ANC)
Land Affairs	Mr Tobie Meyer (NP)
Education	Mr Renier Schoeman (NP)
Safety and Security	Mr Joe Matthews (IFP)
Agriculture	Ms Thoko Msane (ANC)

Select Bibliography

Adam, Heribert and K. Moodley (1993) *The Negotiated Revolution* (Houghton, Jonathan Ball Publishers).

African National Congress (1991) *Constitutional Principles and Structures for a Democratic South Africa* (Bellville, University of the Western Cape).

Asmal, Kader (1990) *Electoral Systems: A Critical Survey* (Bellville, University of the Western Cape).

Bogdanor, Vernon and D. Butler (1983) *Democracy and Elections* (Cambridge, Cambridge University Press).

Butler, David (ed.) (1959) *Elections Abroad* (London, Macmillan).

De Klerk, W (1991) *The Man in his Time: F.W. de Klerk* (Johannesburg, Jonathan Ball Publishers).

Gastrow, Shelagh (1992) *Who's Who in South African Politics* (Johannesburg, Ravan Press).

Giliomee, Hermann and J. Gagiano (eds.) (1990) *The Elusive Search for Peace: South Africa/Israel/Northern Ireland* (Cape Town, Oxford University Press).

Giliomee, Hermann and L. Schlemmer (1989) *From Apartheid to Nation Building* (Cape Town, Oxford University Press).

Giliomee, Hermann and L. Schlemmer (1989) *Negotiating South Africa's*

Future (Johannesburg, Southern Book Publishers).

Friedman, S. (ed.) (1993) *The Long Journey* (Johannesburg, Ravan Press)

Grofman, Bernard and A. Lijphart (1986) *Electoral Laws and their Political Consequences* (New York, Agathon Press).

Horowitz, Donald (1991) *A Democratic South Africa? Constitutional Engineering in a Divided Society* (Cape Town, Oxford University Press).

Johnson, Shaun (1993) *Strange Days Indeed* (London, Bantam Press).

Kotze, Hennie (1992) *President's Council Report on a Proportional Polling System for South Africa in a New Constitutional Dispensation* (Pretoria, Government Printer).

Kotze, Hennie and A. Greyling (1991) *Political Organisations in South Africa A–Z* (Cape Town, Tafelberg).

Lakeman, Enid (1974) *How Democracies Vote* (London, Faber & Faber).

Lijphart, Arend (1985) *Power Sharing in South Africa* (Berkeley, Institute of International Studies).

Lijphart, Arend (1984) *Democracies* (New Haven, Yale University Press).

Lijphart, Arend (1977) *Democracy in Plural Societies* (New Haven, Yale University Press).

Lijphart, Arend and B. Grofman (eds.) (1984) *Choosing an Electoral System* (New York, Praeger).

Lodge, Tom and Bill Nasson et al. (1991) *All, Here, and Now: Black Politics in South Africa in the 1980s* (Cape Town, David Philip).

Mill, J.S. (1888) *On Representative Government* (London, Longmans, Green and Co.).

Niehaus, Carl (1993) *Fighting for Hope* (Cape Town, Human & Rousseau).

Ottoway, David (1994) *Chained Together: Mandela and De Klerk* (New

York, Times Books).

Pakenham, Thomas (1991) *The Scramble for Africa: White Man's Conquest of the Dark Continent from 1876-1912* (New York, Avon Books).

Pogrund, Benjamin (1990) *Sobukwe and Apartheid* (Johannesburg, Jonathan Ball Publishers).

Reynolds, Andrew (1993) *Voting for a New South Africa* (Cape Town, Maskew Miller Longman).

Schrire, Robert (ed.) (1994) *Leadership in the Apartheid State: From Malan to De Klerk* (Cape Town, Oxford University Press).

Schrire, Robert (1990) *Critical Choices for South Africa* (Cape Town, Oxford University Press).

Steytler, Nico, J. Murphy, P. de Vos, M. Rwelamira (eds.) (1994) *Free and Fair Elections* (Kenwyn, Juta & Co.).

Suzman, Helen (1993) *In No Uncertain Terms: A South African Memoir* (New York, Alfred A. Knopf).

Van Rooyen, Johann (1994) *Hard Right: The New White Power in South Africa* (London, I.B. Tauris).